Go Programming Blueprints

Build real-world, production-ready solutions in Go using cutting-edge technology and techniques

Mat Ryer

[PACKT] open source✳
PUBLISHING community experience distilled

BIRMINGHAM - MUMBAI

Go Programming Blueprints

First published: January 2015

Production reference: 1200115

Published by Packt Publishing Ltd.
Livery Place
35 Livery Street
Birmingham B3 2PB, UK.

ISBN 978-1-78398-802-0

www.packtpub.com

Credits

Author
Mat Ryer

Reviewers
Tyler Bunnell

Michael Hamrah

Nimish Parmar

Commissioning Editor
Kunal Parikh

Acquisition Editor
Richard Brookes-Bland

Content Development Editor
Govindan Kurumangattu

Technical Editor
Sebastian Rodrigues

Copy Editor
Vijay Tase

Project Coordinator
Shipra Chawhan

Proofreaders
Simran Bhogal

Maria Gould

Ameesha Green

Paul Hindle

Indexer
Hemangini Bari

Graphics
Abhinash Sahu

Production Coordinator
Komal Ramchandani

Cover Work
Komal Ramchandani

About the Author

Mat Ryer has a family legend (or conspiracy) that tells of him programming computers from the age of 6—he and his father would build games and programs, first BASIC on a ZX Spectrum then later AmigaBASIC and AMOS on their Commodore Amiga. Many hours were spent manually copying out code from the *Amiga Format* magazine, before spending more still tweaking variables or moving GOTO statements around to see what might happen. The same spirit of exploration and obsession with programming led Mat to start work for a local agency in Mansfield, England, when he was 18, where he started to build websites and services.

In 2006, Mat's wife, Laurie, took a job at the Science Museum in London, and so they both left rural Nottinghamshire for the big city, where Mat took a job at BT. It was here that he worked with a talented group of developers and managers on honing agile development skills and developing a light flavor that he still uses today.

After contracting around London for a few years, coding everything from C# and Objective-C to Ruby and JavaScript, Mat noticed a new systems language called Go that Google was pioneering. Because it addressed very pertinent and relevant modern technical challenges, Mat started using it to solve problems while the language was still in beta and he has used it ever since.

In 2012, Mat and Laurie left England to live in Boulder, Colorado, where Mat works on a variety of projects, from big data web services and highly available systems to small side projects and charitable endeavors.

Acknowledgments

I wouldn't have been able to write this book without the help of the wonderful Laurie Edwards, who, while working on her own projects, took the time to keep me organized and focused. Without her continuous and undying support, I dare say, this book (along with every other project I embark on) would never have happened.

Tyler Bunnell (@tylerb on GitHub)—who, believe it or not, I met on Google Code (working on the Goweb project)—is my Go life partner. We have paired on many projects so far, and will no doubt continue to do so into the future, until one of us (him) is tragically killed by the other due to some disagreement over proper use of the sync package! Tyler and I learned Go together, and he was also gracious enough to become a technical reviewer for this book—so in a way, you can blame any mistakes on him!

Other development heroes of mine include Ryan Quinn (@mazondo on GitHub), who seems to build an app a day and is living proof of how building something, however simple, is always better than building nothing. Thanks also go out to Tim Schreiner for engaging in debates with me over the good and bad bits of Go as well as being my go-to guy on matters close to and beyond the fringes of computer science.

Thanks go to the core Go team for building such a fun language and to the entire Go community who have saved me months of development with their contributions.

Special thanks also go to everyone who has supported me and helped me make doing what I love into a career, including but not limited to Nick Ryer (my dad, for getting me into computers in the first place), Maggie Ryer, Chris Ryer, Glenn Wilson, Phil Jackson, Jeff Cavins, Simon Howard, Edd Grant, Alan Meade, Steve Cart, Andy Jackson, Aditya Pradana, Andy Joslin, Simon Howard, Phil Edwards, Tracey Edwards, and all my other great friends and family.

About the Reviewers

Tyler Bunnell (@tylerb on GitHub) is an entrepreneur and developer whose inquisitive personality has enabled him to become an avid problem solver, seeking out knowledge and solutions and always aiming to be innovative and ahead of the curve.

His programming portfolio is interestingly eclectic; he cofounded Mizage, where he created a line of OS X applications, including Divvy, before partnering with a vocal coach to create Voice Tutor for iOS—an application that helps everyone sing without the need for private lessons. In 2012, Tyler took an interest in an emerging language, Go, where he made an immediate impact with contributions to the Go open source community by cofounding popular projects such as Testify, Graceful, and Genny, amongst other things. Most recently, he has turned his attention to an exciting new start-up, but he can't talk about that one just yet.

Michael Hamrah is a software engineer from Brooklyn, New York, who specializes in scalable, distributed systems for the Web with a focus on API design, event-driven asynchronous programming, and data modeling and storage. He works primarily with Scala and Go, and has extensive experience with all levels of the software stack. He can be reached via LinkedIn at https://www.linkedin.com/in/hamrah.

Nimish Parmar has over 10 years of experience building high performance distributed systems. After receiving his bachelor's degree in computer engineering from the University of Mumbai, Nimish completed a master of science in computer science from the University of Southern California. He was the technical reviewer for the book *Amazon Web Services: Migrating your .NET Enterprise Application*, *Packt Publishing*

He's currently working as a senior software engineer at StumbleUpon in San Francisco. Nimish is a die-hard USC Trojans football fan and enjoys snowboarding during winter.

I'd like to thank my parents, Ragini and Bipin. Words can't describe how fortunate I am to have received your endless love and support.

www.PacktPub.com

Support files, eBooks, discount offers, and more

For support files and downloads related to your book, please visit www.PacktPub.com.

Did you know that Packt offers eBook versions of every book published, with PDF and ePub files available? You can upgrade to the eBook version at www.PacktPub.com and as a print book customer, you are entitled to a discount on the eBook copy. Get in touch with us at service@packtpub.com for more details.

At www.PacktPub.com, you can also read a collection of free technical articles, sign up for a range of free newsletters and receive exclusive discounts and offers on Packt books and eBooks.

https://www2.packtpub.com/books/subscription/packtlib

Do you need instant solutions to your IT questions? PacktLib is Packt's online digital book library. Here, you can search, access, and read Packt's entire library of books.

Why subscribe?

- Fully searchable across every book published by Packt
- Copy and paste, print, and bookmark content
- On demand and accessible via a web browser

Free access for Packt account holders

If you have an account with Packt at www.PacktPub.com, you can use this to access PacktLib today and view 9 entirely-free books. Simply use your login credentials for immediate access.

Table of Contents

Preface

I decided to write *Go Programming Blueprints* because I wanted to expel the myth that Go, being a relatively young language and community, is a bad choice for writing and iterating on software quickly. I have a friend who knocks out complete Ruby on Rails apps in a weekend by mashing up pre-existing gems and libraries; Rails as a platform has become known for enabling rapid development. Since I do the same with Go and the ever-growing buffet of open source packages, I wanted to share some real-world examples of how we can quickly build and release software that performs great from day one and is ready to scale when our projects take off in a way that Rails cannot compete with. Of course, most scalability happens outside the language, but features like Go's built-in concurrency mean you can get some very impressive results from even the most basic hardware, giving you a head start when things start to get real.

This book explores five very different projects, any of which could form the basis of a genuine start-up. Whether it's a low-latency chat application, a domain name suggestion tool, a social polling and election service built on Twitter, or a random night out generator powered by Google Places, each chapter touches upon a variety of problems that most products or services written in Go will need to address. The solutions I present in the book are just one of many ways to tackle each project, and I would encourage you to make up your own mind about how I approached them. The concepts are more important than the code itself, but you'll hopefully pick up a few tips and tricks here and there that can go into your Go toolbelt.

The process by which I wrote this book might be interesting because it represents something about the philosophies adopted by many agile developers. I started by giving myself the challenge of building a real deployable product (albeit a simple one; minimum viable product if you will) before getting stuck into it and writing a version 1. Once I got it working, I would rewrite it from scratch. It has been said many times by novelists and journalists that the art of writing is rewriting; I have found this to be true for software as well. The first time we write a piece of code, all we are really doing is learning about the problem and how it might be tackled as well as getting some of our thinking out of our heads and onto paper (or into a text editor). The second time we write it, we are applying our new knowledge to actually solve the problem. If you've never tried this, give it a shot—you might find that the quality of your code shoots up quite dramatically as I did. It doesn't mean the second time will be the last time—software evolves and we should try to keep it as cheap and disposable as possible, so we don't mind throwing pieces away if they go stale or start to get in the way.

I write all of my code following Test-driven Development (TDD) practices, some of which we will do together throughout the chapters and some you'll just see the result of in the final code. All of the test code can be found in the GitHub repositories for this book even if it's not included in print.

Once I had my test-driven second versions completed, I would start writing the chapter describing how and why I did what I did. In most cases, the iterative approach I took is left out of the book because it would just add pages of tweaks and edits, which would likely just become frustrating for the reader. However, on a couple of occasions, we will iterate together to get a feel of how a process of gradual improvements and small iterations (starting and keeping it simple and introducing complexity only when absolutely necessary) can be applied when writing Go packages and programs.

I moved to the United States from England in 2012, but that is not why the chapters are authored in American English; it was a requirement from the publisher. I suppose this book is aimed at an American audience, or perhaps it's because American English is the standard language of computing (in British code, properties that deal with color are spelled without the U). Either way, I apologize in advance for any trans-Atlantic slips; I know how pedantic programmers can be.

Any questions, improvements, suggestions, or debates (I love how opinionated the Go community—as well as the core team and the language itself—is) are more than welcome. These should probably take place in the GitHub issues for the book set up specifically at `https://github.com/matryer/goblueprints` so that everybody can take part.

Finally, I would be thrilled if somebody forms a start-up based on any of these projects, or makes use of them in other places. I would love to hear about it; you can tweet me at @matryer and let me know either way.

What this book covers

Chapter 1, Chat Application with Web Sockets, shows how to build a complete web application that allows multiple people to have a real-time conversation right in their web browser. We see how the net/http package lets us serve HTML pages as well as connect to the client's browser with web sockets.

Chapter 2, Adding Authentication, shows how to add OAuth to our chat application so that we can keep track of who is saying what, but let them log in using Google, Facebook, or GitHub.

Chapter 3, Three Ways to Implement Profile Pictures, explains how to add profile pictures to the chat application taken from either the authentication service, the Gravitar.com web service, or by allowing users to upload their own picture from their hard drive.

Chapter 4, Command-line Tools to Find Domain Names, explores how easy building command-line tools is in Go and puts those skills to use to tackle the problem of finding the perfect domain name for our chat application. It also explores how easy Go makes it to utilize the standard in and standard out pipes to produce some pretty powerful composable tools.

Chapter 5, Building Distributed Systems and Working with Flexible Data, explains how to prepare for the future of democracy by building a highly scalable Twitter polling and vote counting engine powered by NSQ and MongoDB.

Chapter 6, Exposing Data and Functionality through a RESTful Data Web Service API, looks at how to expose the capabilities we built in *Chapter 5, Building Distributed Systems and Working with Flexible Data*, through a JSON web service, specifically how wrapping http.HandlerFunc functions gives us a powerful pipeline pattern.

Chapter 7, Random Recommendations Web Service, shows how to consume the Google Places API to generate a location-based random recommendations API that represents a fun way to explore any area. It also explores why it's important to keep internal data structures private, controlling the public view into the same data, as well as how to implement enumerators in Go.

Chapter 8, Filesystem Backup, helps to build a simple but powerful filesystem backup tool for our code projects and explore interacting with the filesystem using the os package from the Go standard library. It also looks at how Go's interfaces allow simple abstractions to yield powerful results.

Appendix, Good Practices for a Stable Go Environment, teaches us how to install Go from scratch on a new machine and discusses some of the environmental options we have and the impact they might have in the future. We will also consider how collaboration might influence some of our decisions as well as the impact open sourcing our packages might have.

What you need for this book

To compile and run the code from this book, you will need a computer capable of running an operating system that supports the Go toolset, a list of which can be found at `https://golang.org/doc/install#requirements`.

Appendix, Good Practices for a Stable Go Environment, has some useful tips to install Go and set up your development environment including how to work with the GOPATH environment variable.

Who this book is for

This book is for all Go programmers—from beginners looking to explore the language by building real projects to expert gophers with an interest in how the language can be applied in interesting ways.

Conventions

In this book, you will find a number of styles of text that distinguish between different kinds of information. Here are some examples of these styles and an explanation of their meaning.

Code words in text, database table names, folder names, filenames, file extensions, pathnames, dummy URLs, user input, and Twitter handles are shown as follows: "We can use functionality from other packages using the `import` keyword, after we have used `go get` to download them."

A block of code is set as follows:

```
package meander
type Cost int8
```

```
const (
  _ Cost = iota
  Cost1
  Cost2
  Cost3
  Cost4
  Cost5
)
```

When we wish to draw your attention to a particular part of a code block, the relevant lines or items are set in bold:

```
package meander
type Cost int8
const (
  _ Cost = iota
  Cost1
  Cost2
  Cost3
  Cost4
  Cost5
)
```

Any command-line input or output is written as follows:

```
go build -o project && ./project
```

New terms and **important words** are shown in bold. Words that you see on the screen, in menus or dialog boxes for example, appear in the text like this: "Once you install Xcode, you open **Preferences** and navigate to the **Downloads** section.

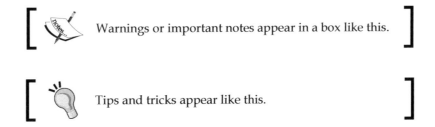

Warnings or important notes appear in a box like this.

Tips and tricks appear like this.

Reader feedback

Feedback from our readers is always welcome. Let us know what you think about this book—what you liked or may have disliked. Reader feedback is important for us to develop titles that you really get the most out of.

To send us general feedback, simply send an email to feedback@packtpub.com, and mention the book title via the subject of your message.

If there is a topic that you have expertise in and you are interested in either writing or contributing to a book, see our author guide on www.packtpub.com/authors.

Customer support

Now that you are the proud owner of a Packt book, we have a number of things to help you to get the most from your purchase.

Downloading the example code

You can download the example code files for all Packt books you have purchased from your account at http://www.packtpub.com. If you purchased this book elsewhere, you can visit http://www.packtpub.com/support and register to have the files e-mailed directly to you. Alternatively, check out the GitHub repository for this book at http://github.com/matryer/goblueprints.

Errata

Although we have taken every care to ensure the accuracy of our content, mistakes do happen. If you find a mistake in one of our books—maybe a mistake in the text or the code—we would be grateful if you would report this to us. By doing so, you can save other readers from frustration and help us improve subsequent versions of this book. If you find any errata, please report them by visiting http://www.packtpub.com/submit-errata, selecting your book, clicking on the **errata submission form** link, and entering the details of your errata. Once your errata are verified, your submission will be accepted and the errata will be uploaded on our website, or added to any list of existing errata, under the Errata section of that title. Any existing errata can be viewed by selecting your title from http://www.packtpub.com/support.

Piracy

Piracy of copyright material on the Internet is an ongoing problem across all media. At Packt, we take the protection of our copyright and licenses very seriously. If you come across any illegal copies of our works, in any form, on the Internet, please provide us with the location address or website name immediately so that we can pursue a remedy.

Please contact us at copyright@packtpub.com with a link to the suspected pirated material.

We appreciate your help in protecting our authors, and our ability to bring you valuable content.

Questions

You can contact us at questions@packtpub.com if you are having a problem with any aspect of the book, and we will do our best to address it.

1
Chat Application with Web Sockets

Go is great for writing high-performance, concurrent server applications and tools, and the Web is the perfect medium over which to deliver them. It would be difficult these days to find a gadget that is not web-enabled and allows us to build a single application that targets almost all platforms and devices.

Our first project will be a web-based chat application that allows multiple users to have a real-time conversation right in their web browser. Idiomatic Go applications are often composed of many packages, which are organized by having code in different folders, and this is also true of the Go standard library. We will start by building a simple web server using the `net/http` package, which will serve the HTML files. We will then go on to add support for web sockets through which our messages will flow.

In languages such as C#, Java, or Node.js, complex threading code and clever use of locks need to be employed in order to keep all clients in sync. As we will see, Go helps us enormously with its built-in channels and concurrency paradigms.

In this chapter, you will learn how to:

- Use the `net/http` package to serve HTTP requests
- Deliver template-driven content to users' browsers
- Satisfy a Go interface to build our own `http.Handler` types
- Use Go's goroutines to allow an application to perform multiple tasks concurrently
- Use channels to share information between running Go routines
- Upgrade HTTP requests to use modern features such as web sockets

- Add tracing to the application to better understand its inner workings
- Write a complete Go package using test-driven development practices
- Return unexported types through exported interfaces

 Complete source code for this project can be found at `https://github.com/matryer/goblueprints/tree/master/chapter1/chat`. The source code was periodically committed so the history in GitHub actually follows the flow of this chapter too.

A simple web server

The first thing our chat application needs is a web server that has two main responsibilities: it must serve the HTML and JavaScript chat clients that run in the user's browser and accept web socket connections to allow the clients to communicate.

 The GOPATH environment variable is covered in detail in *Appendix, Good Practices for a Stable Go Environment*. Be sure to read that first if you need help getting set up.

Create a `main.go` file inside a new folder called `chat` in your GOPATH and add the following code:

```
package main

import (
  "log"
  "net/http"
)

func main() {

  http.HandleFunc("/", func(w http.ResponseWriter, r
*http.Request) {
    w.Write([]byte(`
      <html>
        <head>
          <title>Chat</title>
        </head>
        <body>
          Let's chat!
```

```
      </body>
    </html>
  `))
})
// start the web server
if err := http.ListenAndServe(":8080", nil); err != nil {
  log.Fatal("ListenAndServe:", err)
}
}
```

This is a complete albeit simple Go program that will:

- Listen to the root path using the `net/http` package
- Write out the hardcoded HTML when a request is made
- Start a web server on port `:8080` using the `ListenAndServe` method

The `http.HandleFunc` function maps the path pattern `"/"` to the function we pass as the second argument, so when the user hits `http://localhost:8080/`, the function will be executed. The function signature of `func(w http.ResponseWriter, r *http.Request)` is a common way of handling HTTP requests throughout the Go standard library.

 We are using `package main` because we want to build and run our program from the command line. However, if we were building a reusable chatting package, we might choose to use something different, such as `package chat`.

In a terminal, run the program by navigating to the `main.go` file you just created and execute:

go run main.go

Open a browser to `localhost:8080` to see the **Let's chat!** message.

Having the HTML code embedded within our Go code like this works, but it is pretty ugly and will only get worse as our projects grow. Next, we will see how templates can help us clean this up.

Templates

Templates allow us to blend generic text with specific text, for instance, injecting a user's name into a welcome message. For example, consider the following template:

```
Hello {name}, how are you?
```

We are able to replace the {name} text in the preceding template with the real name of a person. So if Laurie signs in, she might see:

```
Hello Laurie, how are you?
```

The Go standard library has two main template packages: one called text/template for text and one called html/template for HTML. The html/template package does the same as the text version except that it understands the context in which data will be injected into the template. This is useful because it avoids script injection attacks and resolves common issues such as having to encode special characters for URLs.

Initially, we just want to move the HTML code from inside our Go code to its own file, but won't blend any text just yet. The template packages make loading external files very easy, so it's a good choice for us.

Create a new folder under our chat folder called templates and create a chat.html file inside it. We will move the HTML from main.go to this file, but we will make a minor change to ensure our changes have taken effect.

```html
<html>
  <head>
    <title>Chat</title>
  </head>
  <body>
    Let's chat (from template)
  </body>
</html>
```

Now, we have our external HTML file ready to go, but we need a way to compile the template and serve it to the user's browser.

 Compiling a template is a process by which the source template is interpreted and prepared for blending with various data, which must happen before a template can be used but only needs to happen once.

We are going to write our own `struct` type that is responsible for loading, compiling, and delivering our template. We will define a new type that will take a `filename` string, compile the template once (using the `sync.Once` type), keep the reference to the compiled template, and then respond to HTTP requests. You will need to import the `text/template`, `path/filepath`, and `sync` packages in order to build your code.

In `main.go`, insert the following code above the `func main()` line:

```
// templ represents a single template
type templateHandler struct {
   once      sync.Once
   filename  string
   templ     *template.Template
}
// ServeHTTP handles the HTTP request.
func (t *templateHandler) ServeHTTP(w http.ResponseWriter, r
*http.Request) {
   t.once.Do(func() {
      t.templ =
template.Must(template.ParseFiles(filepath.Join("templates",
t.filename)))
   })
   t.templ.Execute(w, nil)
}
```

 Did you know that you could automate the adding and removing of imported packages? See *Appendix, Good Practices for a Stable Go Environment* to learn how to do this.

The `templateHandler` type has a single method called `ServeHTTP` whose signature looks suspiciously like the method we passed to `http.HandleFunc` earlier. This method will load the source file, compile the template and execute it, and write the output to the specified `http.ResponseWriter` object. Because the `ServeHTTP` method satisfies the `http.Handler` interface, we can actually pass it directly to `http.Handle`.

 A quick look at the Go standard library source code, which is located at `http://golang.org/pkg/net/http/#Handler`, will reveal that the interface definition for `http.Handler` specifies that only the `ServeHTTP` method need be present in order for a type to be used to serve HTTP requests by the `net/http` package.

Doing things once

We only need to compile the template once, and there are a few different ways to approach this in Go. The most obvious is to have a NewTemplateHandler function that creates the type and calls some initialization code to compile the template. If we were sure the function would be called by only one goroutine (probably the main one during the setup in the main function), this would be a perfectly acceptable approach. An alternative, which we have employed in the preceding section, is to compile the template once inside the ServeHTTP method. The sync.Once type guarantees that the function we pass as an argument will only be executed once, regardless of how many goroutines are calling ServeHTTP. This is helpful because web servers in Go are automatically concurrent and once our chat application takes the world by storm, we could very well expect to have many concurrent calls to the ServeHTTP method.

Compiling the template inside the ServeHTTP method also ensures that our code does not waste time doing work before it is definitely needed. This lazy initialization approach doesn't save us much in our present case, but in cases where the setup tasks are time- and resource-intensive and where the functionality is used less frequently, it's easy to see how this approach would come in handy.

Using your own handlers

To implement our templateHandler type, we need to update the main body function so that it looks like this:

```
func main() {
  // root
  http.Handle("/", &templateHandler{filename: "chat.html"})
  // start the web server
  if err := http.ListenAndServe(":8080", nil); err != nil {
    log.Fatal("ListenAndServe:", err)
  }
}
```

The templateHandler structure is a valid http.Handler type so we can pass it directly to the http.Handle function and ask it to handle requests that match the specified pattern. In the preceding code, we created a new object of the type templateHandler specifying the filename as chat.html that we then take the address of (using the & **address of** operator) and pass it to the http.Handle function. We do not store a reference to our newly created templateHandler type, but that's OK because we don't need to refer to it again.

In your terminal, exit the program by pressing *Ctrl + C* before re-running it, then refresh your browser and notice the addition of the (from template) text. Now our code is much simpler than an HTML code and free from those ugly blocks.

Properly building and executing Go programs

Running Go programs using a `go run` command is great when our code is made up of a single `main.go` file. However, often we might quickly need to add other files. This requires us to properly build the whole package into an executable binary before running it. This is simple enough, and from now on, this is how you will build and run your programs in a terminal:

```
go build -o {name}
./{name}
```

The `go build` command creates the output binary using all the `.go` files in the specified folder, and the `-o` flag indicates the name of the generated binary. You can then just run the program directly by calling it by name.

For example, in the case of our chat application, we could run:

```
go build -o chat
./chat
```

Since we are compiling templates the first time the page is served, we will need to restart your web server program every time anything changes in order to see the changes take effect.

Modeling a chat room and clients on the server

All users (clients) of our chat application will automatically be placed in one big public room where everyone can chat with everyone else. The `room` type will be responsible for managing client connections and routing messages in and out, while the `client` type represents the connection to a single client.

 Go refers to classes as types and instances of those classes as objects.

To manage our web sockets, we are going to use one of the most powerful aspects of the Go community—open source third-party packages. Every day new packages solving real-world problems are released, ready for you to use in your own projects and even allow you to add features, report and fix bugs, and get support.

 It is often unwise to reinvent the wheel unless you have a very good reason. So before embarking on building a new package, it is worth searching for any existing projects that might have already solved your very problem. If you find one similar project that doesn't quite satisfy your needs, consider contributing to the project and adding features. Go has a particularly active open source community (remember that Go itself is open source) that is always ready to welcome new faces or avatars.

We are going to use Gorilla Project's `websocket` package to handle our server-side sockets rather than write our own. If you're curious about how it works, head over to the project home page on GitHub, `https://github.com/gorilla/websocket`, and browse the open source code.

Modeling the client

Create a new file called `client.go` alongside `main.go` in the `chat` folder and add the following code:

```
package main
import (
  "github.com/gorilla/websocket"
)
// client represents a single chatting user.
type client struct {
  // socket is the web socket for this client.
  socket *websocket.Conn
  // send is a channel on which messages are sent.
  send chan []byte
  // room is the room this client is chatting in.
  room *room
}
```

In the preceding code, socket will hold a reference to the web socket that will allow us to communicate with the client, and the send field is a buffered channel through which received messages are queued ready to be forwarded to the user's browser (via the socket). The room field will keep a reference to the room that the client is chatting in—this is required so that we can forward messages to everyone else in the room.

If you try to build this code, you will notice a few errors. You must ensure that you have called `go get` to retrieve the `websocket` package, which is as easy as opening a terminal and typing the following:

```
go get github.com/gorilla/websocket
```

Building the code again will yield another error:

```
./client.go:17 undefined: room
```

The problem is that we have referred to a `room` type without defining it anywhere. To make the compiler happy, create a file called `room.go` and insert the following placeholder code:

```
package main
type room struct {
  // forward is a channel that holds incoming messages
  // that should be forwarded to the other clients.
  forward chan []byte
}
```

We will improve this definition later once we know a little more about what our room needs to do, but for now, this will allow us to proceed. Later, the `forward` channel is what we will use to send the incoming messages to all other clients.

 You can think of channels as an in-memory thread-safe message queue where senders pass data and receivers read data in a non-blocking, thread-safe way.

In order for a client to do any work, we must define some methods that will do the actual reading and writing to and from the web socket. Adding the following code to `client.go` outside (underneath) the `client` struct will add two methods called `read` and `write` to the `client` type:

```
func (c *client) read() {
  for {
    if _, msg, err := c.socket.ReadMessage(); err == nil {
      c.room.forward <- msg
    } else {
      break
    }
  }
}
```

```
      c.socket.Close()
  }
func (c *client) write() {
   for msg := range c.send {
      if err := c.socket.WriteMessage(websocket.TextMessage, msg);
  err != nil {
         break
      }
   }
   c.socket.Close()
}
```

The `read` method allows our client to read from the socket via the `ReadMessage` method, continually sending any received messages to the `forward` channel on the `room` type. If it encounters an error (such as `'the socket has died'`), the loop will break and the socket will be closed. Similarly, the `write` method continually accepts messages from the `send` channel writing everything out of the socket via the `WriteMessage` method. If writing to the socket fails, the `for` loop is broken and the socket is closed. Build the package again to ensure everything compiles.

Modeling a room

We need a way for clients to join and leave rooms in order to ensure that the `c.room. forward <- msg` code in the preceding section actually forwards the message to all the clients. To ensure that we are not trying to access the same data at the same time, a sensible approach is to use two channels: one that will add a client to the room and another that will remove it. Let's update our `room.go` code to look like this:

```
package main

type room struct {

   // forward is a channel that holds incoming messages
   // that should be forwarded to the other clients.
   forward chan []byte
   // join is a channel for clients wishing to join the room.
   join chan *client
   // leave is a channel for clients wishing to leave the room.
   leave chan *client
   // clients holds all current clients in this room.
   clients map[*client]bool
}
```

We have added three fields: two channels and a map. The `join` and `leave` channels exist simply to allow us to safely add and remove clients from the `clients` map. If we were to access the map directly, it is possible that two Go routines running concurrently might try to modify the map at the same time resulting in corrupt memory or an unpredictable state.

Concurrency programming using idiomatic Go

Now we get to use an extremely powerful feature of Go's concurrency offerings — the `select` statement. We can use `select` statements whenever we need to synchronize or modify shared memory, or take different actions depending on the various activities within our channels.

Beneath the `room` structure, add the following `run` method that contains two of these `select` clauses:

```go
func (r *room) run() {
  for {
    select {
    case client := <-r.join:
      // joining
      r.clients[client] = true
    case client := <-r.leave:
      // leaving
      delete(r.clients, client)
      close(client.send)
    case msg := <-r.forward:
      // forward message to all clients
      for client := range r.clients {
        select {
        case client.send <- msg:
          // send the message
        default:
          // failed to send
          delete(r.clients, client)
          close(client.send)
        }
      }
    }
  }
}
```

Although this might seem like a lot of code to digest, once we break it down a little, we will see that it is fairly simple, although extremely powerful. The top `for` loop indicates that this method will run forever, until the program is terminated. This might seem like a mistake, but remember, if we run this code as a Go routine, it will run in the background, which won't block the rest of our application. The preceding code will keep watching the three channels inside our room: `join`, `leave`, and `forward`. If a message is received on any of those channels, the `select` statement will run the code for that particular case. It is important to remember that it will only run one block of case code at a time. This is how we are able to synchronize to ensure that our `r.clients` map is only ever modified by one thing at a time.

If we receive a message on the `join` channel, we simply update the `r.clients` map to keep a reference of the client that has joined the room. Notice that we are setting the value to `true`. We are using the map more like a slice, but do not have to worry about shrinking the slice as clients come and go through time—setting the value to `true` is just a handy, low-memory way of storing the reference.

If we receive a message on the `leave` channel, we simply delete the `client` type from the map, and close its `send` channel. Closing a channel has special significance in Go, which becomes clear when we look at our final `select` case.

If we receive a message on the `forward` channel, we iterate over all the clients and `send` the message down each client's send channel. Then, the `write` method of our client type will pick it up and send it down the socket to the browser. If the `send` channel is closed, then we know the client is not receiving any more messages, and this is where our second `select` clause (specifically the default case) takes the action of removing the client from the room and tidying things up.

Turning a room into an HTTP handler

Now we are going to turn our `room` type into an `http.Handler` type like we did with the template handler earlier. As you will recall, to do this, we must simply add a method called `ServeHTTP` with the appropriate signature. Add the following code to the bottom of the `room.go` file:

```
const (
  socketBufferSize  = 1024
  messageBufferSize = 256
)
```

```
var upgrader = &websocket.Upgrader{ReadBufferSize:
socketBufferSize, WriteBufferSize: socketBufferSize}
func (r *room) ServeHTTP(w http.ResponseWriter, req *http.Request) {
  socket, err := upgrader.Upgrade(w, req, nil)
  if err != nil {
    log.Fatal("ServeHTTP:", err)
    return
  }
  client := &client{
    socket: socket,
    send:   make(chan []byte, messageBufferSize),
    room:   r,
  }
  r.join <- client
  defer func() { r.leave <- client }()
  go client.write()
  client.read()
}
```

The ServeHTTP method means a room can now act as a handler. We will implement it shortly, but first let's have a look at what is going on in this snippet of code.

In order to use web sockets, we must upgrade the HTTP connection using the websocket.Upgrader type, which is reusable so we need only create one. Then, when a request comes in via the ServeHTTP method, we get the socket by calling the upgrader.Upgrade method. All being well, we then create our client and pass it into the join channel for the current room. We also defer the leaving operation for when the client is finished, which will ensure everything is tidied up after a user goes away.

The write method for the client is then called as a Go routine, as indicated by the three characters at the beginning of the line go (the word go followed by a space character). This tells Go to run the method in a different thread or goroutine.

> Compare the amount of code needed to achieve multithreading or concurrency in other languages with the three key presses that achieve it in Go, and you will see why it has become a favorite among systems developers.

Finally, we call the `read` method in the main thread, which will block operations (keeping the connection alive) until it's time to close it. Adding constants at the top of the snippet is a good practice for declaring values that would otherwise be hardcoded throughout the project. As these grow in number, you might consider putting them in a file of their own, or at least at the top of their respective files so they remain easy to read and modify.

Use helper functions to remove complexity

Our room is almost ready to use, although in order for it to be of any use, the channels and map need to be created. As it is, this could be achieved by asking the developer to use the following code to be sure to do this:

```
r := &room{
  forward: make(chan []byte),
  join:    make(chan *client),
  leave:   make(chan *client),
  clients: make(map[*client]bool),
}
```

Another, slightly more elegant, solution is to instead provide a `newRoom` function that does this for us. This removes the need for others to know about exactly what needs to be done in order for our room to be useful. Underneath the `type room struct` definition, add this function:

```
// newRoom makes a new room that is ready to go.
func newRoom() *room {
  return &room{
    forward: make(chan []byte),
    join:    make(chan *client),
    leave:   make(chan *client),
    clients: make(map[*client]bool),
  }
}
```

Now the users of our code need only call the `newRoom` function instead of the more verbose six lines of code.

Creating and using rooms

Let's update our `main` function in `main.go` to first create and then run a room for everybody to connect to:

```go
func main() {
  r := newRoom()
  http.Handle("/", &templateHandler{filename: "chat.html"})
  http.Handle("/room", r)
  // get the room going
  go r.run()
  // start the web server
  if err := http.ListenAndServe(":8080", nil); err != nil {
    log.Fatal("ListenAndServe:", err)
  }
}
```

We are running the room in a separate Go routine (notice the `go` keyword again) so that the chatting operations occur in the background, allowing our main thread to run the web server. Our server is now finished and successfully built, but remains useless without clients to interact with.

Building an HTML and JavaScript chat client

In order for the users of our chat application to interact with the server and therefore other users, we need to write some client-side code that makes use of the web sockets found in modern browsers. We are already delivering HTML content via the template when users hit the root of our application, so we can enhance that.

Update the `chat.html` file in the `templates` folder with the following markup:

```html
<html>
  <head>
    <title>Chat</title>
    <style>
      input { display: block; }
      ul    { list-style: none; }
    </style>
  </head>
  <body>
    <ul id="messages"></ul>
```

```
<form id="chatbox">
  <textarea></textarea>
  <input type="submit" value="Send" />
  </form>    </body>
</html>
```

The preceding HTML will render a simple web form on the page containing a text area and a **Send** button—this is how our users will submit messages to the server. The messages element in the preceding code will contain the text of the chat messages so that all the users can see what is being said. Next, we need to add some JavaScript to add some functionality to our page. Underneath the form tag, above the closing </body> tag, insert the following code:

```
<script
src="//ajax.googleapis.com/ajax/libs/jquery/1.11.1/jquery.min.js">
</script>
  <script>
    $(function(){
      var socket = null;
      var msgBox = $("#chatbox textarea");
      var messages = $("#messages");
      $("#chatbox").submit(function(){
        if (!msgBox.val()) return false;
        if (!socket) {
          alert("Error: There is no socket connection.");
          return false;
        }
        socket.send(msgBox.val());
        msgBox.val("");
        return false;
      });
      if (!window["WebSocket"]) {
        alert("Error: Your browser does not support web
sockets.")
      } else {
        socket = new WebSocket("ws://localhost:8080/room");
        socket.onclose = function() {
          alert("Connection has been closed.");
        }
        socket.onmessage = function(e) {
          messages.append($("<li>").text(e.data));
        }
      }
```

```
    });
  </script>
```

The `socket = new WebSocket("ws://localhost:8080/room")` line is where we open the socket and add event handlers for two key events: `onclose` and `onmessage`. When the socket receives a message, we use jQuery to append the message to the list element and thus present it to the user.

Submitting the HTML form triggers a call to `socket.send`, which is how we send messages to the server.

Build and run the program again to ensure the templates recompile so these changes are represented.

Navigate to `http://localhost:8080/` in two separate browsers (or two tabs of the same browser) and play with the application. You will notice that messages sent from one client appear instantly in the other clients.

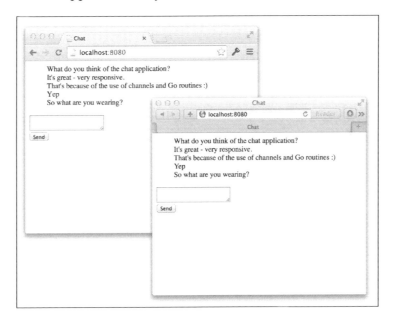

Getting more out of templates

Currently, we are using templates to deliver static HTML, which is nice because it gives us a clean and simple way to separate the client code from the server code. However, templates are actually much more powerful, and we are going to tweak our application to make some more realistic use of them.

The host address of our application (`:8080`) is hardcoded in two places at the moment. The first instance is in `main.go` where we start the web server:

```
if err := http.ListenAndServe(":8080", nil); err != nil {
  log.Fatal("ListenAndServe:", err)
}
```

The second time it is hardcoded in the JavaScript when we open the socket:

```
socket = new WebSocket("ws://localhost:8080/room");
```

Our chat application is pretty stubborn if it insists on only running locally on port 8080, so we are going to use command-line flags to make it configurable and then use the injection capabilities of templates to make sure our JavaScript knows the right host.

Update your `main` function in `main.go`:

```
func main() {
  var addr = flag.String("addr", ":8080", "The addr of the
application.")
  flag.Parse() // parse the flags
  r := newRoom()
  http.Handle("/", &templateHandler{filename: "chat.html"})
  http.Handle("/room", r)
  // get the room going
  go r.run()
  // start the web server
  log.Println("Starting web server on", *addr)
  if err := http.ListenAndServe(*addr, nil); err != nil {
    log.Fatal("ListenAndServe:", err)
  }
}
```

You will need to import the `flag` package in order for this code to build. The definition for the `addr` variable sets up our flag as a string that defaults to `:8080` (with a short description of what the value is intended for). We must call `flag.Parse()` that parses the arguments and extracts the appropriate information. Then, we can reference the value of the host flag by using `*addr`.

> The call to `flag.String` returns a type of `*string`, which is to say it returns the address of a string variable where the value of the flag is stored. To get the value itself (and not the address of the value), we must use the pointer indirection operator, `*`.

We also added a `log.Println` call to output the address in the terminal so we can be sure that our changes have taken effect.

We are going to modify the `templateHandler` type we wrote so that it passes the details of the request as data into the template's `Execute` method. In `main.go`, update the `ServeHTTP` function to pass the request `r` as the `data` argument to the `Execute` method:

```
func (t *templateHandler) ServeHTTP(w http.ResponseWriter, r
*http.Request) {
  t.once.Do(func() {
    t.templ =
template.Must(template.ParseFiles(filepath.Join("templates",
t.filename)))
  })
  t.templ.Execute(w, r)
}
```

This tells the template to render itself using data that can be extracted from `http.Request`, which happens to include the host address that we need.

To use the `Host` value of `http.Request`, we can then make use of the special template syntax that allows us to inject data. Update the line where we create our socket in the `chat.html` file:

```
socket = new WebSocket("ws://{{.Host}}/room");
```

The double curly braces represent an annotation and the way we tell our template source to inject data. `{{.Host}}` is essentially the equivalent of telling it to replace the annotation with the value from `request.Host` (since we passed the request `r` object in as data).

 We have only scratched the surface of the power of the templates built into Go's standard library. The `text/template` package documentation is a great place to learn more about what you can achieve. You can find out more about it at `http://golang.org/pkg/text/template`.

Rebuild and run the chat program again, but this time notice that the chatting operations no longer produce an error, whichever host we specify:

```
go build -o chat
./chat -addr=":3000"
```

View the source of the page in the browser and notice that `{{.Host}}` has been replaced with the actual host of the application. Valid hosts aren't just port numbers; you can also specify the IP addresses or other hostnames—provided they are allowed in your environment, for example, `-addr="192.168.0.1:3000"`.

Tracing code to get a look under the hood

The only way we will know that our application is working is by opening two or more browsers and using our UI to send messages. In other words, we are manually testing our code. This is fine for experimental projects such as our chat application or small projects that aren't expected to grow, but if our code is to have a longer life or be worked on by more than one person, manual testing of this kind becomes a liability. We are not going to tackle **Test-driven Development** (TDD) for our chat program, but we should explore another useful debugging technique called **tracing**.

Tracing is a practice by which we log or print key steps in the flow of a program to make what is going on under the covers visible. In the previous section, we added a `log.Println` call to output the address that the chat program was binding to. In this section, we are going to formalize this and write our own complete tracing package.

We are going to explore TDD practices when writing our tracing code because it is a perfect example of a package that we are likely to reuse, add to, share, and hopefully, even open source.

Writing a package using TDD

Packages in Go are organized into folders, with one package per folder. It is a build error to have differing package declarations within the same folder because all sibling files are expected to contribute to a single package. Go has no concept of subpackages, which means nested packages (in nested folders) exist only for aesthetic or informational reasons but do not inherit any functionality or visibility from super packages. In our chat application, all of our files contributed to the `main` package because we wanted to build an executable tool. Our tracing package will never be run directly, so it can and should use a different package name. We will also need to think about the **Application Programming Interface** (API) of our package, considering how to model a package so that it remains as extensible and flexible as possible for users. This includes the fields, functions, methods, and types that should be exported (visible to the user) and remain hidden for simplicity's sake.

Go uses capitalization of names to denote which items are exported such that names that begin with a capital letter (for example, `Tracer`) are visible to users of a package, and names that begin with a lowercase letter (for example, `templateHandler`) are hidden or private.

Create a new folder called `trace`, which will be the name of our tracing package, alongside the `chat` folder.

Before we jump into the code, let's agree on some design goals for our package by which we can measure success:

- The package should be easy to use
- Unit tests should cover the functionality
- Users should have the flexibility to replace the tracer with their own implementation

Interfaces

Interfaces in Go are an extremely powerful language feature that allow us to define an API without being strict or specific on the implementation details. Wherever possible, describing the basic building blocks of your packages using interfaces usually ends up paying dividends down the road, and this is where we will start for our tracing package.

Create a new file called `tracer.go` inside the `trace` folder and write the following code:

```
package trace
// Tracer is the interface that describes an object capable of
// tracing events throughout code.
type Tracer interface {
  Trace(...interface{})
}
```

The first thing to notice is that we have defined our package as `trace`.

 While it is a good practice to have the folder name match the package name, Go tools do not enforce it, which means you are free to name them differently if it makes sense. Remember, when people import your package, they will type the name of the folder, and if suddenly a package with a different name is imported, it could get confusing.

Our `Tracer` type (the capital `T` means we intend this to be a publicly visible type) is an interface that describes a single method called `Trace`. The `...interface{}` argument type states that our `Trace` method will accept zero or more arguments of any type. You might think that this is redundant since the method should just take a single string (we want to just trace out some string of characters, don't we?). However, consider functions such as `fmt.Sprint` and `log.Fatal`, both of which follow a pattern littered through to Go's standard library that provides a helpful shortcut when trying to communicate multiple things in one go. Wherever possible, we should follow such patterns and practices because we want our own APIs to be familiar and clear to the Go community.

Unit tests

We promised ourselves we would follow test-driven practices, but interfaces are simply definitions that do not provide any implementation and so cannot be directly tested. But we are about to write a real implementation of a `Tracer` method, and we will indeed write the tests first.

Create a new file called `tracer_test.go` in the `trace` folder and insert the following scaffold code:

```
package trace
import (
  "testing"
)
func TestNew(t *testing.T) {
  t.Error("We haven't written our test yet")
}
```

Testing was built into the Go tool chain from the very beginning, making writing automatable tests a first-class citizen. The test code lives alongside the production code in files suffixed with `_test.go`. The Go tools will treat any function that starts with `Test` (taking a single `*testing.T` argument) as a unit test, and it will be executed when we run our tests. To run them for this package, navigate to the `trace` folder in a terminal and do the following:

```
go test
```

You will see that our tests fail because of our call to `t.Error` in the body of our `TestNew` function:

```
--- FAIL: TestNew (0.00 seconds)
```

```
    tracer_test.go:8: We haven't written our test yet
FAIL
exit status 1
FAIL    trace    0.011s
```

 Clearing the terminal before each test run is a great way to make sure you aren't confusing previous runs with the most recent one. On Windows, you can use the `cls` command; on Unix machines, the `clear` command does the same thing.

Obviously, we haven't properly written our test and we don't expect it to pass yet, so let's update the `TestNew` function:

```go
func TestNew(t *testing.T) {
  var buf bytes.Buffer
  tracer := New(&buf)
  if tracer == nil {
    t.Error("Return from New should not be nil")
  } else {
    tracer.Trace("Hello trace package.")
    if buf.String() != "Hello trace package.\n" {
      t.Errorf("Trace should not write '%s'.", buf.String())
    }
  }
}
```

Most packages throughout the book are available from the Go standard library, so you can add an `import` statement for the appropriate package in order to access the package. Others are external, and that's when you need to use `go get` to download them before they can be imported. For this case, you'll need to add `import "bytes"` to the top of the file.

We have started designing our API by becoming the first user of it. We want to be able to capture the output of our tracer in a `bytes.Buffer` so that we can then ensure that the string in the buffer matches the expected value. If it does not, a call to `t.Errorf` will fail the test. Before that, we check to make sure the return from a made-up `New` function is not `nil`; again, if it is, the test will fail because of the call to `t.Error`.

Red-green testing

Running `go test` now actually produces an error; it complains that there is no `New` function. We haven't made a mistake here; we are following a practice known as red-green testing. Red-green testing proposes that we first write a unit test, see it fail (or produce an error), write the minimum amount of code possible to make that test pass, and rinse and repeat it again. The key point here being that we want to make sure the code we add is actually doing something as well as ensuring that the test code we write is testing something meaningful.

Consider a meaningless test for a minute:

```
if true == true {
  t.Error("True should be true")
}
```

It is logically impossible for true to not be true (if true ever equals false, it's time to get a new computer), and so our test is pointless. If a test or claim cannot fail, there is no value whatsoever to be found in it.

Replacing `true` with a variable that you expect to be set to `true` under certain conditions would mean that such a test can indeed fail (like when the code being tested is misbehaving) — at this point, you have a meaningful test that is worth contributing to the code base.

You can treat the output of `go test` like a to-do list, solving only one problem at a time. Right now, the complaint about the missing `New` function is all we will address. In the `trace.go` file, let's add the minimum amount of code possible to progress with things; add the following snippet underneath the interface type definition:

```
func New() {}
```

Running `go test` now shows us that things have indeed progressed, albeit not very far. We now have two errors:

```
./tracer_test.go:11: too many arguments in call to New
```

```
./tracer_test.go:11: New(&buf) used as value
```

The first error tells us that we are passing arguments to our `New` function, but the `New` function doesn't accept any. The second error says that we are using the return of the `New` function as a value, but that the `New` function doesn't return anything. You might have seen this coming, and indeed as you gain more experience writing test-driven code, you will most likely jump over such trivial details. However, to properly illustrate the method, we are going to be pedantic for a while. Let's address the first error by updating our `New` function to take in the expected argument:

```
func New(w io.Writer) {}
```

We are taking an argument that satisfies the `io.Writer` interface, which means that the specified object must have a suitable `Write` method.

 Using existing interfaces, especially ones found in the Go standard library, is an extremely powerful and often necessary way to ensure that your code is as flexible and elegant as possible.

Accepting `io.Writer` means that the user can decide where the tracing output will be written. This output could be the standard output, a file, network socket, `bytes.Buffer` as in our test case, or even some custom-made object, provided it implements the `Write` method of the `io.Writer` interface

Running `go test` again shows us that we have resolved the first error and we only need add a return type in order to progress past our second error:

```
func New(w io.Writer) Tracer {}
```

We are stating that our `New` function will return a `Tracer`, but we do not return anything, which `go test` happily complains about:

`./tracer.go:13: missing return at end of function`

Fixing this is easy; we can just return `nil` from the `New` function:

```
func New(w io.Writer) Tracer {
   return nil
}
```

Of course, our test code has asserted that the return should not be `nil`, so `go test` now gives us a failure message:

`tracer_test.go:14: Return from New should not be nil`

 You can see how a strict adherence to the red-green principle can get a little tedious, but it is vital that we do not jump too far ahead. If we were to write a lot of implementation code in one go, we will very likely have code that is not covered by a unit test.

The ever-thoughtful core team has even solved this problem for us by providing code coverage statistics which we can generate by running the following command:

`go test -cover`

Provided that all tests pass, adding the `-cover` flag will tell us how much of our code was touched during the execution of the tests. Obviously, the closer we get to 100 percent the better.

Implementing the interface

To satisfy this test, we need something that we can properly return from the New method because Tracer is only an interface and we have to return something real. Let's add an implementation of a tracer to our tracer.go file:

```
type tracer struct {
  out io.Writer
}

func (t *tracer) Trace(a ...interface{}) {}
```

Our implementation is extremely simple; the tracer type has an io.Writer field called out which is where we will write the trace output to. And the Trace method exactly matches the method required by the Tracer interface, although it doesn't do anything yet.

Now we can finally fix the New method:

```
func New(w io.Writer) Tracer {
  return &tracer{out: w}
}
```

Running go test again shows us that our expectation was not met because nothing was written during our call to Trace:

tracer_test.go:18: Trace should not write ''.

Let's update our Trace method to write the blended arguments to the specified io.Writer field:

```
func (t *tracer) Trace(a ...interface{}) {
  t.out.Write([]byte(fmt.Sprint(a...)))
  t.out.Write([]byte("\n"))
}
```

When the Trace method is called, we call Write on the io.Writer stored in the out field and use fmt.Sprint to format the a arguments. We convert the string return type from fmt.Sprint to string and then to []byte because that is what is expected by the io.Writer interface.

Have we finally satisfied our test?

go test -cover

PASS

```
coverage: 100.0% of statements
ok      trace   0.011s
```

Congratulations! We have successfully passed our test and have `100.0%` test coverage. Once we have finished our glass of champagne, we can take a minute to consider something very interesting about our implementation.

Unexported types being returned to users

The `tracer` struct type we wrote is unexported because it begins with a lowercase `t`, so how is it that we are able to return it from the exported `New` function? After all, doesn't the user receive the returned object? This is perfectly acceptable and valid Go code; the user will only ever see an object that satisfies the `Tracer` interface and will never even know about our private `tracer` type. Since they only ever interact with the interface anyway, it wouldn't matter if our `tracer` implementation exposed other methods or fields; they would never be seen. This allows us to keep the public API of our package clean and simple.

This hidden implementation technique is used throughout the Go standard library, for example, the `ioutil.NopCloser` method is a function that turns a normal `io.Reader` into `io.ReadCloser` whereas the `Close` method does nothing (used for when `io.Reader` objects that don't need to be closed are passed into functions that require `io.ReadCloser` types). The method returns `io.ReadCloser` as far as the user is concerned, but under the hood, there is a secret `nopCloser` type hiding the implementation details.

 To see this for yourself, browse the Go standard library source code at `http://golang.org/src/pkg/io/ioutil/ioutil.go` and search for the `nopCloser` struct.

Using our new trace package

Now that we have completed the first version of our `trace` package, we can use it in our chat application in order to better understand what is going on when users send messages through the user interface.

In `room.go`, let's import our new package and make some calls to the `Trace` method. The path to the `trace` package we just wrote will depend on your `GOPATH` environment variable because the import path is relative to the `$GOPATH/src` folder. So if you create your `trace` package in `$GOPATH/src/mycode/trace`, then you would need to import `mycode/trace`.

Update the room type and the run() method like this:

```go
type room struct {
  // forward is a channel that holds incoming messages
  // that should be forwarded to the other clients.
  forward chan []byte
  // join is a channel for clients wishing to join the room.
  join chan *client
  // leave is a channel for clients wishing to leave the room.
  leave chan *client
  // clients holds all current clients in this room.
  clients map[*client]bool
  // tracer will receive trace information of activity
  // in the room.
  tracer trace.Tracer
}
func (r *room) run() {
  for {
    select {
    case client := <-r.join:
      // joining
      r.clients[client] = true
      r.tracer.Trace("New client joined")
    case client := <-r.leave:
      // leaving
      delete(r.clients, client)
      close(client.send)
      r.tracer.Trace("Client left")
    case msg := <-r.forward:
      r.tracer.Trace("Message received: ", string(msg))
      // forward message to all clients
      for client := range r.clients {
        select {
        case client.send <- msg:
          // send the message
          r.tracer.Trace(" -- sent to client")
        default:
          // failed to send
          delete(r.clients, client)
          close(client.send)
          r.tracer.Trace(" -- failed to send, cleaned up client")
        }
      }
    }
  }
}
```

We added a `trace.Tracer` field to our `room` type and then made periodic calls to the `Trace` method peppered throughout the code. If we run our program and try to send messages, you'll notice that the application panics because the `tracer` field is `nil`. We can remedy this for now by making sure we create and assign an appropriate object when we create our `room` type. Update the `main.go` file to do this:

```
r := newRoom()
r.tracer = trace.New(os.Stdout)
```

We are using our `New` method to create an object that will send the output to the `os.Stdout` standard output pipe (this is a technical way of saying we want it to print the output to our terminal).

Now rebuild and run the program and use two browsers to play with the application, and notice that the terminal now has some interesting trace information for us:

```
New client joined
New client joined
Message received: Hello Chat
  -- sent to client
  -- sent to client
Message received: Good morning :)
  -- sent to client
  -- sent to client
Client left
Client left
```

Now we are able to use the debug information to get an insight into what the application is doing, which will assist us when developing and supporting our project.

Making tracing optional

Once the application is released, the sort of tracing information we are generating will be pretty useless if it's just printed out to some terminal somewhere, or even worse, if it creates a lot of noise for our systems administrators. Also, remember that when we don't set a tracer for our `room` type, our code panics, which isn't a very user-friendly situation. To resolve these two issues, we are going to enhance our `trace` package with a `trace.Off()` method that will return an object that satisfies the `Tracer` interface but will not do anything when the `Trace` method is called.

Let's add a test that calls the Off function to get a silent tracer before making a call to Trace to ensure the code doesn't panic. Since the tracing won't happen, that's all we can do in our test code. Add the following test function to the tracer_test.go file:

```go
func TestOff(t *testing.T) {
    var silentTracer Tracer = Off()
    silentTracer.Trace("something")
}
```

To make it pass, add the following code to the tracer.go file:

```go
type nilTracer struct{}
func (t *nilTracer) Trace(a ...interface{}) {}
// Off creates a Tracer that will ignore calls to Trace.
func Off() Tracer {
    return &nilTracer{}
}
```

Our nilTracer struct has defined a Trace method that does nothing, and a call to the Off() method will create a new nilTracer struct and return it. Notice that our nilTracer struct differs from our tracer struct in that it doesn't take an io.Writer; it doesn't need one because it isn't going to write anything.

Now let's solve our second problem by updating our newRoom method in the room. go file:

```go
func newRoom() *room {
    return &room{
        forward: make(chan []byte),
        join:    make(chan *client),
        leave:   make(chan *client),
        clients: make(map[*client]bool),
        tracer:  trace.Off(),
    }
}
```

By default, our room type will be created with a nilTracer struct and any calls to Trace will just be ignored. You can try this out by removing the r.tracer = trace. New(os.Stdout) line from the main.go file: notice that nothing gets written to the terminal when you use the application and there is no panic.

Clean package APIs

A quick glance at the API (in this context, the exposed variables, methods, and types) for our trace package highlights that a simple and obvious design has emerged:

- The New() method
- The Off() method
- The Tracer interface

I would be very confident to give this package to a Go programmer without any documentation or guidelines, and I'm pretty sure they would know what do to with it.

 In Go, adding documentation is as simple as adding comments to the line before each item. The blog post on the subject is a worthwhile read (http://blog.golang.org/godoc-documenting-go-code), where you can see a copy of the hosted source code for tracer.go that is an example of how you might annotate the trace package. For more information, refer to github.com/matryer/goblueprints/blob/master/chapter1/trace/tracer.go.

Summary

In this chapter, we developed a complete concurrent chat application and our own simple package to trace the flow of our programs to help us better understand what is going on under the hood.

We used the net/http package to quickly build what turned out to be a very powerful concurrent HTTP web server. In one particular case, we then upgraded the connection to open a web socket between the client and server. This means that we can easily and quickly communicate messages to the user's web browser without having to write messy polling code. We explored how templates are useful to separate the code from the content as well as to allow us to inject data into our template source, which let us make the host address configurable. Command-line flags helped us give simple configuration control to the people hosting our application while also letting us specify sensible defaults.

Our chat application made use of Go's powerful concurrency capabilities that allowed us to write clear *threaded* code in just a few lines of idiomatic Go. By controlling the coming and going of clients through channels, we were able to set synchronization points in our code that prevented us from corrupting memory by attempting to modify the same objects at the same time.

We learned how interfaces such as `http.Handler` and our own `trace.Tracer` allow us to provide disparate implementations without having to touch the code that makes use of them, and in some cases, without having to expose even the name of the implementation to our users. We saw how just by adding a `ServeHTTP` method to our `room` type, we turned our custom room concept into a valid HTTP handler object, which managed our web socket connections.

We aren't actually very far away from being able to properly release our application, except for one major oversight: you cannot see who sent each message. We have no concept of users or even user names, and for a real chat application, this is not acceptable.

In the next chapter, we will add the names of the people responding to their messages in order to make them feel like they are having a real conversation with other humans.

2

Adding Authentication

The chat application we built in the previous chapter focused on high-performance transmission of messages from the clients to the server and back again, but our users have no way of knowing who they are talking to. One solution to this problem is building of some kind of signup and login functionality and letting our users create accounts and authenticate themselves before they can open the chat page.

Whenever we are about to build something from scratch, we must ask ourselves how others have solved this problem before (it is extremely rare to encounter genuinely original problems), and whether any open solutions or standards already exist that we can make use of. Authorization and authentication are hardly new problems, especially in the world of the Web, with many different protocols out there to choose from. So how do we decide on the best option to pursue? As always, we must look at this question from the point of view of the user.

A lot of websites these days allow you to sign in using your accounts existing elsewhere on a variety of social media or community websites. This saves users the tedious job of entering all their account information over and over again as they decide to try out different products and services. It also has a positive effect on the conversion rates for new sites.

In this chapter, we will enhance our chat codebase to add authentication, which will allow our users to sign in using Google, Facebook, or GitHub and you'll see how easy it is to add other sign-in portals too. In order to join the chat, users must first sign in. Following this, we will use the authorized data to augment our user experience so everyone knows who is in the room, and who said what.

In this chapter, you will learn to:

- Use the decorator pattern to wrap `http.Handler` types to add additional functionality to handlers
- Serve HTTP endpoints with dynamic paths

- Use the Gomniauth open source project to access authentication services
- Get and set cookies using the `http` package
- Encode objects as Base64 and back to normal again
- Send and receive JSON data over a web socket
- Give different types of data to templates
- Work with channels of your own types

Handlers all the way down

For our chat application, we implemented our own `http.Handler` type in order to easily compile, execute, and deliver HTML content to browsers. Since this is a very simple but powerful interface, we are going to continue to use it wherever possible when adding functionality to our HTTP processing.

In order to determine whether a user is authenticated, we will create an authentication wrapper handler that performs the check, and passes execution on to the inner handler only if the user is authenticated.

Our wrapper handler will satisfy the same `http.Handler` interface as the object inside it, allowing us to wrap any valid handler. In fact, even the authentication handler we are about to write could be later encapsulated inside a similar wrapper if needed.

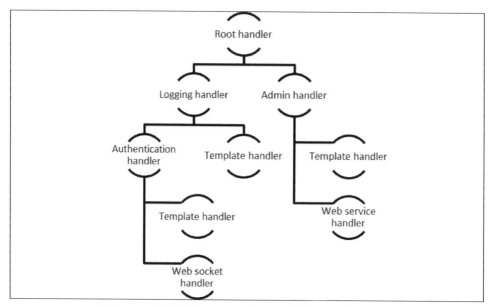

Diagram of a chaining pattern when applied to HTTP handlers

The preceding figure shows how this pattern could be applied in a more complicated HTTP handler scenario. Each object implements the `http.Handler` interface, which means that object could be passed into the `http.Handle` method to directly handle a request, or it can be given to another object, which adds some kind of extra functionality. The `Logging` handler might write to a logfile before and after the `ServeHTTP` method is called on the inner handler. Because the inner handler is just another `http.Handler`, any other handler can be wrapped in (or decorated with) the `Logging` handler.

It is also common for an object to contain logic that decides which inner handler should be executed. For example, our authentication handler will either pass the execution to the wrapped handler, or handle the request itself by issuing a redirect to the browser.

That's plenty of theory for now; let's write some code. Create a new file called `auth.go` in the `chat` folder:

```go
package main
import (
  "net/http"
)
type authHandler struct {
  next http.Handler
}
func (h *authHandler) ServeHTTP(w http.ResponseWriter, r
*http.Request) {
  if _, err := r.Cookie("auth"); err == http.ErrNoCookie {
    // not authenticated
    w.Header().Set("Location", "/login")
    w.WriteHeader(http.StatusTemporaryRedirect)
  } else if err != nil {
    // some other error
    panic(err.Error())
  } else {
    // success - call the next handler
    h.next.ServeHTTP(w, r)
  }
}
func MustAuth(handler http.Handler) http.Handler {
  return &authHandler{next: handler}
}
```

The authHandler type not only implements the ServeHTTP method (which satisfies the http.Handler interface) but also stores (wraps) http.Handler in the next field. Our MustAuth helper function simply creates authHandler that wraps any other http.Handler. Let's tweak the following root mapping line:

```
http.Handle("/", &templateHandler{filename: "chat.html"})
```

Let's change the first argument to make it explicit about the page meant for chatting. Next, let's use the MustAuth function to wrap templateHandler for the second argument:

```
http.Handle("/chat", MustAuth(&templateHandler{filename:
"chat.html"}))
```

Wrapping templateHandler with the MustAuth function will cause execution to run first through our authHandler, and only to templateHandler if the request is authenticated.

The ServeHTTP method in our authHandler will look for a special cookie called auth, and use the Header and WriteHeader methods on http.ResponseWriter to redirect the user to a login page if the cookie is missing.

Build and run the chat application and try to hit http://localhost:8080/chat:

```
go build -o chat
./chat -host=":8080"
```

 You need to delete your cookies to clear out previous auth tokens, or any other cookies that might be left over from other development projects served through localhost.

If you look in the address bar of your browser, you will notice that you are immediately redirected to the /login page. Since we cannot handle that path yet, you'll just get a **404 page not found** error.

Making a pretty social sign-in page

So far we haven't paid much attention to making our application look nice, after all this book is about Go and not user-interface development. However, there is no excuse for building ugly apps, and so we will build a social sign-in page that is as pretty as it is functional.

Bootstrap is a frontend framework used to develop responsive projects on the Web. It provides CSS and JavaScript code that solve many user-interface problems in a consistent and good-looking way. While sites built using Bootstrap all tend to look the same (although there are plenty of ways in which the UI can be customized), it is a great choice for early versions of apps, or for developers who don't have access to designers.

If you build your application using the semantic standards set forth by Bootstrap, it becomes easy for you to make a Bootstrap theme for your site or application and you know it will slot right into your code.

We will use the version of Bootstrap hosted on a CDN so we don't have to worry about downloading and serving our own version through our chat application. This means that in order to render our pages properly, we will need an active Internet connection, even during development.

If you prefer to download and host your own copy of Bootstrap, you can do so. Keep the files in an `assets` folder and add the following call to your `main` function (it uses `http.Handle` to serve the assets via your application):

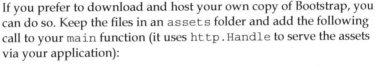

```
http.Handle("/assets/", http.StripPrefix("/assets",
http.FileServer(http.Dir("/path/to/assets/"))))
```

Notice how the `http.StripPrefix` and `http.FileServer` functions return objects that satisfy the `http.Handler` interface as per the decorator pattern that we implement with our `MustAuth` helper function.

In `main.go`, let's add an endpoint for the login page:

```
http.Handle("/chat", MustAuth(&templateHandler{filename:
"chat.html"}))
http.Handle("/login", &templateHandler{filename: "login.html"})
http.Handle("/room", r)
```

Obviously, we do not want to use the `MustAuth` method for our login page because it will cause an infinite redirection loop.

Create a new file called `login.html` inside our `templates` folder, and insert the following HTML code:

```
<html>
  <head>
    <title>Login</title>
    <link rel="stylesheet"
```

```
        href="//netdna.bootstrapcdn.com/bootstrap/3.1.1/css/
        bootstrap.min.css">
   </head>
   <body>
     <div class="container">
       <div class="page-header">
         <h1>Sign in</h1>
       </div>
       <div class="panel panel-danger">
         <div class="panel-heading">
           <h3 class="panel-title">In order to chat, you must be
             signed in</h3>
         </div>
         <div class="panel-body">
           <p>Select the service you would like to sign in
             with:</p>
           <ul>
             <li>
               <a href="/auth/login/facebook">Facebook</a>
             </li>
             <li>
               <a href="/auth/login/github">GitHub</a>
             </li>
             <li>
               <a href="/auth/login/google">Google</a>
             </li>
           </ul>
         </div>
       </div>
     </div>
   </body>
</html>
```

Restart the web server and navigate to `http://localhost:8080/login`. You will notice that it now displays our sign-in page:

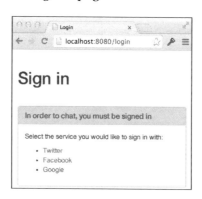

Endpoints with dynamic paths

Pattern matching for the `http` package in the Go standard library isn't the most comprehensive and fully featured implementation out there. For example, Ruby on Rails makes it much easier to have dynamic segments inside the path:

```
"auth/:action/:provider_name"
```

This then provides a data map (or dictionary) containing the values that the framework automatically extracted from the matched path. So if you visit `auth/login/google`, then `params[:provider_name]` would equal `google`, and `params[:action]` would equal `login`.

The most the `http` package lets us specify by default is a path prefix, which we can do by leaving a trailing slash at the end of the pattern:

```
"auth/"
```

We would then have to manually parse the remaining segments to extract the appropriate data. This is acceptable for relatively simple cases, which suits our needs for the time being since we only need to handle a few different paths such as:

- `/auth/login/google`
- `/auth/login/facebook`
- `/auth/callback/google`
- `/auth/callback/facebook`

 If you need to handle more advanced routing situations, you might want to consider using dedicated packages such as Goweb, Pat, Routes, or mux. For extremely simple cases such as ours, the built-in capabilities will do.

We are going to create a new handler that powers our login process. In `auth.go`, add the following `loginHandler` code:

```go
// loginHandler handles the third-party login process.
// format: /auth/{action}/{provider}
func loginHandler(w http.ResponseWriter, r *http.Request) {
  segs := strings.Split(r.URL.Path, "/")
  action := segs[2]
  provider := segs[3]
  switch action {
  case "login":
    log.Println("TODO handle login for", provider)
```

```
default:
    w.WriteHeader(http.StatusNotFound)
    fmt.Fprintf(w, "Auth action %s not supported", action)
    }
}
```

In the preceding code, we break the path into segments using `strings.Split` before pulling out the values for `action` and `provider`. If the action value is known, we will run the specific code; otherwise, we will write out an error message and return an `http.StatusNotFound` status code (which in the language of HTTP status code, is a `404` code).

We will not bullet-proof our code right now but it's worth noticing that if someone hits `loginHandler` with too few segments, our code will panic because it expects `segs[2]` and `segs[3]` to exist.

For extra credit, see whether you can protect against this and return a nice error message instead of a panic if someone hits `/auth/nonsense`.

Our `loginHandler` is only a function and not an object that implements the `http.Handler` interface. This is because, unlike other handlers, we don't need it to store any state. The Go standard library supports this, so we can use the `http.HandleFunc` function to map it in a way similar to how we used `http.Handle` earlier. In `main.go`, update the handlers:

```
http.Handle("/chat", MustAuth(&templateHandler{filename:
"chat.html"}))
http.Handle("/login", &templateHandler{filename: "login.html"})
http.HandleFunc("/auth/", loginHandler)
http.Handle("/room", r)
```

Rebuild and run the chat application:

```
go build -o chat
./chat -host=":8080"
```

Hit the following URLs and notice the output logged in the terminal:

- `http://localhost:8080/auth/login/google` outputs `TODO handle login for google`

- `http://localhost:8080/auth/login/facebook` outputs `TODO handle login for facebook`

We have successfully implemented a dynamic path-matching mechanism that so far just prints out to-do messages; next we need to write code that integrates with the authentication services.

OAuth2

OAuth2 is an open authentication and authorization standard designed to allow resource owners to give clients delegated access to private data (such as wall posts or tweets) via an access token exchange handshake. Even if you do not wish to access the private data, OAuth2 is a great option that allows people to sign in using their existing credentials, without exposing those credentials to a third-party site. In this case, we are the third party and we want to allow our users to sign in using services that support OAuth2.

From a user's point of view, the OAuth2 flow is:

1. A user selects provider with whom they wish to sign in to the client app.

2. The user is redirected to the provider's website (with a URL that includes the client app ID) where they are asked to give permission to the client app.

3. The user signs in from the OAuth2 service provider and accepts the permissions requested by the third-party application.

4. The user is redirected back to the client app with a request code.

5. In the background, the client app sends the grant code to the provider, who sends back an auth token.

6. The client app uses the access token to make authorized requests to the provider, such as to get user information or wall posts.

To avoid reinventing the wheel, we will look at a few open source projects that have already solved this problem for us.

Open source OAuth2 packages

Andrew Gerrand has been working on the core Go team since February 2010, that is two years before Go 1.0 was officially released. His `goauth2` package (see `https://code.google.com/p/goauth2/`) is an elegant implementation of the OAuth2 protocol written entirely in Go.

Andrew's project inspired Gomniauth (see `https://github.com/stretchr/gomniauth`). An open source Go alternative to Ruby's `omniauth` project, Gomniauth provides a unified solution to access different OAuth2 services. In the future, when OAuth3 (or whatever next-generation authentication protocol it is) comes out, in theory, Gomniauth could take on the pain of implementing the details, leaving the user code untouched.

For our application, we will use Gomniauth to access OAuth services provided by Google, Facebook, and GitHub, so make sure you have it installed by running the following command:

```
go get github.com/stretchr/gomniauth
```

 Some of the project dependencies of Gomniauth are kept in Bazaar repositories, so you'll need to head over to `http://wiki.bazaar.canonical.com` to download them.

Tell the authentication providers about your app

Before we ask an authentication provider to help our users sign in, we must tell them about our application. Most providers have some kind of web tool or console where you can create applications to kick-start the process. Here's one from Google:

In order to identify the client application, we need to create a client ID and secret. Despite the fact that OAuth2 is an open standard, each provider has their own language and mechanism to set things up, so you will most likely have to play around with the user interface or the documentation to figure it out in each case.

At the time of writing this, in **Google Developer Console**, you navigate to **APIs & auth | Credentials** and click on the **Create new Client ID** button.

In most cases, for added security, you have to be explicit about the host URLs from where requests will come. For now, since we're hosting our app locally on `localhost:8080`, you should use that. You will also be asked for a redirect URI that is the endpoint in our chat application and to which the user will be redirected after successfully signing in. The callback will be another action on our `loginHandler`, so the redirection URL for the Google client will be `http://localhost:8080/auth/callback/google`.

Once you finish the authentication process for the providers you want to support, you will be given a client ID and secret for each provider. Make a note of these, because we will need them when we set up the providers in our chat application.

> If we host our application on a real domain, we have to create new client IDs and secrets, or update the appropriate URL fields on our authentication providers to ensure that they point to the right place. Either way, it's not bad practice to have a different set of development and production keys for security.

Implementing external logging in

In order to make use of the projects, clients, or accounts that we created on the authentication provider sites, we have to tell Gomniauth which providers we want to use, and how we will interact with them. We do this by calling the `WithProviders` function on the primary Gomniauth package. Add the following code snippet to `main.go` (just underneath the `flag.Parse()` line towards the top of the `main` function):

```
// set up gomniauth
gomniauth.SetSecurityKey("some long key")
gomniauth.WithProviders(
  facebook.New("key", "secret",
    "http://localhost:8080/auth/callback/facebook"),
  github.New("key", "secret",
    "http://localhost:8080/auth/callback/github"),
  google.New("key", "secret",
    "http://localhost:8080/auth/callback/google"),
)
```

You should replace the `key` and `secret` placeholders with the actual values you noted down earlier. The third argument represents the callback URL that should match the ones you provided when creating your clients on the provider's website. Notice the second path segment is `callback`; while we haven't implemented this yet, this is where we handle the response from the authentication process.

As usual, you will need to ensure all the appropriate packages are imported:

```
import (
  "github.com/stretchr/gomniauth/providers/facebook"
  "github.com/stretchr/gomniauth/providers/github"
  "github.com/stretchr/gomniauth/providers/google"
)
```

Gomniauth requires the `SetSecurityKey` call because it sends state data between the client and server along with a signature checksum, which ensures that the state values haven't been tempered with while transmitting. The security key is used when creating the hash in a way that it is almost impossible to recreate the same hash without knowing the exact security key. You should replace `some long key` with a security hash or phrase of your choice.

Logging in

Now that we have configured Gomniauth, we need to redirect users to the provider's authentication page when they land on our `/auth/login/{provider}` path. We just have to update our `loginHandler` function in `auth.go`:

```
func loginHandler(w http.ResponseWriter, r *http.Request) {
  segs := strings.Split(r.URL.Path, "/")
  action := segs[2]
  provider := segs[3]
  switch action {
  case "login":
    provider, err := gomniauth.Provider(provider)
    if err != nil {
      log.Fatalln("Error when trying to get provider", provider,
"-", err)
    }
    loginUrl, err := provider.GetBeginAuthURL(nil, nil)
    if err != nil {
```

```
        log.Fatalln("Error when trying to GetBeginAuthURL for",
    provider, "-", err)
        }
        w.Header.Set("Location",loginUrl)
        w.WriteHeader(http.StatusTemporaryRedirect)
      default:
        w.WriteHeader(http.StatusNotFound)
        fmt.Fprintf(w, "Auth action %s not supported", action)
      }
    }
```

We do two main things here. First, we use the gomniauth.Provider function to get the provider object that matches the object specified in the URL (such as google or github). Then we use the GetBeginAuthURL method to get the location where we must send users in order to start the authentication process.

> The GetBeginAuthURL(nil, nil) arguments are for the state and options respectively, which we are not going to use for our chat application.
>
> The first argument is a state map of data that is encoded, and signed and sent to the authentication provider. The provider doesn't do anything with the state, it just sends it back to our callback endpoint. This is useful if, for example, we want to redirect the user back to the original page they were trying to access before the authentication process intervened. For our purpose, we have only the /chat endpoint, so we don't need to worry about sending any state.
>
> The second argument is a map of additional options that will be sent to the authentication provider, which somehow modifies the behavior of the authentication process. For example, you can specify your own scope parameter, which allows you to make a request for permission to access additional information from the provider. For more information about the available options, search for OAuth2 on the Internet or read the documentation for each provider, as these values differ from service to service.

If our code gets no error from the GetBeginAuthURL call, we simply redirect the user's browser to the returned URL.

Rebuild and run the chat application:

```
go build -o chat
./chat -host=":8080"
```

Open the main chat page by accessing `http://localhost:8080/chat`. As we aren't logged in yet, we are redirected to our sign-in page. Click on the Google option to sign in using your Google account, and you will notice that you are presented with a Google-specific sign-in page (if you are not already signed in to Google). Once you are signed in, you will be presented with a page asking you to give permission for our chat application before you can view basic information about your account:

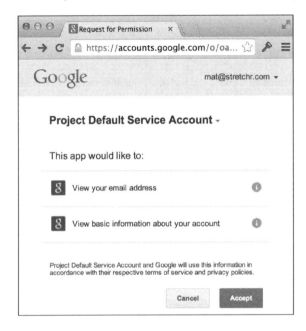

This is the same flow that users of our chat application will experience when signing in.

Click on **Accept** and you will notice that you are redirected back to our application code, but presented with an `Auth action callback not supported` error. This is because we haven't yet implemented the callback functionality in `loginHandler`.

Handling the response from the provider

Once the user clicks on **Accept** on the provider's website (or if they click on the equivalent of **Cancel**), they will be redirected back to the callback endpoint in our application.

A quick glance at the complete URL that comes back shows us the grant code that the provider has given us.

```
http://localhost:8080/auth/callback/google?code=4/Q92xJ-
BQfoX6PHhzkjhgtyfLc0Ylm.QqV4u9AbA9sYguyfbjFEsNoJKMOjQI
```

We don't have to worry about what to do with this code because Gomniauth will process the OAuth URL parameters for us (by sending the grant code to Google servers and exchanging it for an access token as per the OAuth specification), so we can simply jump to implementing our callback handler. However, it's worth knowing that this code will be exchanged by the authentication provider for a token that allows us to access private user data. For added security, this additional step happens behind the scenes, from server to server rather than in the browser.

In `auth.go`, we are ready to add another switch case to our action path segment. Insert the following code above the default case:

```
case "callback":

  provider, err := gomniauth.Provider(provider)
  if err != nil {
    log.Fatalln("Error when trying to get provider", provider, "-
", err)
  }

  creds, err :=
provider.CompleteAuth(objx.MustFromURLQuery(r.URL.RawQuery))
  if err != nil {
    log.Fatalln("Error when trying to complete auth for",
provider, "-", err)
  }

  user, err := provider.GetUser(creds)
  if err != nil {
    log.Fatalln("Error when trying to get user from", provider, "-
", err)
  }

  authCookieValue := objx.New(map[string]interface{}{
    "name": user.Name(),
  }).MustBase64()
  http.SetCookie(w, &http.Cookie{
    Name:   "auth",
    Value: authCookieValue,
    Path:   "/"})

  w.Header()["Location"] = []string{"/chat"}
  w.WriteHeader(http.StatusTemporaryRedirect)
```

When the authentication provider redirects the users back after they have granted permission, the URL specifies that it is a callback action. We look up the authentication provider as we did before, and call its `CompleteAuth` method. We parse the `RawQuery` from the `http.Request` (the `GET` request that the user's browser is now making) into `objx.Map` (the multi-purpose map type that Gomniauth uses) and the `CompleteAuth` method uses the URL query parameter values to complete the authentication handshake with the provider. All being well, we will be given some authorized credentials with which we access our user's basic data. We then use the `GetUser` method for the provider and Gomniauth uses the specified credentials to access some basic information about the user.

Once we have the user data, we Base64-encode the `Name` field in a JSON object and store it as the value to our `auth` cookie for later use.

 Base64-encoding of data ensures it won't contain any special or unpredictable characters, like passing data in a URL or storing it in a cookie. Remember that although Base64-encoded data looks encrypted, it is not—you can easily decode Base64-encoded data back into the original text with little effort. There are online tools that do this for you.

After setting the cookie, we redirect the user to the chat page, which we can safely assume was the original destination.

Once you build and run the code again and hit the `/chat` page, you will notice that the signup flow works, and we are finally allowed back to the chat page. Most browsers have an inspector or a console—a tool that allows you to view the cookies that the server has sent you—that you can use to see whether the `auth` cookie has appeared:

```
go build -o chat
./chat -host=":8080"
```

In our case, the cookie value is `eyJuYW1lIjoiTWF0IFJ5ZXIifQ==`, which is a Base64-encoded version of `{"name":"Mat Ryer"}`. Remember, we never typed in a name in our chat application; instead, Gomniauth asked Google for a name when we opted to sign in with Google. Storing non-signed cookies like this is fine for incidental information such as a user's name, however, you should avoid storing any sensitive information using non-signed cookies, as it's easy for people to access and change the data.

Presenting the user data

Having the user data inside a cookie is a good start, but nontechnical people will never even know it's there, so we must bring the data to the fore. We will do this by enhancing our templateHandler method that first passes the user data into the template's Execute method; this allows us to use template annotations in our HTML to display the user data to the users.

Update the ServeHTTP method of our templateHandler in main.go:

```
func (t *templateHandler) ServeHTTP(w http.ResponseWriter, r
*http.Request) {
  t.once.Do(func() {
    t.templ =
template.Must(template.ParseFiles(filepath.Join("templates",
t.filename)))
  })
  data := map[string]interface{}{
    "Host": r.Host,
  }
  if authCookie, err := r.Cookie("auth"); err == nil {
    data["UserData"] = objx.MustFromBase64(authCookie.Value)
  }

  t.templ.Execute(w, data)
}
```

Instead of just passing the entire http.Request object to our template as data, we are creating a new map[string]interface{} definition for a data object that potentially has two fields: Host and UserData (the latter will only appear if an auth cookie is present). By specifying the map type followed by curly braces, we are able to add the Host entry at the same time as making our map. We then pass this new data object as the second argument to the Execute method on our template.

Now we add an HTML file to our template source to display the name. Update the chatbox form in chat.html:

```
<form id="chatbox">
  {{.UserData.name}}:<br/>
  <textarea></textarea>
  <input type="submit" value="Send" />
</form>
```

The `{{.UserData.name}}` annotation tells the template engine to insert our user's name before the `textarea` control.

 Since we're using the `objx` package, don't forget to run `go get` `http://github.com/stretchr/objx`, and import it.

Rebuild and run the chat application again, and you will notice the addition of your name before the chat box:

```
go build -o chat
./chat -host=":8080"
```

Augmenting messages with additional data

So far, our chat application has only transmitted messages as slices of bytes or `[]` `byte` types between the client and the server; therefore, our forward channel for our room has the `chan []byte` type. In order to send data (such as who sent it and when) in addition to the message itself, we enhance our forward channel and also how we interact with the web socket on both ends.

Define a new type that will replace the `[]byte` slice by creating a new file called `message.go` in the `chat` folder:

```
package main
import (
  "time"
)
// message represents a single message
type message struct {
  Name    string
  Message string
  When    time.Time
}
```

The `message` type will encapsulate the message string itself, but we have also added the `Name` and `When` fields that respectively hold the user's name and a timestamp of when the message was sent.

Since the `client` type is responsible for communicating with the browser, it needs to transmit and receive more than just the single message string. As we are talking to a JavaScript application (that is the chat client running in the browser) and the Go standard library has a great JSON implementation, this seems the perfect choice to encode additional information in the messages. We will change the `read` and `write` methods in `client.go` to use the `ReadJSON` and `WriteJSON` methods on the socket, and we will encode and decode our new `message` type:

```go
func (c *client) read() {
  for {
    var msg *message
    if err := c.socket.ReadJSON(&msg); err == nil {
      msg.When = time.Now()
      msg.Name = c.userData["name"].(string)
      c.room.forward <- msg
    } else {
      break
    }
  }
  c.socket.Close()
}
func (c *client) write() {
  for msg := range c.send {
    if err := c.socket.WriteJSON(msg); err != nil {
      break
    }
  }
  c.socket.Close()
}
```

When we receive a message from the browser, we will expect to populate only the `Message` field, which is why we set the `When` and `Name` fields ourselves in the preceding code.

You will notice that when you try to build the preceding code, it complains about a few things. The main reason is that we are trying to send a `*message` object down our `forward` and `send chan []byte` channels. This is not allowed until we change the type of the channel. In `room.go`, change the `forward` field to be of type `chan *message`, and do the same for the `send chan` type in `client.go`.

We must update the code that initializes our channels since the types have now changed. Alternatively, you can wait for the compiler to raise these issues and fix them as you go. In room.go, you need to make the following changes:

- Change forward: make(chan []byte) to forward: make(chan *message)

- Change r.tracer.Trace("Message received: ", string(msg)) to r.tracer.Trace("Message received: ", msg.Message)

- Change send: make(chan []byte, messageBufferSize) to send: make(chan *message, messageBufferSize)

The compiler will also complain about the lack of user data on a client, which is a fair point because the client type has no idea about the new user data we have added to the cookie. Update the client struct to include a new map[string]interface{} called userData:

```
// client represents a single chatting user.
type client struct {
  // socket is the web socket for this client.
  socket *websocket.Conn
  // send is a channel on which messages are sent.
  send chan *message
  // room is the room this client is chatting in.
  room *room
  // userData holds information about the user
  userData map[string]interface{}
}
```

The user data comes from the client cookie that we access through the http.Request objects's Cookie method. In room.go, update ServeHTTP with the following changes:

```
func (r *room) ServeHTTP(w http.ResponseWriter, req *http.Request) {
  socket, err := upgrader.Upgrade(w, req, nil)
  if err != nil {
    log.Fatal("ServeHTTP:", err)
    return
  }

  authCookie, err := req.Cookie("auth")
  if err != nil {
    log.Fatal("Failed to get auth cookie:", err)
    return
  }
```

```
client := &client{
  socket:   socket,
  send:     make(chan *message, messageBufferSize),
  room:     r,
  userData: objx.MustFromBase64(authCookie.Value),
}
r.join <- client
defer func() { r.leave <- client }()
go client.write()
client.read()
}
```

We use the `Cookie` method on the `http.Request` type to get our user data before passing it to the client. We are using the `objx.MustFromBase64` method to convert our encoded cookie value back into a usable map object.

Now that we have changed the type being sent and received on the socket from `[]byte` to `*message`, we must tell our JavaScript client that we are sending JSON instead of just a plain string. Also we must ask that it send JSON back to the server when a user submits a message. In `chat.html`, first update the `socket.send` call:

```
socket.send(JSON.stringify({"Message": msgBox.val()}));
```

We are using `JSON.stringify` to serialize the specified JSON object (containing just the `Message` field) into a string, which is then sent to the server. Our Go code will decode (or unmarshal) the JSON string into a `message` object, matching the field names from the client JSON object with those of our `message` type.

Finally, update the `socket.onmessage` callback function to expect JSON, and also add the name of the sender to the page:

```
socket.onmessage = function(e) {
  var msg = eval("("+e.data+")");
  messages.append(
    $("<li>").append(
      $("<strong>").text(msg.Name + ": "),
      $("<span>").text(msg.Message)
    )
  );
}
```

In the preceding code snippet, we've used JavaScript's `eval` function to turn the JSON string into a JavaScript object, and then access the fields to build up the elements needed to properly display them.

Build and run the application, and if you can, log in with two different accounts in two different browsers (or invite a friend to help you test it):

```
go build -o chat
./chat -host=":8080"
```

The following screenshot shows the chat application's browser chat screens:

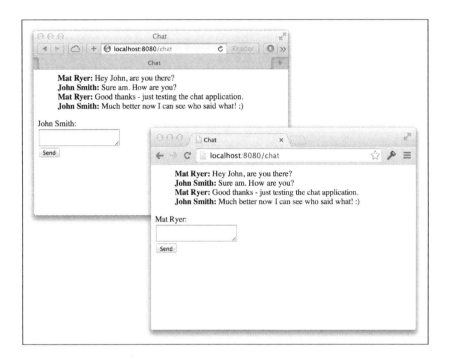

Summary

In this chapter, we added a useful and necessary feature to our chat application by asking users to authenticate themselves using OAuth2 service providers, before allowing them to join the conversation. We made use of several open source packages such as Objx and Gomniauth, which dramatically reduced the amount of multi-server complexity we would otherwise need to deal with.

We implemented a pattern when we wrapped http.Handler types to allow us to easily specify which paths require the user to be authenticated, and which were available even without an auth cookie. Our MustAuth helper function allowed us to generate the wrapper types in a fluent and simple way, without adding clutter and confusion to our code.

We saw how to use cookies and Base64-encoding to safely (although not securely) store the state of particular users in their browser, and to make use of that data over normal connections and through web sockets. We took more control of the data available to our templates in order to provide the name of the user to the UI, and saw how to only provide certain data under specific conditions.

Since we needed to send and receive additional information over the web socket, we learned how easy it was to change channels of native types into channels that work with types of our own such as our `message` type. We also learned how to transmit JSON objects over the socket, rather than just slices of bytes. Thanks to the type safety of Go, and the ability to specify types for channels, the compiler helps ensure that we do not send anything other than `message` objects through `chan *message`. Attempting to do so would result in a compiler error, alerting us to the fact right away.

To see the name of the person chatting is a great leap forward in usability from the application we built in the previous chapter, but it's very formal and might not attract modern users of the Web, who are used to a much more visual experience. We are missing pictures of people chatting, and in the next chapter, we will explore different ways in which we can allow users to better represent themselves in our application.

As an extra assignment, see if you can make use of the `time.Time` field that we put into the `message` type to tell users when the messages were sent.

3
Three Ways to Implement Profile Pictures

So far, our chat application has made use of the OAuth2 protocol to allow users to sign in to our application so that we know who is saying what. In this chapter, we are going to add profile pictures to make the chatting experience more engaging.

We will look at the following ways to add pictures or avatars alongside the messages in our application:

- Using the avatar picture provided by the authentication server
- Using the `Gravatar.com` web service to look up a picture by the user's e-mail address
- Allowing the user to upload their own picture and host it themselves

The first two options allow us to delegate the hosting of pictures to a third party—either an authentication service or `Gravatar.com`—which is great because it reduces the cost of hosting our application (in terms of storage costs and bandwidth, since the user's browsers will actually download the pictures from the servers of the authenticating service, not ours). The third option requires us to host pictures ourselves at a location that is web accessible.

These options aren't mutually exclusive; you will most likely use some combination of them in a real-world production application. Towards the end of the chapter, we will see how the flexible design that emerges allows us to try each implementation in turn, until we find an appropriate avatar.

We are going to be agile with our design throughout this chapter, doing the minimum work needed to accomplish each milestone. This means that at the end of each section, we will have working implementations that are demonstrable in the browser. This also means that we will refactor code as and when we need to and discuss the rationale behind the decisions we make as we go.

Specifically, in this chapter, you will learn the following:

- What are good practices to get additional information from authentication services, even when there are no standards in place
- When it is appropriate to build abstractions into our code
- How Go's zero-initialization pattern can save time and memory
- How reusing an interface allows us to work with collections and individual objects in the same way as the existing interface did
- How to use the `Gravatar.com` web service
- How to do MD5 hashing in Go
- How to upload files over HTTP and store them on a server
- How to serve static files through a Go web server
- How to use unit tests to guide the refactoring of code
- How and when to abstract functionality from `struct` types into interfaces

Avatars from the authentication server

It turns out that most authentication servers already have images for their users, and they make them available through the protected user resource that we already know how to access in order to get our users' names. To use this avatar picture, we need to get the URL from the provider, store it in the cookie for our user, and send it through a web socket so that every client can render the picture alongside the corresponding message.

Getting the avatar URL

The schema for user or profile resources is not part of the OAuth2 spec, which means that each provider is responsible for deciding how to represent that data. Indeed, providers do things differently, for example, the avatar URL in a GitHub user resource is stored in a field called `avatar_url`, whereas in Google, the same field is called `picture`. Facebook goes even further by nesting the avatar URL value in a `url` field inside an object called `picture`. Luckily, Gomniauth abstracts this for us; its `GetUser` call on a provider standardizes the interface to get common fields.

In order to make use of the avatar URL field, we need to go back and store its information in our cookie. In `auth.go`, look inside the `callback` action switch case and update the code that creates the `authCookieValue` object as follows:

```
authCookieValue := objx.New(map[string]interface{}{
  "name":       user.Name(),
  "avatar_url": user.AvatarURL(),
}).MustBase64()
```

The `AvatarURL` method called in the preceding code will return the appropriate URL value which we then store in the `avatar_url` field which will be stored in the cookie.

Gomniauth defines a `User` type of interface and each provider implements their own version. The generic `map[string]interface{}` data returned from the authentication server is stored inside each object, and the method calls access the appropriate value using the right field name for that provider. This approach — describing the way information is accessed without being strict about implementation details — is a great use of interfaces in Go.

Transmitting the avatar URL

We need to update our `message` type so that it can also carry with it the avatar URL. In `message.go`, add the `AvatarURL` string field:

```
type message struct {
  Name      string
  Message   string
  When      time.Time
  AvatarURL string
}
```

So far, we have not actually assigned a value to `AvatarURL` like we do for the `Name` field, so we must update our `read` method in `client.go`:

```
func (c *client) read() {
  for {
    var msg *message
    if err := c.socket.ReadJSON(&msg); err == nil {
      msg.When = time.Now()
      msg.Name = c.userData["name"].(string)
      if avatarUrl, ok := c.userData["avatar_url"]; ok {
        msg.AvatarURL = avatarUrl.(string)
      }
      c.room.forward <- msg
    } else {
```

```
        break
      }
    }
  }
  c.socket.Close()
}
```

All we have done here is we took the value from the `userData` field that represents what we put into the cookie and assigned it to the appropriate field in `message` if the value was present in the map. We will now take the additional step of checking whether the value is present because we cannot guarantee that the authentication service will provide a value for this field. And since it could be `nil`, it might cause a panic to assign it to a `string` type if it's actually missing.

Adding the avatar to the user interface

Now that our JavaScript client gets an avatar URL value via the socket, we can use it to display the image alongside the messages. We do this by updating the `socket.onmessage` code in `chat.html`:

```
socket.onmessage = function(e) {
  var msg = eval("("+e.data+")");
  messages.append(
    $("<li>").append(
      $("<img>").css({
        width:50,
        verticalAlign:"middle"
      }).attr("src", msg.AvatarURL),
      $("<strong>").text(msg.Name + ": "),
      $("<span>").text(msg.Message)
    )
  );
}
```

When we receive a message, we will insert an `img` tag with the source set to the `AvatarURL` field from the message. We will use jQuery's `css` method to force a width of `50` pixels. This protects us from massive pictures spoiling our interface and allows us to align the image to the middle of the surrounding text.

If we build and run our application having logged in with a previous version, you will find that the `auth` cookie that doesn't contain the avatar URL is still there. We are not asked to sign in again (since we are already logged in), and the code that adds the `avatar_url` field never gets a chance to run. We could delete our cookie and refresh the page, but we would have to keep doing so whenever we make changes during development. Let's solve this problem properly by adding a logout feature.

Logging out

The simplest way to log a user out is to get rid of the `auth` cookie and redirect the user to the chat page, which will in turn cause a redirect to the login page since we just removed the cookie. We do this by adding a new `HandleFunc` call to `main.go`:

```
http.HandleFunc("/logout", func(w http.ResponseWriter, r
*http.Request) {
  http.SetCookie(w, &http.Cookie{
    Name:   "auth",
    Value:  "",
    Path:   "/",
    MaxAge: -1,
  })
  w.Header()["Location"] = []string{"/chat"}
  w.WriteHeader(http.StatusTemporaryRedirect)
})
```

The preceding handler function uses `http.SetCookie` to update the cookie setting `MaxAge` to `-1`, which indicates that it should be deleted immediately by the browser. Not all browsers are forced to delete the cookie, which is why we also provide a new `Value` setting of an empty string, thus removing the user data that would previously have been stored.

As an additional assignment, you can bulletproof your app a little by updating the first line in `ServeHTTP` for your `authHandler` in `auth.go` to make it cope with the empty-value case as well as the missing-cookie case:

```
if cookie, err := r.Cookie("auth"); err ==
http.ErrNoCookie || cookie.Value == ""
```

Instead of ignoring the return of `r.Cookie`, we keep a reference to the returned cookie (if there was actually one) and also add an additional check to see whether the `Value` string of the cookie is empty or not.

Before we continue, let's add a `Sign Out` link to make it even easier to get rid of the cookie, and also to allow our users to log out. In `chat.html`, update the `chatbox` form to insert a simple HTML link to the new `/logout` handler:

```
<form id="chatbox">
  {{.UserData.name}}:<br/>
  <textarea></textarea>
  <input type="submit" value="Send" />
  or <a href="/logout">sign out</a>
</form>
```

Now build and run the application and open a browser to `localhost:8080/chat`:

```
go build -o chat
./chat -host=:8080
```

Log out if you need to and log back in. When you click on **Send**, you will see your avatar picture appear next to your messages.

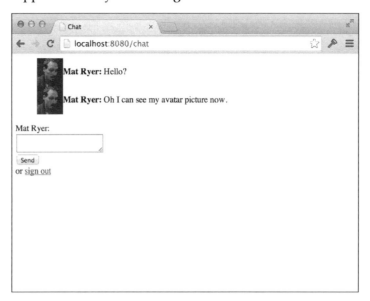

Making things prettier

Our application is starting to look a little ugly, and it's time to do something about it. In the previous chapter, we implemented the Bootstrap library into our login page, and we are now going to extend its use to our chat page. We will make three changes in `chat.html`: include Bootstrap and tweak the CSS styles for our page, change the markup for our form, and tweak how we render messages on the page.

First, let's update the `style` tag at the top of the page and insert a `link` tag above it to include Bootstrap:

```
<link rel="stylesheet"
href="//netdna.bootstrapcdn.com/bootstrap/3.1.1/css/bootstrap.min.
css">
<style>
  ul#messages        { list-style: none; }
  ul#messages li     { margin-bottom: 2px; }
```

```
    ul#messages li img { margin-right: 10px; }
  </style>
```

Next, let's replace the markup at the top of the `body` tag (before the `script` tags) with the following code:

```
<div class="container">
  <div class="panel panel-default">
    <div class="panel-body">
      <ul id="messages"></ul>
    </div>
  </div>
  <form id="chatbox" role="form">
    <div class="form-group">
      <label for="message">Send a message as
        {{.UserData.name}}</label> or <a href="/logout">Sign
        out</a>
      <textarea id="message" class="form-control"></textarea>
    </div>
    <input type="submit" value="Send" class="btn btn-default" />
  </form>
</div>
```

This markup follows Bootstrap standards of applying appropriate classes to various items, for example, the `form-control` class neatly formats elements within `form` (you can check out the Bootstrap documentation for more information on what these classes do).

Finally, let's update our `socket.onmessage` JavaScript code to put the sender's name as the `title` attribute for our image. This makes our app display the image when you hover the mouse over it rather than displaying it next to every message:

```
socket.onmessage = function(e) {
  var msg = eval("("+e.data+")");
  messages.append(
    $("<li>").append(
      $("<img>").attr("title", msg.Name).css({
        width:50,
        verticalAlign:"middle"
      }).attr("src", msg.AvatarURL),
      $("<span>").text(msg.Message)
    )
  );
}
```

Build and run the application and refresh your browser to see whether a new design appears:

```
go build -o chat
./chat -host=:8080
```

The preceding command shows the following output:

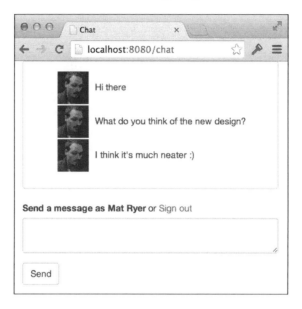

With relatively few changes to the code, we have dramatically improved the look and feel of our application.

Implementing Gravatar

Gravatar is a web service that allows users to upload a single profile picture and associate it with their e-mail address to make it available from any website. Developers, like us, can access those images for our application, just by performing a GET operation on a specific API endpoint. In this section, we will see how to implement Gravatar rather than use the picture provided by the authentication service.

Abstracting the avatar URL process

Since we have three different ways of obtaining the avatar URL in our application, we have reached the point where it would be sensible to learn how to abstract the functionality in order to cleanly implement the options. Abstraction refers to a process in which we separate the idea of something from its specific implementation. `http.Handler` is a great example of how a handler will be used along with its ins and outs, without being specific about what action is taken by each handler.

In Go, we start to describe our idea of getting an avatar URL by defining an interface. Let's create a new file called `avatar.go` and insert the following code:

```go
package main
import (
  "errors"
)
// ErrNoAvatar is the error that is returned when the
// Avatar instance is unable to provide an avatar URL.
var ErrNoAvatarURL = errors.New("chat: Unable to get an avatar
URL.")
// Avatar represents types capable of representing
// user profile pictures.
type Avatar interface {
  // GetAvatarURL gets the avatar URL for the specified client,
  // or returns an error if something goes wrong.
  // ErrNoAvatarURL is returned if the object is unable to get
  // a URL for the specified client.
  GetAvatarURL(c *client) (string, error)
}
```

The `Avatar` interface describes the `GetAvatarURL` method that a type must satisfy in order to be able to get avatar URLs. We took the client as an argument so that we know for which user to return the URL. The method returns two arguments: a string (which will be the URL if things go well) and an error in case something goes wrong.

One of the things that could go wrong is simply that one of the specific implementations of `Avatar` is unable to get the URL. In that case, `GetAvatarURL` will return the `ErrNoAvatarURL` error as the second argument. The `ErrNoAvatarURL` error therefore becomes a part of the interface; it's one of the possible returns from the method and something that users of our code should probably explicitly handle. We mention this in the comments part of the code for the method, which is the only way to communicate such design decisions in Go.

Because the error is initialized immediately using errors.New and stored in the ErrNoAvatarURL variable, only one of these objects will ever be created; passing the pointer of the error as a return is very inexpensive. This is unlike Java's checked exceptions — which serve a similar purpose — where expensive exception objects are created and used as part of the control flow.

The authentication service and avatar's implementation

The first implementation of Avatar we write will replace the existing functionality where we hardcoded the avatar URL obtained from the authentication service. Let's use a **Test-driven Development (TDD)** approach so we can be sure our code works without having to manually test it. Let's create a new file called avatar_test.go in the chat folder:

```go
package main
import "testing"
func TestAuthAvatar(t *testing.T) {
  var authAvatar AuthAvatar
  client := new(client)
  url, err := authAvatar.GetAvatarURL(client)
  if err != ErrNoAvatarURL {
    t.Error("AuthAvatar.GetAvatarURL should return ErrNoAvatarURL
when no value present")
  }
  // set a value
  testUrl := "http://url-to-gravatar/"
  client.userData = map[string]interface{}{"avatar_url": testUrl}
  url, err = authAvatar.GetAvatarURL(client)
  if err != nil {
    t.Error("AuthAvatar.GetAvatarURL should return no error when
value present")
  } else {
    if url != testUrl {
      t.Error("AuthAvatar.GetAvatarURL should return correct URL")
    }
  }
}
```

This test file contains a test for our as-of-yet nonexistent AuthAvatar type's GetAvatarURL method. First, it uses a client with no user data and ensures that the ErrNoAvatarURL error is returned. After setting a suitable value, our test calls the method again—this time to assert that it returns the correct value. However, building this code fails because the AuthAvatar type doesn't exist, so we'll declare authAvatar next.

Before we write our implementation, it's worth noticing that we only declare the authAvatar variable as the AuthAvatar type, but never actually assign anything to it so its value remains nil. This is not a mistake; we are actually making use of Go's zero-initialization (or default initialization) capabilities. Since there is no state needed for our object (we will pass client as an argument), there is no need to waste time and memory on initializing an instance of it. In Go, it is acceptable to call a method on a nil object, provided that the method doesn't try to access a field. When we actually come to writing our implementation, we will look at a way in which we can ensure this is the case.

Let's head back over to avatar.go and make our test pass. Add the following code to the bottom of the file:

```
type AuthAvatar struct{}
var UseAuthAvatar AuthAvatar
func (_ AuthAvatar) GetAvatarURL(c *client) (string, error) {
  if url, ok := c.userData["avatar_url"]; ok {
    if urlStr, ok := url.(string); ok {
      return urlStr, nil
    }
  }
  return "", ErrNoAvatarURL
}
```

Here, we define our AuthAvatar type as an empty struct and define the implementation of the GetAvatarURL method. We also create a handy variable called UseAuthAvatar that has the AuthAvatar type but which remains of nil value. We can later assign the UseAuthAvatar variable to any field looking for an Avatar interface type.

Normally, the receiver of a method (the type defined in parentheses before the name) will be assigned to a variable so that it can be accessed in the body of the method. Since, in our case, we assume the object can have nil value, we can use an underscore to tell Go to throw away the reference. This serves as an added reminder to ourselves that we should avoid using it.

The body of our implementation is otherwise relatively simple: we are safely looking for the value of `avatar_url` and ensuring it is a string before returning it. If anything fails along the way, we return the `ErrNoAvatarURL` error as defined in the interface.

Let's run the tests by opening a terminal and then navigating to the `chat` folder and typing the following:

```
go test
```

All being well, our tests will pass and we will have successfully created our first `Avatar` implementation.

Using an implementation

When we use an implementation, we could refer to either the helper variables directly or create our own instance of the interface whenever we need the functionality. However, this would defeat the very object of the abstraction. Instead, we use the `Avatar` interface type to indicate where we need the capability.

For our chat application, we will have a single way to obtain an avatar URL per chat room. So let's update the `room` type so it can hold an `Avatar` object. In `room.go`, add the following field definition to the type `room struct`:

```
// avatar is how avatar information will be obtained.
avatar Avatar
```

Update the `newRoom` function so we can pass in an `Avatar` implementation for use; we will just assign this implementation to the new field when we create our `room` instance:

```
// newRoom makes a new room that is ready to go.
func newRoom(avatar Avatar) *room {
  return &room{
    forward: make(chan *message),
    join:    make(chan *client),
    leave:   make(chan *client),
    clients: make(map[*client]bool),
    tracer:  trace.Off(),
    avatar:  avatar,
  }
}
```

Building the project now will highlight the fact that the call to `newRoom` in `main.go` is broken because we have not provided an `Avatar` argument; let's update it by passing in our handy `UseAuthAvatar` variable as follows:

```
r := newRoom(UseAuthAvatar)
```

We didn't have to create an instance of `AuthAvatar`, so no memory was allocated. In our case, this doesn't result in great savings (since we only have one room for our whole application), but imagine the size of the potential savings if our application has thousands of rooms. The way we named the `UseAuthAvatar` variable means that the preceding code is very easy to read and it also makes our intention obvious.

Thinking about code readability is important when designing interfaces. Consider a method that takes a Boolean input—just passing in true or false hides the real meaning if you don't know the argument names. Consider defining a couple of helper constants as in the following short example:

```
func move(animated bool) { /* ... */ }
const Animate = true
const DontAnimate = false
```

Think about which of the following calls to move are easier to understand:

```
move(true)
move(false)
move(Animate)
move(DontAnimate)
```

All that is left now is to change `client` to use our new `Avatar` interface. In `client.go`, update the `read` method as follows:

```go
func (c *client) read() {
  for {
    var msg *message
    if err := c.socket.ReadJSON(&msg); err == nil {
      msg.When = time.Now()
      msg.Name = c.userData["name"].(string)
      msg.AvatarURL, _ = c.room.avatar.GetAvatarURL(c)
      c.room.forward <- msg
    } else {
      break
    }
  }
  c.socket.Close()
}
```

Here, we are asking the `avatar` instance on `room` to get the avatar URL for us instead of extracting it from `userData` ourselves.

When you build and run the application, you will notice that (although we have refactored things a little) the behavior and user experience hasn't changed at all. This is because we told our room to use the `AuthAvatar` implementation.

Now let's add another implementation to the room.

Gravatar implementation

The Gravatar implementation in `Avitar` will do the same job as the `AuthAvatar` implementation, except it will generate a URL for a profile picture hosted on `Gravatar.com`. Let's start by adding a test to our `avatar_test.go` file:

```go
func TestGravatarAvatar(t *testing.T) {
  var gravatarAvitar GravatarAvatar
  client := new(client)
  client.userData = map[string]interface{}{"email":
"MyEmailAddress@example.com"}
  url, err := gravatarAvitar.GetAvatarURL(client)
  if err != nil {
    t.Error("GravatarAvitar.GetAvatarURL should not return an
error")
  }
  if url !=
"//www.gravatar.com/avatar/0bc83cb571cd1c50ba6f3e8a78ef1346" {
    t.Errorf("GravatarAvitar.GetAvatarURL wrongly returned %s",
url)
  }
}
```

Gravatar uses a hash of the e-mail address to generate a unique ID for each profile picture, so we set up a client and ensure `userData` contains an e-mail address. Next, we call the same `GetAvatarURL` method, but this time on an object that has the `GravatarAvatar` type. We then assert that a correct URL was returned. We already know this is the appropriate URL for the specified e-mail address because it is listed as an example in the Gravatar documentation—a great strategy to ensure our code is doing what it should be.

Recall that all the source code for this book is available on GitHub. You can save time on building the preceding core by copying and pasting bits and pieces from `https://github.com/matryer/goblueprints`. Hardcoding things such as the base URL is not usually a good idea; we have hardcoded throughout the book to make the code snippets easier to read and more obvious, but you are welcome to extract them as you go along if you like.

Running these tests (with `go test`) obviously causes errors because we haven't defined our types yet. Let's head back to `avatar.go` and add the following code while being sure to import the `io` package:

```
type GravatarAvatar struct{}
var UseGravatar GravatarAvatar
func (_ GravatarAvatar) GetAvatarURL(c *client) (string, error) {
  if email, ok := c.userData["email"]; ok {
    if emailStr, ok := email.(string); ok {
      m := md5.New()
      io.WriteString(m, strings.ToLower(emailStr))
      return fmt.Sprintf("//www.gravatar.com/avatar/%x",
m.Sum(nil)), nil
    }
  }
  return "", ErrNoAvatarURL
}
```

We used the same pattern as we did for `AuthAvatar`: we have an empty struct, a helpful `UseGravatar` variable, and the `GetAvatarURL` method implementation itself. In this method, we follow Gravatar's guidelines to generate an MD5 hash from the e-mail address (after we ensured it was lowercase) and append it to the hardcoded base URL.

It is very easy to achieve hashing in Go, thanks to the hard work put in by the writers of the Go standard library. The `crypto` package has an impressive array of cryptography and hashing capabilities—all very easy to use. In our case, we create a new `md5` hasher; because the hasher implements the `io.Writer` interface, we can use `io.WriteString` to write a string of bytes to it. Calling `Sum` returns the current hash for the bytes written.

> You might have noticed that we end up hashing the e-mail address every time we need the avatar URL. This is pretty inefficient, especially at scale, but we should prioritize getting stuff done over optimization. If we need to, we can always come back later and change the way this works.

Running the tests now shows us that our code is working, but we haven't yet included an e-mail address in the `auth` cookie. We do this by locating the code where we assign to the `authCookieValue` object in `auth.go` and updating it to grab the `Email` value from Gomniauth:

```
authCookieValue := objx.New(map[string]interface{}{
  "name":       user.Name(),
```

```
    "avatar_url": user.AvatarURL(),
    "email":     user.Email(),
}).MustBase64()
```

The final thing we must do is tell our room to use the Gravatar implementation instead of the `AuthAvatar` implementation. We do this by calling `newRoom` in `main.go` and making the following change:

```
r := newRoom(UseGravatar)
```

Build and run the chat program once again and head to the browser. Remember, since we have changed the information stored in the cookie, we must sign out and sign back in again in order to see our changes take effect.

Assuming you have a different image for your Gravatar account, you will notice that the system is now pulling the image from Gravatar instead of the authentication provider. Using your browser's inspector or debug tool will show you that the `src` attribute of the `img` tag has indeed changed.

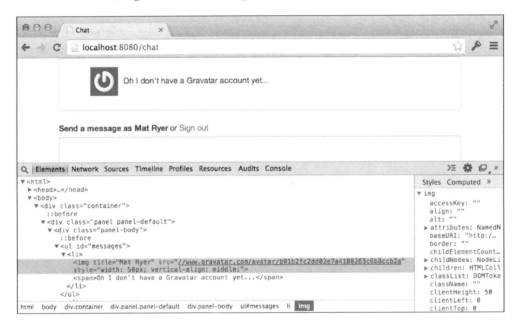

If you don't have a Gravatar account, you'll likely see a default placeholder image in place of your profile picture.

Uploading an avatar picture

In the third and final approach of uploading a picture, we will look at how to allow users to upload an image from their local hard drive to use as their profile picture when chatting. We will need a way to associate a file with a particular user to ensure that we associate the right picture with the corresponding messages.

User identification

In order to uniquely identify our users, we are going to copy Gravatar's approach by hashing their e-mail address and using the resulting string as an identifier. We will store the user ID in the cookie along with the rest of the user-specific data. This will actually have the added benefit of removing from `GravatarAuth` the inefficiency associated with continuous hashing.

In `auth.go`, replace the code that creates the `authCookieValue` object with the following code:

```
m := md5.New()
io.WriteString(m, strings.ToLower(user.Name()))
userId := fmt.Sprintf("%x", m.Sum(nil))
// save some data
authCookieValue := objx.New(map[string]interface{}{
  "userid":     userId,
  "name":       user.Name(),
  "avatar_url": user.AvatarURL(),
  "email":      user.Email(),
}).MustBase64()
```

Here we have hashed the e-mail address and stored the resulting value in the `userid` field at the point at which the user logs in. Henceforth, we can use this value in our Gravatar code instead of hashing the e-mail address for every message. To do this, first we update the test by removing the following line from `avatar_test.go`:

```
client.userData = map[string]interface{}{"email":
"MyEmailAddress@example.com"}
```

We then replace the preceding line with this line:

```
client.userData = map[string]interface{}{"userid":
"0bc83cb571cd1c50ba6f3e8a78ef1346"}
```

We no longer need to set the email field since it is not used; instead, we just have to set an appropriate value to the new userid field. However, if you run go test in a terminal, you will see this test fail.

To make the test pass, in avatar.go, update the GetAvatarURL method for the GravatarAuth type:

```
func (_ GravatarAvatar) GetAvatarURL(c *client) (string, error) {
  if userid, ok := c.userData["userid"]; ok {
    if useridStr, ok := userid.(string); ok {
      return "//www.gravatar.com/avatar/" + useridStr, nil
    }
  }
  return "", ErrNoAvatarURL
}
```

This won't change the behavior, but it allows us to make an unexpected optimization, which is a great example of why you shouldn't optimize code too early—the inefficiencies that you spot early on may not last long enough to warrant the effort required to fix them.

An upload form

If our users are to upload a file as their avatar, they need a way to browse their local hard drive and submit the file to the server. We facilitate this by adding a new template-driven page. In the chat/templates folder, create a file called upload.html:

```
<html>
  <head>
    <title>Upload</title>
    <link rel="stylesheet"
      href="//netdna.bootstrapcdn.com/bootstrap/3.1.1/css/
      bootstrap.min.css">
  </head>
  <body>
    <div class="container">
      <div class="page-header">
        <h1>Upload picture</h1>
      </div>
      <form role="form" action="/uploader"
        enctype="multipart/form-data" method="post">
        <input type="hidden" name="userid"
          value="{{.UserData.userid}}" />
```

```
        <div class="form-group">
          <label for="message">Select file</label>
          <input type="file" name="avatarFile" />
        </div>
        <input type="submit" value="Upload" class="btn " />
      </form>
    </div>
  </body>
</html>
```

We used Bootstrap again to make our page look nice and also to make it fit in with the other pages. However, the key point to note here is the HTML form that will provide the user interface necessary for uploading files. The action points to /uploader, the handler for which we have yet to implement, and the enctype attribute must be multipart/form-data so the browser can transmit binary data over HTTP. Then, there is an input element of the type file, which will contain the reference to the file we want to upload. Notice also that we have included the userid value from the UserData map as a hidden input—this will tell us which user is uploading a file. It is important that the name attributes are correct, as this is how we will refer to the data when we implement our handler on the server.

Let's now map the new template to the /upload path in main.go:

```
http.Handle("/upload", &templateHandler{filename: "upload.html"})
```

Handling the upload

When the user clicks on **Upload** after selecting a file, the browser will send the data for the file as well as the user ID to /uploader, but right now, that data doesn't actually go anywhere. We will implement a new HandlerFunc that is capable of receiving the file, reading the bytes that are streamed through the connection, and saving it as a new file on the server. In the chat folder, let's create a new folder called avatars—this is where we will save the avatar image files.

Next, create a new file called upload.go and insert the following code—make sure to add the appropriate package name and imports (which are ioutils, net/http, io, and path):

```
func uploaderHandler(w http.ResponseWriter, req *http.Request) {
  userId := req.FormValue("userid")
  file, header, err := req.FormFile("avatarFile")
  if err != nil {
    io.WriteString(w, err.Error())
    return
  }
```

```
    data, err := ioutil.ReadAll(file)
    if err != nil {
      io.WriteString(w, err.Error())
      return
    }
    filename := path.Join("avatars", userId+path.Ext(header.Filename))
    err = ioutil.WriteFile(filename, data, 0777)
    if err != nil {
      io.WriteString(w, err.Error())
      return
    }
    io.WriteString(w, "Successful")
}
```

Here, first `uploaderHandler` uses the `FormValue` method on `http.Request` to get the user ID that we placed in the hidden input in our HTML form. Then it gets an `io.Reader` type capable of reading the uploaded bytes by calling `req.FormFile`, which returns three arguments. The first argument represents the file itself with the `multipart.File` interface type, which is also an `io.Reader`. The second is a `multipart.FileHeader` object that contains metadata about the file, such as the filename. And finally, the third argument is an error that we hope will have a `nil` value.

What do we mean when we say that the `multipart.File` interface type is also an `io.Reader`? Well, a quick glance at the documentation at `http://golang.org/pkg/mime/multipart/#File` makes it clear that the type is actually just a wrapper interface for a few other more general interfaces. This means that a `multipart.File` type can be passed to methods that require `io.Reader`, since any object that implements `multipart.File` must therefore implement `io.Reader`.

Embedding standard library interfaces to describe new concepts is a great way to make sure your code works in as many contexts as possible. Similarly, you should try to write code that uses the simplest interface type you can find, ideally from the standard library. For example, if you wrote a method that needed to read the contents of a file, you could ask the user to provide an argument of the type `multipart.File`. However, if you ask for `io.Reader` instead, your code will become significantly more flexible because any type that has the appropriate `Read` method can be passed in, which includes user-defined types too.

The `ioutil.ReadAll` method will just keep reading from the specified `io.Reader` until all of the bytes have been received, so this is where we actually receive the stream of bytes from the client. We then use `path.Join` and `path.Ext` to build a new filename using `userid`, and copy the extension from the original filename that we can get from `multipart.FileHeader`.

We then use the `ioutil.WriteFile` method to create a new file in the `avatars` folder. We use `userid` in the filename to associate the image with the correct user, much in the same way as Gravatar does. The `0777` value specifies that the new file we create has full file permissions, which is a good default setting if you're not sure what other permissions should be set.

If an error occurs at any stage, our code will write it out to the response, which will help us debug it, or it will write **Successful** if everything went well.

In order to map this new handler function to /uploader, we need to head back to `main.go` and add the following line to `func main`:

```
http.HandleFunc("/uploader", uploaderHandler)
```

Now build and run the application and remember to log out and log back in again to give our code a chance to upload the `auth` cookie.

```
go build -o chat
./chat -host=:8080
```

Open `http://localhost:8080/upload` and click on **Choose File**, then select a file from your hard drive and click on **Upload**. Navigate to your `chat/avatars` folder and you will notice that the file was indeed uploaded and renamed to the value of your `userid` field.

Serving the images

Now that we have a place to keep our users' avatar images on the server, we need a way to make them accessible to the browser. We do this by using the `net/http` package's built-in file server. In `main.go`, add the following code:

```
http.Handle("/avatars/",
  http.StripPrefix("/avatars/",
    http.FileServer(http.Dir("./avatars"))))
```

This is actually a single line of code that has been broken up to improve readability. The `http.Handle` call should feel familiar: we are specifying that we want to map the `/avatars/` path with the specified handler—this is where things get interesting. Both `http.StripPrefix` and `http.FileServer` return `Handler`, and they make use of the decorator pattern we learned about in the previous chapter. The `StripPrefix` function takes `Handler` in, modifies the path by removing the specified prefix, and passes functionality onto an inner handler. In our case, the inner handler is an `http.FileServer` handler that will simply serve static files, provide index listings, and generate the `404 Not Found` error if it cannot find the file. The `http.Dir` function allows us to specify which folder we want to expose publicly.

If we didn't strip the `/avatars/` prefix from the requests with `http.StripPrefix`, the file server would look for another folder called `avatars` inside the actual `avatars` folder, that is, `/avatars/avatars/filename` instead of `/avatars/filename`.

Let's build the program and run it before opening `http://localhost:8080/avatars/` in a browser. You'll notice that the file server has generated a listing of the files inside our `avatars` folder. Clicking on a file will either download the file, or in the case of an image, simply display it. If you haven't done so already, go to `http://localhost:8080/upload` and upload a picture, then head back to the listing page and click on it to see it in the browser.

The Avatar implementation for local files

The final piece to making filesystem avatars work is to write an implementation of our `Avatar` interface that generates URLs that point to the filesystem endpoint we created in the last section.

Let's add a test function to our `avatar_test.go` file:

```
func TestFileSystemAvatar(t *testing.T) {

    // make a test avatar file
    filename := path.Join("avatars", "abc.jpg")
    ioutil.WriteFile(filename, []byte{}, 0777)
    defer func() { os.Remove(filename) }()

    var fileSystemAvatar FileSystemAvatar
    client := new(client)
    client.userData = map[string]interface{}{"userid": "abc"}
    url, err := fileSystemAvatar.GetAvatarURL(client)
    if err != nil {
      t.Error("FileSystemAvatar.GetAvatarURL should not return an
error")
```

```
    }
    if url != "/avatars/abc.jpg" {
        t.Errorf("FileSystemAvatar.GetAvatarURL wrongly returned %s",
url)
    }
}
```

This test is similar to, but slightly more involved than, the `GravatarAvatar` test because we are also creating a test file in our `avatars` folder and deleting it afterwards.

The `defer` keyword is a great way to ensure the code runs regardless of what happens in the rest of the function. Even if our test code panics, the deferred functions will still be called.

The rest of the test is simple: we set a `userid` field in `client.userData` and call `GetAvatarURL` to ensure we get back the right value. Of course, running this test will fail, so let's go and add the following code to make it pass in `avatar.go`:

```
type FileSystemAvatar struct{}
var UseFileSystemAvatar FileSystemAvatar
func (_ FileSystemAvatar) GetAvatarURL(c *client) (string, error) {
    if userid, ok := c.userData["userid"]; ok {
        if useridStr, ok := userid.(string); ok {
            return "/avatars/" + useridStr + ".jpg", nil
        }
    }
    return "", ErrNoAvatarURL
}
```

As we see here, to generate the correct URL, we simply get the `userid` value and build the final string by adding the appropriate segments together. You may have noticed that we have hardcoded the file extension to `.jpg`, which means that the initial version of our chat application will only support JPEGs.

Supporting only JPEGs might seem like a half-baked solution, but following Agile methodologies, this is perfectly fine; after all, custom JPEG profile pictures are better than no custom profile pictures at all.

Let's see our new code in action by updating `main.go` to use our new `Avatar` implementation:

```
r := newRoom(UseFileSystemAvatar)
```

Now build and run the application as usual and go to `http://localhost:8080/upload` and use a web form to upload a JPEG image to use as your profile picture. To make sure it's working correctly, choose a unique image that isn't your Gravatar picture or the image from the authentication service. Once you see the successful message after clicking on **Upload**, go to `http://localhost:8080/chat` and post a message. You will notice that the application has indeed used the profile picture that you uploaded.

To change your profile picture, go back to the `/upload` page and upload a different picture, then jump back to the `/chat` page and post more messages.

Supporting different file types

To support different file types, we have to make our `GetAvatarURL` method for the `FileSystemAvatar` type a little smarter.

Instead of just blindly building the string, we will use the very useful `ioutil.ReadDir` method to get a listing of the files. The listing also includes directories, so we will use the `IsDir` method to determine whether we should skip it or not.

We will then check to see whether each file starts with the `userid` field (remember that we named our files in this way) by a call to `path.Match`. If the filename matches the `userid` field, then we have found the file for that user and we return the path. If anything goes wrong or if we can't find the file, we return the `ErrNoAvatarURL` error as usual.

Update the appropriate method in `avatar.go` with the following code:

```go
func (_ FileSystemAvatar) GetAvatarURL(c *client) (string, error) {
  if userid, ok := c.userData["userid"]; ok {
    if useridStr, ok := userid.(string); ok {
      if files, err := ioutil.ReadDir("avatars"); err == nil {
        for _, file := range files {
          if file.IsDir() {
            continue
          }
          if match, _ := path.Match(useridStr+"*", file.Name());
match {
            return "/avatars/" + file.Name(), nil
          }
        }
      }
    }
  }
  return "", ErrNoAvatarURL
}
```

Delete all the files in the `avatar` folder to prevent confusion and rebuild the program. This time upload an image of a different type and notice that our application has no difficulty handling it.

Refactoring and optimizing our code

When we look back at how our `Avatar` type is used, you will notice that every time someone sends a message, the application makes a call to `GetAvatarURL`. In our latest implementation, each time the method is called, we iterate over all the files in the `avatars` folder. For a particularly chatty user, this could mean that we end up iterating over and over again many times a minute. This is an obvious waste of resources and would, at some point very soon, become a scaling problem.

Instead of getting the avatar URL for every message, we will get it only once when the user first logs in and cache it in the `auth` cookie. Unfortunately, our `Avatar` interface type requires that we pass in a `client` object to the `GetAvatarURL` method and we do not have such an object at the point at which we are authenticating the user.

So did we make a mistake when we designed our `Avatar` interface? While this is a natural conclusion to come to, in fact we did the right thing. We designed the solution with the best information we had available at the time and therefore had a working chat application much sooner than if we'd tried to design for every possible future case. Software evolves and almost always changes during the development process and will definitely change throughout the lifetime of the code.

Replacing concrete types with interfaces

We have concluded that our `GetAvatarURL` method depends on a type that is not available to us at the point we need it, so what would be a good alternative? We could pass each required field as a separate argument but this would make our interface brittle, since as soon as an `Avatar` implementation needs a new piece of information, we'd have to change the method signature. Instead, we will create a new type that will encapsulate the information our `Avatar` implementations need while conceptually remaining decoupled from our specific case.

In `auth.go`, add the following code to the top of the page (underneath the `package` keyword of course):

```
import gomniauthcommon "github.com/stretchr/gomniauth/common"
type ChatUser interface {
  UniqueID() string
  AvatarURL() string
}
```

```
type chatUser struct {
  gomniauthcommon.User
  uniqueID string
}
func (u chatUser) UniqueID() string {
  return u.uniqueID
}
```

Here, the `import` statement imported the `common` package from Gomniauth and at the same time gave it a specific name through which it will be accessed: `gomniauthcommon`. This isn't entirely necessary since we have no package name conflicts. However, it makes the code easier to understand.

In the preceding code snippet, we also defined a new interface type called `ChatUser`, which exposes the information needed in order for our `Avatar` implementations to generate the correct URLs. Then, we defined an actual implementation called `chatUser` (notice the lowercase starting letter) that implements the interface. It also makes use of a very interesting feature in Go: type embedding. We actually embedded the interface type `gomniauth/common.User`, which means that our `struct` implements the interface automatically.

You may have noticed that we only actually implemented one of the two required methods to satisfy our `ChatUser` interface. We got away with this because the Gomniauth `User` interface happens to define the same `AvatarURL` method. In practice, when we instantiate our `chatUser` struct—provided we set an appropriate value for the implied Gomniauth `User` field—our object implements both Gomniauth's `User` interface and our own `ChatUser` interface at the same time.

Changing interfaces in a test-driven way

Before we can use our new type, we must update the `Avatar` interface and appropriate implementations to make use of it. As we will follow TDD practices, we are going to make these changes in our test file, see compiler errors when we try to build our code, and see failing tests once we fix those errors before finally making the tests pass.

Open `avatar_test.go` and replace `TestAuthAvatar` with the following code:

```
func TestAuthAvatar(t *testing.T) {
  var authAvatar AuthAvatar
  testUser := &gomniauthtest.TestUser{}
  testUser.On("AvatarURL").Return("", ErrNoAvatarURL)
```

```
testChatUser := &chatUser{User: testUser}
url, err := authAvatar.GetAvatarURL(testChatUser)
if err != ErrNoAvatarURL {
  t.Error("AuthAvatar.GetAvatarURL should return ErrNoAvatarURL
when no value present")
}
testUrl := "http://url-to-gravatar/"
testUser = &gomniauthtest.TestUser{}
testChatUser.User = testUser
testUser.On("AvatarURL").Return(testUrl, nil)
url, err = authAvatar.GetAvatarURL(testChatUser)
if err != nil {
  t.Error("AuthAvatar.GetAvatarURL should return no error when
value present")
} else {
  if url != testUrl {
    t.Error("AuthAvatar.GetAvatarURL should return correct URL")
  }
}
}
```

> You will also need to import the gomniauth/test package as gomniauthtest like we did in the last section.

Using our new interface before we have defined it is a good way to check the sanity of our thinking, which is another advantage of practicing TDD. In this new test, we create TestUser provided by Gomniauth and embed it into a chatUser type. We then pass the new chatUser type into our GetAvatarURL calls and make the same assertions about output as we always have done.

> Gomniauth's TestUser type is interesting as it makes use of the Testify package's mocking capabilities. See https://github.com/stretchr/testify for more information.
>
> The On and Return methods allow us to tell TestUser what to do when specific methods are called. In the first case, we tell the AvatarURL method to return the error, and in the second case, we ask it to return the testUrl value, which simulates the two possible outcomes we are covering in this test.

Updating the `TestGravatarAvatar` and `TestFileSystemAvatar` tests is much simpler because they rely only on the `UniqueID` method, the value of which we can control directly.

Replace the other two tests in `avatar_test.go` with the following code:

```
func TestGravatarAvatar(t *testing.T) {
  var gravatarAvitar GravatarAvatar
  user := &chatUser{uniqueID: "abc"}
  url, err := gravatarAvitar.GetAvatarURL(user)
  if err != nil {
    t.Error("GravatarAvitar.GetAvatarURL should not return an
error")
  }
  if url != "//www.gravatar.com/avatar/abc" {
    t.Errorf("GravatarAvitar.GetAvatarURL wrongly returned %s",
url)
  }
}
func TestFileSystemAvatar(t *testing.T) {
  // make a test avatar file
  filename := path.Join("avatars", "abc.jpg")
  ioutil.WriteFile(filename, []byte{}, 0777)
  defer func() { os.Remove(filename) }()
  var fileSystemAvatar FileSystemAvatar
  user := &chatUser{uniqueID: "abc"}
  url, err := fileSystemAvatar.GetAvatarURL(user)
  if err != nil {
    t.Error("FileSystemAvatar.GetAvatarURL should not return an
error")
  }
  if url != "/avatars/abc.jpg" {
    t.Errorf("FileSystemAvatar.GetAvatarURL wrongly returned %s",
url)
  }
}
```

Of course, this test code won't even compile because we are yet to update our `Avatar` interface. In `avatar.go`, update the `GetAvatarURL` signature in the `Avatar` interface type to take a `ChatUser` type rather than a `client` type:

```
GetAvatarURL(ChatUser) (string, error)
```

 Note that we are using the `ChatUser` interface (uppercase starting letter) rather than our internal `chatUser` implementation struct—after all, we want to be flexible about the types our `GetAvatarURL` methods accept.

Trying to build this will reveal that we now have broken implementations because all the `GetAvatarURL` methods are still asking for a `client` object.

Fixing existing implementations

Changing an interface like the one we have is a good way to automatically find the parts of our code that have been affected because they will cause compiler errors. Of course, if we were writing a package that other people would use, we would have to be far stricter towards changing the interfaces.

We are now going to update the three implementation signatures to satisfy the new interface and change the method bodies to make use of the new type. Replace the implementation for `FileSystemAvatar` with the following:

```
func (_ FileSystemAvatar) GetAvatarURL(u ChatUser) (string, error) {
  if files, err := ioutil.ReadDir("avatars"); err == nil {
    for _, file := range files {
      if file.IsDir() {
        continue
      }
      if match, _ := path.Match(u.UniqueID()+"*", file.Name());
match {
        return "/avatars/" + file.Name(), nil
      }
    }
  }
  return "", ErrNoAvatarURL
}
```

The key change here is that we no longer access the `userData` field on the client, and instead just call `UniqueID` directly on the `ChatUser` interface.

Next, we update the `AuthAvatar` implementation with the following code:

```
func (_ AuthAvatar) GetAvatarURL(u ChatUser) (string, error) {
  url := u.AvatarURL()
  if len(url) > 0 {
    return url, nil
  }
  return "", ErrNoAvatarURL
}
```

Our new design is proving to be much simpler; it's always a good thing if we can reduce the amount of code needed. The preceding code makes a call to get the `AvatarURL` value, and provided it isn't empty (or `len(url) > 0`), we return it; else, we return the `ErrNoAvatarURL` error instead.

Finally, update the `GravatarAvatar` implementation:

```
func (_ GravatarAvatar) GetAvatarURL(u ChatUser) (string, error) {
  return "//www.gravatar.com/avatar/" + u.UniqueID(), nil
}
```

Global variables versus fields

So far, we have assigned the `Avatar` implementation to the `room` type, which enables us to use different avatars for different rooms. However, this has exposed an issue: when our users sign in, there is no concept of which room they are headed to so we cannot know which `Avatar` implementation to use. Because our application only supports a single room, we are going to look at another approach toward selecting implementations: the use of global variables.

A global variable is simply a variable that is defined outside any type definition and is accessible from every part of the package (and from outside the package if it's exported). For a simple configuration, such as which type of `Avatar` implementation to use, they are an easy and simple solution. Underneath the `import` statements in `main.go`, add the following line:

```
// set the active Avatar implementation
var avatars Avatar = UseFileSystemAvatar
```

This defines `avatars` as a global variable that we can use when we need to get the avatar URL for a particular user.

Implementing our new design

We need to change the code that calls `GetAvatarURL` for every message to just access the value that we put into the `userData` cache (via the `auth` cookie). Change the line where `msg.AvatarURL` is assigned, as follows:

```
if avatarUrl, ok := c.userData["avatar_url"]; ok {
  msg.AvatarURL = avatarUrl.(string)
}
```

Find the code inside `loginHandler` in `auth.go` where we call `provider.GetUser` and replace it down to where we set the `authCookieValue` object with the following code:

```
user, err := provider.GetUser(creds)
if err != nil {
  log.Fatalln("Error when trying to get user from", provider, "-",
err)
}
```

```
chatUser := &chatUser{User: user}
m := md5.New()
io.WriteString(m, strings.ToLower(user.Name()))
chatUser.uniqueID = fmt.Sprintf("%x", m.Sum(nil))
avatarURL, err := avatars.GetAvatarURL(chatUser)
if err != nil {
  log.Fatalln("Error when trying to GetAvatarURL", "-", err)
}
```

Here, we created a new `chatUser` variable while setting the `User` field (which represents the embedded interface) to the `User` value returned from Gomniauth. We then saved the `userid` MD5 hash to the `uniqueID` field.

The call to `avatars.GetAvatarURL` is where all of our hard work has paid off, as we now get the avatar URL for the user far earlier in the process. Update the `authCookieValue` line in `auth.go` to cache the avatar URL in the cookie and remove the e-mail address since it is no longer needed:

```
authCookieValue := objx.New(map[string]interface{}{
  "userid":     chatUser.uniqueID,
  "name":       user.Name(),
  "avatar_url": avatarURL,
}).MustBase64()
```

However expensive the work that the `Avatar` implementation needs to do, like iterating over files on the filesystem, it is mitigated by the fact that the implementation only does so when the user first logs in, and not every time they send a message.

Tidying up and testing

Finally, we get to snip away some of the fat that has accumulated during our refactoring process.

Since we no longer store the `Avatar` implementation in `room`, let's remove the field and all references to it from the type. In `room.go`, delete the `avatar Avatar` definition from the `room` struct and update the `newRoom` method:

```
func newRoom() *room {
  return &room{
    forward: make(chan *message),
    join:    make(chan *client),
    leave:   make(chan *client),
    clients: make(map[*client]bool),
    tracer:  trace.Off(),
  }
}
```

> Remember to use the compiler as your to-do list where possible, and follow the errors to find where you have impacted other code.

In `main.go`, remove the parameter passed into the `newRoom` function call since we are using our global variable instead of this one.

After this exercise, the end user experience remains unchanged. Usually, when refactoring the code, it is the internals that are modified while the public-facing interface remains stable and unchanged.

> It's usually a good idea to run tools such as `golint` and `go vet` against your code as well to make sure it follows good practices and doesn't contain any Go faux pas such as missing comments or badly named functions.

Combining all three implementations

To close this chapter off with a bang, we will implement a mechanism in which each `Avatar` implementation takes a turn in trying to get the value. If the first implementation returns the `ErrNoAvatarURL` error, we will try the next and so on until we find a useable value.

In `avatar.go`, underneath the `Avatar` type, add the following type definition:

```
type TryAvatars []Avatar
```

The `TryAvatars` type is simply a slice of `Avatar` objects; therefore, we will add the following `GetAvatarURL` method:

```
func (a TryAvatars) GetAvatarURL(u ChatUser) (string, error) {
  for _, avatar := range a {
    if url, err := avatar.GetAvatarURL(u); err == nil {
      return url, nil
    }
  }
  return "", ErrNoAvatarURL
}
```

This means that `TryAvatars` is now a valid `Avatar` implementation and can be used in place of any specific implementation. In the preceding method, we iterated over the slice of `Avatar` objects in an order, calling `GetAvatarURL` for each one. If no error is returned, we return the URL; otherwise, we carry on looking. Finally, if we are unable to find a value, we just return `ErrNoAvatarURL` as per the interface design.

Update the `avatars` global variable in `main.go` to use our new implementation:

```
var avatars Avatar = TryAvatars{
   UseFileSystemAvatar,
   UseAuthAvatar,
   UseGravatar}
```

Here we created a new instance of our `TryAvatars` slice type while putting the other `Avatar` implementations inside it. The order matters since it iterates over the objects in the order in which they appear in the slice. So, first our code will check to see whether the user has uploaded a picture; if they haven't, the code will check whether the authentication service has a picture for us to use. If both the approaches fail, a Gravatar URL will be generated, which in the worst case (for example, if the user hasn't added a Gravatar picture), will render a default placeholder image.

To see our new functionality in action, perform the following steps:

1. Build and rerun the application:
    ```
    go build -o chat
    ./chat -host=:8080
    ```
2. Log out by visiting `http://localhost:8080/logout`.
3. Delete all the pictures from the `avatars` folder.
4. Log back in by navigating to `http://localhost:8080/chat`.
5. Send some messages and take note of your profile picture.
6. Visit `http://localhost:8080/upload` and upload a new profile picture.
7. Log out again and log back in as before.
8. Send some more messages and notice that your profile picture has updated.

Summary

In this chapter, we added three different implementations of profile pictures to our chat application. First we asked the authentication service to provide a URL for us to use. We did this by using Gomniauth's abstraction of the user resource data, which we then included as part of the user interface every time a user would send a message. Using Go's zero (or default) initialization pattern, we were able to refer to different implementations of our `Avatar` interface without actually creating any instances.

We stored data in a cookie for when the user would log in. Therefore, and also given the fact that cookies persist between builds of our code, we added a handy logout feature to help us validate our changes, which we also exposed to our users so that they could log out too. Other small changes to the code and the inclusion of Bootstrap on our chat page dramatically improved the look and feel of our application.

We used MD5 hashing in Go to implement the `Gravatar.com` API by hashing the e-mail address that the authentication service provided. If the e-mail address is not known to Gravatar, they will deliver a nice default placeholder image for us, which means our user interface will never be broken due to missing images.

We then built and completed an upload form and associated the server functionality that saved uploaded pictures in the `avatars` folder. We saw how to expose the saved uploaded pictures to users via the standard library's `http.FileServer` handler. As this introduced inefficiencies in our design by causing too much filesystem access, we refactored our solution with the help of our unit tests. By moving the `GetAvatarURL` call to the point at which users log in, rather than every time a message is sent, we made our code significantly more scalable.

Our special `ErrNoAvatarURL` error type was used as part of our interface design to allow us to inform the calling code when it was not possible to obtain an appropriate URL—this became particularly useful when we created our `Avatars` slice type. By implementing the `Avatar` interface on a slice of `Avatar` types, we were able to make a new implementation that took turns trying to get a valid URL from each of the different options available, starting with the filesystem, then the authentication service, and finally Gravatar. We achieved this with zero impact on how the user would interact with the interface. If an implementation returned `ErrNoAvatarURL`, we tried the next one.

Our chat application is ready to go live so we can invite our friends and have a real conversation. But first we need to choose a domain name to host it at, something we will look at in the next chapter.

4

Command-line Tools to Find Domain Names

The chat application we built in the previous chapters is ready to take the world by storm, but not before we give it a home on the Internet. Before we invite our friends to join the conversation, we need to pick a valid, catchy, and available domain name that we can point to the server running our Go code. Instead of sitting in front of our favorite domain name provider for hours on end trying different names, we are going to develop a few command-line tools that will help us find the right one. As we do so, we will see how the Go standard library allows us to interface with the terminal and other executing applications, as well as explore some patterns and practices to build command-line programs.

In this chapter, you will learn:

- How to build complete command-line applications with as little as a single code file

- How to ensure that the tools we build can be composed with other tools using standard streams

- How to interact with a simple third-party JSON RESTful API

- How to utilize the standard in and out pipes in Go code

- How to read from a streaming source one line at a time

- How to build a WHOIS client to look up domain information

- How to store and use sensitive or deployment-specific information in environment variables

Pipe design for command-line tools

We are going to build a series of command-line tools that use the standard streams (`stdin` and `stdout`) to communicate with the user and with other tools. Each tool will take input line by line via the standard in pipe, process it in some way, and then print the output line by line to the standard out pipe for the next tool or for the user.

By default, the standard input is connected to the user's keyboard, and the standard output is printed to the terminal from which the command was run; however, both can be redirected using redirection metacharacters. It's possible to throw the output away by redirecting it to `NUL` on Windows or `/dev/null` on Unix machines, or redirecting it to a file, which will cause the output to be saved to the disk. Alternatively, you can pipe (using the | pipe character) the output of one program into the input of another; it is this feature that we will make use of in order to connect our various tools together. For example, you could pipe the output from one program to the input of another program in a terminal by using this code:

```
one | two
```

Our tools will work with lines of strings where each line (separated by a linefeed character) represents one string. When run without any pipe redirection, we will be able to interact directly with the programs using the default in and out, which will be useful when testing and debugging our code.

Five simple programs

In this chapter, we will build five small programs that we will combine together at the end. The key features of the programs are as follows:

- **Sprinkle**: This program will add some web-friendly sprinkle words to increase the chances of finding available domain names

- **Domainify**: This program will ensure words are acceptable for a domain name by removing unacceptable characters and replacing spaces with hyphens and adding an appropriate top-level domain (such as `.com` and `.net`) to the end

- **Coolify**: This program will make a boring old normal word into Web 2.0 by fiddling around with vowels

- **Synonyms**: This program will use a third-party API to find synonyms

- **Available**: This program will check to see whether the domain is available or not using an appropriate WHOIS server

Five programs might seem like a lot for one chapter, but don't forget how small entire programs can be in Go.

Sprinkle

Our first program augments incoming words with some sugar terms in order to improve the odds of finding available names. Many companies use this approach to keep the core messaging consistent while being able to afford the .com domain. For example, if we pass in the word chat, it might pass out chatapp; alternatively, if we pass in talk, we may get back talk time.

Go's math/rand package allows us to break away from the predictability of computers to give a chance or opportunity to get involved in our program's process and make our solution feel a little more intelligent than it actually is.

To make our Sprinkle program work, we will:

- Define an array of transformations using a special constant to indicate where the original word will appear
- Use the bufio package to scan input from stdin and fmt.Println to write output to stdout
- Use the math/rand package to randomly select which transformation to apply to the word, such as appending "app" or prefixing the term with "get"

 All of our programs will reside in the $GOPATH/src directory. For example, if your GOPATH is ~/Work/projects/go, you would create your program folders in the ~/Work/projects/go/src folder.

In the $GOPATH/src directory, create a new folder called sprinkle and add a main. go file containing the following code:

```
package main
import (
  "bufio"
  "fmt"
  "math/rand"
  "os"
  "strings"
  "time"
)
const otherWord = "*"
var transforms = []string{
  otherWord,
  otherWord,
  otherWord,
  otherWord,
  otherWord + "app",
  otherWord + "site",
```

```go
      otherWord + "time",
      "get" + otherWord,
      "go" + otherWord,
      "lets " + otherWord,
  }
  func main() {
    rand.Seed(time.Now().UTC().UnixNano())
    s := bufio.NewScanner(os.Stdin)
    for s.Scan() {
      t := transforms[rand.Intn(len(transforms))]
      fmt.Println(strings.Replace(t, otherWord, s.Text(), -1))
    }
  }
```

From now on, it is assumed that you will sort out the appropriate import statements yourself. If you need assistance, refer to the tips provided in *Appendix, Good Practices for a Stable Go Environment.*

The preceding code represents our complete Sprinkle program. It defines three things: a constant, a variable, and the obligatory main function, which serves as the entry point to Sprinkle. The otherWord constant string is a helpful token that allows us to specify where the original word should occur in each of our possible transformations. It lets us write code such as otherWord+"extra", which makes it clear that, in this particular case, we want to add the word extra to the end of the original word.

The possible transformations are stored in the transforms variable that we declare as a slice of strings. In the preceding code, we defined a few different transformations such as adding app to the end of a word or lets before it. Feel free to add some more in there; the more creative, the better.

In the main function, the first thing we do is use the current time as a random seed. Computers can't actually generate random numbers, but changing the seed number for the random algorithms gives the illusion that it can. We use the current time in nanoseconds because it's different each time the program is run (provided the system clock isn't being reset before each run).

We then create a bufio.Scanner object (called bufio.NewScanner) and tell it to read input from os.Stdin, which represents the standard in stream. This will be a common pattern in our five programs since we are always going to read from standard in and write to standard out.

The bufio.Scanner object actually takes io.Reader as its input source, so there is a wide range of types that we could use here. If you were writing unit tests for this code, you could specify your own io.Reader for the scanner to read from, removing the need for you to worry about simulating the standard input stream.

As the default case, the scanner allows us to read, one at a time, blocks of bytes separated by defined delimiters such as a carriage return and linefeed characters. We can specify our own split function for the scanner or use one of the options built in the standard library. For example, there is bufio.ScanWords that scans individual words by breaking on whitespace rather than linefeeds. Since our design specifies that each line must contain a word (or a short phrase), the default line-by-line setting is ideal.

A call to the Scan method tells the scanner to read the next block of bytes (the next line) from the input, and returns a bool value indicating whether it found anything or not. This is how we are able to use it as the condition for the for loop. While there is content to work on, Scan returns true and the body of the for loop is executed, and when Scan reaches the end of the input, it returns false, and the loop is broken. The bytes that have been selected are stored in the Bytes method of the scanner, and the handy Text method that we use converts the []byte slice into a string for us.

Inside the for loop (so for each line of input), we use rand.Intn to select a random item from the transforms slice, and use strings.Replace to insert the original word where the otherWord string appears. Finally, we use fmt.Println to print the output to the default standard output stream.

Let's build our program and play with it:

```
go build -o sprinkle
./sprinkle
```

Once the program is running, since we haven't piped any content in, or specified a source for it to read from, we will use the default behavior where it reads the user input from the terminal. Type in chat and hit return. The scanner in our code notices the linefeed character at the end of the word and runs the code that transforms it, outputting the result. For example, if you type chat a few times, you might see output like:

```
chat
go chat
chat
lets chat
chat
chat app
```

Sprinkle never exits (meaning the `Scan` method never returns `false` to break the loop) because the terminal is still running; in normal execution, the in pipe will be closed by whatever program is generating the input. To stop the program, hit *Ctrl + C.*

Before we move on, let's try running Sprinkle specifying a different input source, we are going to use the `echo` command to generate some content, and pipe it into our Sprinkle program using the pipe character:

```
echo "chat" | ./sprinkle
```

The program will randomly transform the word, print it out, and exit since the `echo` command generates only one line of input before terminating and closing the pipe.

We have successfully completed our first program, which has a very simple but useful function, as we will see.

Exercise – configurable transformations

As an extra assignment, rather than hardcoding the `transformations` array as we have done, see if you can externalize it into a text file or database.

Domainify

Some of the words that output from Sprinkle contain spaces and perhaps other characters that are not allowed in domains, so we are going to write a program, called Domainify, that converts a line of text into an acceptable domain segment and add an appropriate **Top-level Domain (TLD)** to the end. Alongside the `sprinkle` folder, create a new one called `domainify`, and add a `main.go` file with the following code:

```go
package main
var tlds = []string{"com", "net"}
const allowedChars = "abcdefghijklmnopqrstuvwxyz0123456789_-"
func main() {
  rand.Seed(time.Now().UTC().UnixNano())
  s := bufio.NewScanner(os.Stdin)
  for s.Scan() {
    text := strings.ToLower(s.Text())
    var newText []rune
    for _, r := range text {
      if unicode.IsSpace(r) {
        r = '-'
      }
      if !strings.ContainsRune(allowedChars, r) {
        continue
      }
```

```
        newText = append(newText, r)
    }
    fmt.Println(string(newText) + "." +
            tlds[rand.Intn(len(tlds))])
  }
}
```

You will notice a few similarities between the Domainify and Sprinkle programs: we set the random seed using `rand.Seed`, generate a `NewScanner` method wrapping the `os.Stdin` reader, and scan each line until there is no more input.

We then convert the text to lowercase and build up a new slice of `rune` types called `newText`. The `rune` types consist only of characters that appear in the `allowedChars` string, which `strings.ContainsRune` lets us know. If `rune` is a space that we determine by calling `unicode.IsSpace`, we replace it with a hyphen, which is an acceptable practice in domain names.

> Ranging over a string returns the index of each character and a `rune` type, which is a numerical value (specifically `int32`) representing the character itself. For more information about runes, characters, and strings, refer to `http://blog.golang.org/strings`.

Finally, we convert `newText` from a `[]`rune slice to a string and add either `.com` or `.net` to the end before printing it out using `fmt.Println`.

Build and run Domainify:

```
go build -o domainify
./domainify
```

Type in some of these options to see how `domainify` reacts:

- `Monkey`
- `Hello Domainify`
- `"What's up?"`
- `One (two) three!`

You can see that, for example, `One (two) three!` might yield `one-two-three.com`.

We are now going to compose Sprinkle and Domainify to see them work together. In your terminal, navigate to the parent folder (probably `$GOPATH/src`) of `sprinkle` and `domainify`, and run the following command:

```
./sprinkle/sprinkle | ./domainify/domainify
```

Here we ran the Sprinkle program and piped the output into the Domainify program. By default, `sprinkle` uses the terminal as the input and `domanify` outputs to the terminal. Try typing in `chat` a few times again, and notice the output is similar to what Sprinkle was outputting previously, except now the words are acceptable for domain names. It is this piping between programs that allows us to compose command-line tools together.

Exercise – making top-level domains configurable

Only supporting `.com` and `.net` top-level domains is fairly limiting. As an additional assignment, see if you can accept a list of TLDs via a command-line flag.

Coolify

Often domain names for common words such as `chat` are already taken and a common solution is to play around with the vowels in the words. For example, we might remove the `a` leaving `cht` (which is actually less likely to be available), or add an `a` to produce `chaat`. While this clearly has no actual effect on coolness, it has become a popular, albeit slightly dated, way to secure domain names that still sound like the original word.

Our third program, Coolify, will allow us to play with the vowels of words that come in via the input, and write the modified versions to the output.

Create a new folder called `coolify` alongside `sprinkle` and `domainify`, and create the `main.go` code file with the following code:

```
package main
const (
  duplicateVowel bool   = true
  removeVowel    bool   = false
)
func randBool() bool {
  return rand.Intn(2) == 0
}
func main() {
  rand.Seed(time.Now().UTC().UnixNano())
  s := bufio.NewScanner(os.Stdin)
  for s.Scan() {
    word := []byte(s.Text())
    if randBool() {
      var vI int = -1
```

```
      for i, char := range word {
        switch char {
        case 'a', 'e', 'i', 'o', 'u', 'A', 'E', 'I', 'O', 'U':
          if randBool() {
            vI = i
          }
        }
      }
      if vI >= 0 {
        switch randBool() {
        case duplicateVowel:
          word = append(word[:vI+1], word[vI:]...)
        case removeVowel:
          word = append(word[:vI], word[vI+1:]...)
        }
      }
    }
    fmt.Println(string(word))
  }
}
```

While the preceding Coolify code looks very similar to the codes of Sprinkle and Domainify, it is slightly more complicated. At the very top of the code we declare two constants, duplicateVowel and removeVowel, that help make Coolify code more readable. The switch statement decides whether we duplicate or remove a vowel. Also, using these constants, we are able to express our intent very clearly, rather than using just true or false.

We then define the randBool helper function that just randomly returns true or false by asking the rand package to generate a random number, and checking whether if that number comes out as zero. It will be either 0 or 1, so there's a 50/50 chance of it being true.

The main function for Coolify starts the same way as the main functions for Sprinkle and Domainify — by setting the rand.Seed method and creating a scanner of the standard input stream before executing the loop body for each line of input. We call randBool first to decide whether we are even going to mutate a word or not, so Coolify will only affect half of the words passed through it.

We then iterate over each rune in the string and look for a vowel. If our randBool method returns true, we keep the index of the vowel character in the vI variable. If not, we keep looking through the string for another vowel, which allows us to randomly select a vowel from the words rather than always modifying the same one.

Once we have selected a vowel, we then use `randBool` again to randomly decide what action to take.

This is where the helpful constants come in; consider the following alternative switch statement:

```
switch randBool() {
case true:
  word = append(word[:vI+1], word[vI:]...)
case false:
  word = append(word[:vI], word[vI+1:]...)
}
```

In the preceding code snippet, it's difficult to tell what is going on because `true` and `false` don't express any context. On the other hand, using `duplicateVowel` and `removeVowel` tells anyone reading the code what we mean by the result of `randBool`.

The three dots following the slices cause each item to pass as a separate argument to the `append` function. This is an idiomatic way of appending one slice to another. Inside the `switch` case, we do some slice manipulation to either duplicate the vowel or remove it altogether. We are reslicing our `[]byte` slice and using the `append` function to build a new one made up of sections of the original word. The following diagram shows which sections of the string we access in our code:

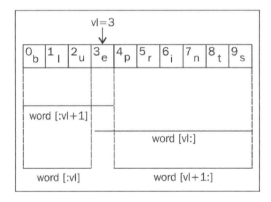

If we take the value `blueprints` as an example word, and assume that our code selected the first `e` character as the vowel (so that `vI` is 3), we can see what each new slice of word represents in this table:

Code	Value	Description
`word[:vI+1]`	`blue`	Describes a slice from the beginning of the word slice to the selected vowel. The `+1` is required because the value following the colon does not include the specified index; rather it slices up to that value.
`word[vI:]`	`eprints`	Describes a slice starting at and including the selected vowel to the end of the slice.
`word[:vI]`	`blu`	Describes a slice from the beginning of the word slice up to, but not including, the selected vowel.
`word[vI+1:]`	`prints`	Describes a slice from the item following the selected vowel to the end of the slice.

After we modify the word, we print it out using `fmt.Println`.

Let's build Coolify and play with it to see what it can do:

```
go build -o coolify
./coolify
```

When Coolify is running, try typing `blueprints` to see what sort of modifications it comes up with:

```
blueprnts
bleprints
bluepriints
blueprnts
blueprints
bluprints
```

Let's see how Coolify plays with Sprinkle and Domainify by adding their names to our pipe chain. In the terminal, navigate back (using the `cd` command) to the parent folder and run the following commands:

```
./coolify/coolify | ./sprinkle/sprinkle | ./domainify/domainify
```

We will first spice up a word with extra pieces and make it cooler by tweaking the vowels before finally transforming it into a valid domain name. Play around by typing in a few words and seeing what suggestions our code makes.

Synonyms

So far, our programs have only modified words, but to really bring our solution to life, we need to be able to integrate a third-party API that provides word synonyms. This allows us to suggest different domain names while retaining the original meaning. Unlike Sprinkle and Domainify, Synonyms will write out more than one response for each word given to it. Our architecture of piping programs together means this is no problem; in fact we do not even have to worry about it since each of the three programs is capable of reading multiple lines from the input source.

The Big Hugh Thesaurus at `bighughlabs.com` has a very clean and simple API that allows us to make a single HTTP GET request in order to look up synonyms.

 If in the future the API we are using changes or disappears (after all, this is the Internet!), you will find some options at `https://github.com/matryer/goblueprints`.

Before you can use the Big Hugh Thesaurus, you'll need an API key, which you can get by signing up to the service at `http://words.bighugelabs.com/`.

Using environment variables for configuration

Your API key is a sensitive piece of configuration information that you won't want to share with others. We could store it as `const` in our code, but that would not only mean we couldn't share our code without sharing our key (not good, especially if you love open source projects), but also, and perhaps more importantly, you would have to recompile your project if the key expires or if you want to use a different one.

A better solution is using an environment variable to store the key, as this will allow you to easily change it if you need to. You could also have different keys for different deployments; perhaps you have one key for development or testing and another for production. This way, you can set a specific key for a particular execution of code, so you can easily switch keys without having to change your system-level settings. Either way, different operating systems deal with environment variables in similar ways, so they are a perfect choice if you are writing cross-platform code.

Create a new environment variable called BHT_APIKEY and set your API key as its value.

 For machines running a bash shell, you can modify your ~/.bashrc file or similar to include export commands such as:

export BHT_APIKEY=abc123def456ghi789jkl

On Windows machines, you can navigate to the properties of your computer and look for **Environment Variables** in the **Advanced** section.

Consuming a web API

Making a request for http://words.bighugelabs.com/apisample.php?v=2&format=json in a web browser shows us what the structure of JSON response data looks like when finding synonyms for the word love:

```
{
    "noun":{
        "syn":[
            "passion",
            "beloved",
            "dear"
        ]
    },
    "verb":{
        "syn":[
            "love",
            "roll in the hay",
            "make out"
        ],
        "ant":[
            "hate"
        ]
    }
}
```

The real API returns a lot more actual words than what is printed here, but the structure is the important thing. It represents an object where the keys describe the types of words (verbs, nouns, and so on) and values are objects that contain arrays of strings keyed on syn or ant (for synonym and antonym respectively); it is the synonyms we are interested in.

To turn this JSON string data into something we can use in our code, we must decode it into structures of our own using capabilities found in the `encoding/json` package. Because we're writing something that could be useful outside the scope of our project, we will consume the API in a reusable package rather than directly in our program code. Create a new folder called `thesaurus` alongside your other program folders (in `$GOPATH/src`) and insert the following code into a new `bighugh.go` file:

```go
package thesaurus
import (
  "encoding/json"
  "errors"
  "net/http"
)
type BigHugh struct {
  APIKey string
}
type synonyms struct {
  Noun *words `json:"noun"`
  Verb *words `json:"verb"`
}
type words struct {
  Syn []string `json:"syn"`
}
func (b *BigHugh) Synonyms(term string) ([]string, error) {
  var syns []string
  response, err := http.Get("http://words.bighugelabs.com/api/2/"
+ b.APIKey + "/" + term + "/json")
  if err != nil {
     return syns, errors.New("bighugh: Failed when looking for
synonyms for \"" + term + "\"" + err.Error())
  }
  var data synonyms
  defer response.Body.Close()
  if err := json.NewDecoder(response.Body).Decode(&data); err !=
nil {
     return syns, err
  }
  syns = append(syns, data.Noun.Syn...)
  syns = append(syns, data.Verb.Syn...)
  return syns, nil
}
```

In the preceding code, the BigHugh type we define houses the necessary API key and provides the Synonyms method that will be responsible for doing the work of accessing the endpoint, parsing the response, and returning the results. The most interesting parts of this code are the synonyms and words structures. They describe the JSON response format in Go terms, namely an object containing noun and verb objects, which in turn contain a slice of strings in a variable called Syn. The tags (strings in backticks following each field definition) tell the encoding/json package which fields to map to which variables; this is required since we have given them different names.

> Typically, JSON keys have lowercase names, but we have to use capitalized names in our structures so that the encoding/json package knows that the fields exist. If we didn't, the package would simply ignore the fields. However, the types themselves (synonyms and words) do not need to be exported.

The Synonyms method takes a term argument and uses http.Get to make a web request to the API endpoint in which the URL contains not only the API key value, but also the term value itself. If the web request fails for some reason, we will make a call to log.Fatalln, which writes the error out to the standard error stream and exits the program with a non-zero exit code (actually an exit code of 1) — this indicates that an error has occurred.

If the web request is successful, we pass the response body (another io.Reader) to the json.NewDecoder method and ask it to decode the bytes into the data variable that is of our synonyms type. We defer the closing of the response body in order to keep memory clean before using Go's built-in append function to concatenate both noun and verb synonyms to the syns slice that we then return.

Although we have implemented the BigHugh thesaurus, it isn't the only option out there, and we can express this by adding a Thesaurus interface to our package. In the thesaurus folder, create a new file called thesaurus.go, and add the following interface definition to the file:

```
package thesaurus
type Thesaurus interface {
  Synonyms(term string) ([]string, error)
}
```

This simple interface just describes a method that takes a term string and returns either a slice of strings containing the synonyms, or an error (if something goes wrong). Our BigHugh structure already implements this interface, but now other users could add interchangeable implementations for other services, such as Dictionary.com or the Merriam-Webster Online service.

Next we are going to use this new package in a program. Change directory in terminal by backing up a level to $GOPATH/src, create a new folder called synonyms, and insert the following code into a new main.go file you will place in that folder:

```go
func main() {
  apiKey := os.Getenv("BHT_APIKEY")
  thesaurus := &thesaurus.BigHugh{APIKey: apiKey}
  s := bufio.NewScanner(os.Stdin)
  for s.Scan() {
    word := s.Text()
    syns, err := thesaurus.Synonyms(word)
    if err != nil {
      log.Fatalln("Failed when looking for synonyms for
\""+word+"\"", err)
    }
    if len(syns) == 0 {
      log.Fatalln("Couldn't find any synonyms for \"" + word +
"\"")
    }
    for _, syn := range syns {
      fmt.Println(syn)
    }
  }
}
```

When you manage your imports again, you will have written a complete program capable of looking up synonyms for words by integrating the Big Huge Thesaurus API.

In the preceding code, the first thing our main function does is get the BHT_APIKEY environment variable value via the os.Getenv call. To bullet proof your code, you might consider double-checking to ensure this value is properly set, and report an error if it is not. For now, we will assume that everything is configured properly.

Next, the preceding code starts to look a little familiar since it scans each line of input again from os.Stdin and calls the Synonyms method to get a list of replacement words.

Let's build a program and see what kind of synonyms the API comes back with when we input the word chat:

```
go build -o synonyms
./synonyms
chat
confab
```

```
confabulation

schmooze

New World chat

Old World chat

conversation

thrush

wood warbler

chew the fat

shoot the breeze

chitchat

chatter
```

The results you get will most likely differ from what we have listed here since we're hitting a live API, but the important aspect here is that when we give a word or term as input to the program, it returns a list of synonyms as output, one per line.

 Try chaining your programs together in various orders to see what result you get. Regardless, we will do this together later in the chapter.

Getting domain suggestions

By composing the four programs we have built so far in this chapter, we already have a useful tool for suggesting domain names. All we have to do now is run the programs while piping the output into input in the appropriate way. In a terminal, navigate to the parent folder and run the following single line:

```
./synonyms/synonyms | ./sprinkle/sprinkle | ./coolify/coolify |
./domainify/domainify
```

Because the synonyms program is first in our list, it will receive the input from the terminal (whatever the user decides to type in). Similarly, because domainify is last in the chain, it will print its output to the terminal for the user to see. At each step, the lines of words will be piped through the other programs, giving them each a chance to do their magic.

Type in some words to see some domain suggestions, for example, if you type chat and hit return, you might see:

```
getcnfab.com

confabulationtim.com

getschmoozee.net
```

```
schmosee.com
neew-world-chatsite.net
oold-world-chatsite.com
conversatin.net
new-world-warblersit.com
gothrush.net
lets-wood-wrbler.com
chw-the-fat.com
```

The number of suggestions you get will actually depend on the number of synonyms, since it is the only program that generates more lines of output than we give it.

We still haven't solved our biggest problem—the fact that we have no idea whether the suggested domain names are actually available or not, so we still have to sit and type each of them into a website. In the next section, we will address this issue.

Available

Our final program, Available, will connect to a WHOIS server to ask for details about domains passed into it—of course, if no details are returned, we can safely assume that the domain is available for purchase. Unfortunately, the WHOIS specification (see `http://tools.ietf.org/html/rfc3912`) is very small and contains no information about how a WHOIS server should reply when you ask it for details about a domain. This means programmatically parsing the response becomes a messy endeavor. To address this issue for now, we will integrate with only a single WHOIS server that we can be sure will have No match somewhere in the response when it has no records for the domain.

 A more robust solution might be to have a WHOIS interface with well-defined structures for the details, and perhaps an error message for the cases when the domain doesn't exist—with different implementations for different WHOIS servers. As you can imagine, it's quite a project; perfect for an open source effort.

Create a new folder called `available` alongside the others in `$GOPATH/src` and add a `main.go` file
in it containing the following function code:

```go
func exists(domain string) (bool, error) {
  const whoisServer string = "com.whois-servers.net"
  conn, err := net.Dial("tcp", whoisServer+":43")
  if err != nil {
    return false, err
```

```
    }
    defer conn.Close()
    conn.Write([]byte(domain + "\r\n"))
    scanner := bufio.NewScanner(conn)
    for scanner.Scan() {
      if strings.Contains(strings.ToLower(scanner.Text()), "no
match") {
        return false, nil
      }
    }
    return true, nil
  }
```

The `exists` function implements what little there is in the WHOIS specification by opening a connection to port `43` on the specified `whoisServer` instance with a call to `net.Dial`. We then defer the closing of the connection, which means that however the function exits (successfully or with an error, or even a panic), `Close()` will still be called on the connection `conn`. Once the connection is open, we simply write the domain followed by `\r\n` (the carriage return and line feed characters). This is all the specification tells us, so we are on our own from now on.

Essentially, we are looking for some mention of no match in the response, and that is how we will decide whether a domain exists or not (`exists` in this case is actually just asking the WHOIS server if it has a record for the domain we specified). We use our favorite `bufio.Scanner` method to help us iterate over the lines in the response. Passing the connection into `NewScanner` works because `net.Conn` is actually an `io.Reader` too. We use `strings.ToLower` so we don't have to worry about case sensitivity, and `strings.Contains` to see if any of the lines contains the no match text. If it does, we return `false` (since the domain doesn't exist), otherwise we return `true`.

The `com.whois-servers.net` WHOIS service supports domain names for `.com` and `.net`, which is why the Domainify program only adds these types of domains. If you used a server that had WHOIS information for a wider selection of domains, you could add support for additional TLDs.

Let's add a `main` function that uses our `exists` function to check to see whether the incoming domains are available or not. The check mark and cross mark symbols in the following code are optional—if your terminal doesn't support them you are free to substitute them with simple `Yes` and `No` strings.

Add the following code to `main.go`:

```
var marks = map[bool]string{true: "✓", false: "✗"}
func main() {
  s := bufio.NewScanner(os.Stdin)
```

```
  for s.Scan() {
    domain := s.Text()
    fmt.Print(domain, " ")
    exist, err := exists(domain)
    if err != nil {
      log.Fatalln(err)
    }
    fmt.Println(marks[!exist])
    time.Sleep(1 * time.Second)
  }
}
```

In the preceding code for the `main` function, we simply iterate over each line coming in via `os.Stdin`, printing out the domain with `fmt.Print` (but not `fmt.Println`, as we do not want the linefeed yet), calling our `exists` function to see whether the domain exists or not, and printing out the result with `fmt.Println` (because we *do* want a linefeed at the end).

Finally, we use `time.Sleep` to tell the process to do nothing for 1 second in order to make sure we take it easy on the WHOIS server.

Most WHOIS servers will be limited in various ways in order to prevent you from taking up too much resources. So slowing things down is a sensible way to make sure we don't make the remote servers angry.

Consider what this also means for unit tests. If a unit test was actually making real requests to a remote WHOIS server, every time your tests run, you will be clocking up stats against your IP address. A much better approach would be to stub the WHOIS server to simulate real responses.

The `marks` map at the top of the preceding code is a nice way to map the Boolean response from `exists` to human-readable text, allowing us to just print the response in a single line using `fmt.Println(marks[!exist])`. We are saying not exist because our program is checking whether the domain is available or not (logically the opposite of whether it exists in the WHOIS server or not).

We can use the check and cross characters in our code happily because all Go code files are UTF-8 compliant—the best way to actually get these characters is to search the Web for them, and use copy and paste to bring them into code; else there are platform-dependent ways to get such special characters.

After fixing the `import` statements for the `main.go` file, we can try out Available to see whether domain names are available or not:

```
go build -o available
./available
```

Once Available is running, type in some domain names:

```
packtpub.com
packtpub.com ✗
google.com
google.com ✗
madeupdomain1897238746234.net
madeupdomain1897238746234.net ✓
```

As you can see, for domains that are obviously not available, we get our little cross mark, but when we make up a domain name using random numbers, we see that it is indeed available.

Composing all five programs

Now that we have completed all five of our programs, it's time to put them all together so that we can use our tool to find an available domain name for our chat application. The simplest way to do this is to use the technique we have been using throughout this chapter: using pipes in a terminal to connect the output and input.

In the terminal, navigate to the parent folder of the five programs and run the following single line of code:

```
./synonyms/synonyms | ./sprinkle/sprinkle | ./coolify/coolify |
./domainify/domainify | ./available/available
```

Once the programs are running, type in a starting word and see how it generates suggestions before checking their availability.

For example, typing in `chat` might cause the programs to take the following actions:

1. The word `chat` goes into `synonyms` and out comes a series of synonyms:
   ° confab
   ° confabulation
   ° schmooze

2. The synonyms flow into `sprinkle` where they are augmented with web-friendly prefixes and suffixes such as:

    ○ `confabapp`

    ○ `goconfabulation`

    ○ `schmooze time`

3. These new words flow into `coolify`, where the vowels are potentially tweaked:

    ○ `confabaapp`

    ○ `goconfabulatioon`

    ○ `schmoooze time`

4. The modified words then flow into `domainify` where they are turned into valid domain names:

    ○ `confabaapp.com`

    ○ `goconfabulatioon.net`

    ○ `schmooze-time.com`

5. Finally, the domain names flow into `available` where they are checked against the WHOIS server to see whether somebody has already taken the domain or not:

    ○ `confabaapp.com` ✗

    ○ `goconfabulatioon.net` ✓

    ○ `schmooze-time.com` ✓

One program to rule them all

Running our solution by piping programs together is an elegant architecture, but it doesn't have a very elegant interface. Specifically, whenever we want to run our solution, we have to type the long messy line where each program is listed separated by pipe characters. In this section, we are going to write a Go program that uses the `os/exec` package to run each subprogram while piping the output from one into the input of the next as per our design.

Create a new folder called `domainfinder` alongside the other five programs, and create another new folder called `lib` inside that folder. The `lib` folder is where we will keep builds of our subprograms, but we don't want to be copying and pasting them every time we make a change. Instead, we will write a script that builds the subprograms and copies the binaries to the `lib` folder for us.

Create a new file called `build.sh` on Unix machines or `build.bat` for Windows and insert the following code:

```bash
#!/bin/bash
echo Building domainfinder...
go build -o domainfinder
echo Building synonyms...
cd ../synonyms
go build -o ../domainfinder/lib/synonyms
echo Building available...
cd ../available
go build -o ../domainfinder/lib/available
cd ../build
echo Building sprinkle...
cd ../sprinkle
go build -o ../domainfinder/lib/sprinkle
cd ../build
echo Building coolify...
cd ../coolify
go build -o ../domainfinder/lib/coolify
cd ../build
echo Building domainify...
cd ../domainify
go build -o ../domainfinder/lib/domainify
cd ../build
echo Done.
```

The preceding script simply builds all of our subprograms (including `domainfinder`, which we are yet to write) telling `go build` to place them in our `lib` folder. Be sure to give the new script execution rights by doing `chmod +x build.sh`, or something similar. Run this script from a terminal and look inside the `lib` folder to ensure that it has indeed placed the binaries for our subprograms in there.

 Don't worry about the `no buildable Go source files` error for now, it's just Go telling us that the `domainfinder` program doesn't have any `.go` files to build.

Create a new file called `main.go` inside `domainfinder` and insert the following code in the file:

```go
package main
var cmdChain = []*exec.Cmd{
    exec.Command("lib/synonyms"),
    exec.Command("lib/sprinkle"),
```

```
        exec.Command("lib/coolify"),
        exec.Command("lib/domainify"),
        exec.Command("lib/available"),
}
func main() {

    cmdChain[0].Stdin = os.Stdin
    cmdChain[len(cmdChain)-1].Stdout = os.Stdout

    for i := 0; i < len(cmdChain)-1; i++ {
        thisCmd := cmdChain[i]
        nextCmd := cmdChain[i+1]
        stdout, err := thisCmd.StdoutPipe()
        if err != nil {
            log.Fatalln(err)
        }
        nextCmd.Stdin = stdout
    }

    for _, cmd := range cmdChain {
        if err := cmd.Start(); err != nil {
            log.Fatalln(err)
        } else {
            defer cmd.Process.Kill()
        }
    }

    for _, cmd := range cmdChain {
        if err := cmd.Wait(); err != nil {
            log.Fatalln(err)
        }
    }

}
```

The os/exec package gives us everything we need to work with running external programs or commands from within Go programs. First, our cmdChain slice contains *exec.Cmd commands in the order in which we want to join them together.

At the top of the main function, we tie the Stdin (standard in stream) of the first program to the os.Stdin stream for this program, and the Stdout (standard out stream) of the last program to the os.Stdout stream for this program. This means that, like before, we will be taking input through the standard input stream and writing output to the standard output stream.

Our next block of code is where we join the subprograms together by iterating over each item and setting its `Stdin` to the `Stdout` of the program before it.

The following table shows each program, with a description of where it gets its input from, and where its output goes:

Program	Input (Stdin)	Output (Stdout)
synonyms	The same `Stdin` as `domainfinder`	sprinkle
sprinkle	synonyms	coolify
coolify	sprinkle	domainify
domainify	coolify	available
available	domainify	The same `Stdout` as `domainfinder`

We then iterate over each command calling the `Start` method, which runs the program in the background (as opposed to the `Run` method which will block our code until the subprogram exits—which of course is no good since we have to run five programs at the same time). If anything goes wrong, we bail with `log.Fatalln`, but if the program starts successfully, we then defer a call to kill the process. This helps us ensure the subprograms exit when our `main` function exits, which will be when the `domainfinder` program ends.

Once all of the programs are running, we then iterate over every command again and wait for it to finish. This is to ensure that `domainfinder` doesn't exit early and kill off all the subprograms too soon.

Run the `build.sh` or `build.bat` script again and notice that the `domainfinder` program has the same behavior as we have seen before, with a much more elegant interface.

Summary

In this chapter, we learned how five small command-line programs can, when composed together, produce powerful results while remaining modular. We avoided tightly coupling our programs so they are still useful in their own right. For example, we can use our available program just to check if domain names we manually enter are available or not, or we can use our `synonyms` program just as a command-line thesaurus.

We learned how standard streams could be used to build different flows of these types of programs, and how redirection of the standard input and the standard output lets us play around with different flows very easily.

We learned how simple it is in Go to consume a JSON RESTful APIs web service when we needed to get synonyms from the Big Hugh Thesaurus. We kept it simple at first by coding it inline and later refactoring the code to abstract the `Thesaurus` type into its own package, which is ready to share. We also consumed a non-HTTP API when we opened a connection to the WHOIS server and wrote data over raw TCP.

We saw how the `math/rand` package can bring a little variety and unpredictability, by allowing us to use pseudo random numbers and decisions in our code, which meant that each time we run our program, we get different results.

Finally, we built our `domainfinder` super program that composes all the subprograms together giving our solution a simple, clean, and elegant interface.

5
Building Distributed Systems and Working with Flexible Data

In this chapter, we will explore transferrable skills that allow us to use schemaless data and distributed technologies to solve big data problems. The system we will build in this chapter will prepare us for a future where democratic elections all happen online—on Twitter of course. Our solution will collect and count votes by querying Twitter's streaming API for mentions of specific hashtags, and each component will be capable of horizontally scaling to meet demand. Our use case is a fun and interesting one, but the core concepts we'll learn and specific technology choices we'll make are the real focus of this chapter. The ideas discussed here are directly applicable to any system that needs true-scale capabilities.

 Horizontal scaling refers to adding nodes, such as physical machines, to a system in order to improve its availability, performance, and/ or capacity. Big data companies such as Google can scale by adding affordable and easy-to-obtain hardware (commonly referred to as commodity hardware) due to the way they write their software and architect their solutions. Vertical scaling is synonymous with increasing the resource available to a single node, such as adding additional RAM to a box, or a processor with more cores.

In this chapter, you will:

- Learn about distributed NoSQL datastores; specifically how to interact with MongoDB
- Learn about distributed messaging queues; specifically Bit.ly's NSQ and how to use the `go-nsq` package to easily publish and subscribe to events

- Stream live tweet data through Twitter's streaming APIs and manage long running net connections
- Learn about how to properly stop programs with many internal goroutines
- Learn how to use low memory channels for signaling

System design

Having a basic design sketched out is often useful, especially in distributed systems where many components will be communicating with each other in different ways. We don't want to spend too long on this stage because our design is likely to evolve as we get stuck into the details, but we will look at a high-level outline so we can discuss the constituents and how they fit together.

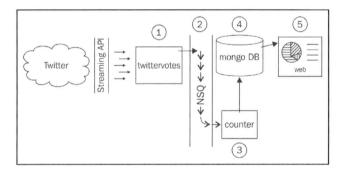

The preceding image shows the basic overview of the system we are going to build:

- Twitter is the social media network we all know and love.
- Twitter's streaming API allows long-running connections where tweet data is streamed as quickly as possible.
- `twittervotes` is a program we will write that reads tweets and pushes the votes into the messaging queue. `twittervotes` pulls the relevant tweet data, figures out what is being voted for (or rather, which options are mentioned), and pushes the vote into NSQ.
- NSQ is an open source, real-time distributed messaging platform designed to operate at scale, built and maintained by Bit.ly. NSQ carries the message across its instances making it available to anyone who has expressed an interest in the vote data.

- counter is a program we will write that listens out for votes on the messaging queue, and periodically saves the results in the MongoDB database. counter receives the vote messages from NSQ and keeps an in-memory tally of the results, periodically pushing an update to persist the data.
- MongoDB is an open source document database designed to operate at scale.
- web is a web server program that will expose the live results that we will write in the next chapter.

It could be argued that a single Go program could be written that reads the tweets, counts the votes, and pushes them to a user interface but such a solution, while being a great proof of concept, would be very limited in scale. In our design, any one of the components can be horizontally scaled as the demand for that particular capability increases. If we have relatively few polls, but lots of people viewing the data, we can keep the twittervotes and counter instances down and add more web and MongoDB nodes, or vice versa if the situation is reversed.

Another key advantage to our design is redundancy; since we can have many instances of our components working at the same time, if one of our boxes disappears (due to a system crash or power cut, for example) the others can pick up the slack. Modern architectures often distribute such a system over the geographical expanse to protect from local natural disasters too. All of these options are available to use if we build our solution in this way.

We chose the specific technologies in this chapter because of their links to Go (NSQ, for example, is written entirely in Go), and the availability of well-tested drivers and packages. Conceptually, however, you can drop in a variety of alternatives as you see fit.

Database design

We will call our MongoDB database ballots. It will contain a single collection called polls which is where we will store the poll details, such as the title, the options, and the results (in a single JSON document). The code for a poll will look something like this:

```
{
  "_id": "???",
  "title": "Poll title",
  "options": ["one", "two", "three"],
  "results": {
    "one": 100,
    "two": 200,
    "three": 300
  }
}
```

The _id field is automatically generated by MongoDB and will be how we identify each poll. The options field contains an array of string options; these are the hashtags we will look for on Twitter. The results field is a map where the key represents the option, and the value represents the total number of votes for each item.

Installing the environment

The code we write in this chapter has real external dependencies that we need to get set up before we can start to build our system.

 Be sure to check out the chapter notes at https://github.com/ matryer/goblueprints if you get stuck on installing any of the dependencies.

In most cases, services such as mongod and nsqd will have to be started before we can run our programs. Since we are writing components of a distributed system, we will have to run each program at the same time, which is as simple as opening many terminal windows.

NSQ

NSQ is a messaging queue that allows one program to send messages or events to another, or to many other programs running either locally on the same machine, or on different nodes connected by a network. NSQ guarantees the delivery of messages, which means it keeps undelivered messages cached until all interested parties have received them. This means that, even if we stop our counter program, we won't miss any votes. You can contrast this capability with fire-and-forget message queues where information is deemed out-of-date, and therefore is forgotten if it isn't delivered in time, and where the sender of the messages doesn't care if the consumer received them or not.

A message queue abstraction allows you to have different components of a system running in different places, provided they have network connectivity to the queue. Your programs are decoupled from others; instead, your designs start to care about the ins and outs of specialized micro-services, rather than the flow of data through a monolithic program.

NSQ transfers raw bytes, which means it is up to us how we encode data into those bytes. For example, we could encode the data as JSON or in a binary format depending on our needs. In our case, we are going to send the vote option as a string without any additional encoding, since we are only sharing a single data field.

Open `http://nsq.io/deployment/installing.html` in a browser (or search `install nsq`) and follow the instructions for your environment. You can either download pre-compiled binaries or build your own from the source. If you have homebrew installed, installing NSQ is as simple as typing:

```
brew install nsq
```

Once you have installed NSQ, you will need to add the `bin` folder to your PATH environment variable so that the tools are available in a terminal.

To validate that NSQ is properly installed, open a terminal and run `nsqlookupd`; if the program successfully starts, you should see some output similar to the following:

```
nsqlookupd v0.2.27 (built w/go1.3)
TCP: listening on [::]:4160
HTTP: listening on [::]:4161
```

We are going to use the default ports to interact with NSQ so take note of the TCP and HTTP ports listed in the output, as we will be referring to them in our code.

Press *Ctrl + C* to stop the process for now; we'll start them properly later.

The key tools from the NSQ install that we are going to use are `nsqlookupd` and `nsqd`. The `nsqlookupd` program is a daemon that manages topology information about the distributed NSQ environment; it keeps track of all the `nsqd` producers for specific topics and provides interfaces for clients to query such information. The `nsqd` program is a daemon that does the heavy lifting for NSQ such as receiving, queuing, and delivering messages from and to interested parties. For more information and background on NSQ, visit `http://nsq.io/`.

NSQ driver for Go

The NSQ tools themselves are written in Go, so it is logical that the Bit.ly team already has a Go package that makes interacting with NSQ very easy. We will need to use it, so in a terminal, get it using `go get`:

```
go get github.com/bitly/go-nsq
```

MongoDB

MongoDB is a document database, which basically allows you to store and query JSON documents and the data within them. Each document goes into a collection that can be used to group the documents together without enforcing any schema on the data inside them. Unlike rows in a traditional RDBMS such as Oracle, Microsoft SQL Server, or MySQL, it is perfectly acceptable for documents to have a different shape. For example, a `people` collection can contain the following three JSON documents at the same time:

```
{"name":"Mat","lang":"en","points":57}
{"name":"Laurie","position":"Scrum Master"}
{"position":"Traditional Manager","exists":false}
```

This flexibility allows data with varying structure to coexist without impacting performance or wasting space. It is also extremely useful if you expect your software to evolve over time, as we really always should.

MongoDB was designed to scale while also remaining very easy to work with on single-box install such as our development machine. When we host our application for production, we would likely install a more complex multi-sharded, replicated system, which is distributed across many nodes and locations, but for now, just running `mongod` will do.

Head over to `http://www.mongodb.org/downloads` to grab the latest version of MongoDB and install it, making sure to register the `bin` folder with your PATH environment variable as usual.

To validate that MongoDB is successfully installed, run the `mongod` command, then hit *Ctrl + C* to stop it for now.

MongoDB driver for Go

Gustavo Niemeyer has done a great job in simplifying interactions with MongoDB with his `mgo` (pronounced "mango") package hosted at `http://labix.org/mgo`, which is *go gettable* with the following command:

```
go get gopkg.in/mgo.v2
```

Starting the environment

Now that we have all the pieces we need installed, we need to start our environment. In this section, we are going to:

- Start `nsqlookupd` so that our `nsqd` instances are discoverable
- Start `nsqd` and tell it which `nsqlookupd` to use
- Start `mongod` for data services

Each of these daemons should run in their own terminal window, which will make it easy for us to stop them by just hitting *Ctrl + C*.

Remember the page number for this section as you will likely revisit it a few times as you work through this chapter.

In a terminal window, run:

```
nsqlookupd
```

Take note of the TCP port, which by default is `4160`, and in another terminal window, run:

```
nsqd --lookupd-tcp-address=localhost:4160
```

Make sure the port number in the `--lookupd-tcp-address` flag matches the TCP port of the `nsqlookupd` instance. Once you start `nsqd`, you will notice some output is printed to the terminal from both `nsqlookupd` and `nsqd`; this indicates that the two processes are talking to each other.

In yet another window or tab, start MongoDB by running:

```
mongod --dbpath ./db
```

The `dbpath` flag tells MongoDB where to store the data files for our database. You can pick any location you like, but you'll have to make sure the folder exists before `mongod` will run.

By deleting the `dbpath` folder at any time, you can effectively erase all data and start afresh. This is especially useful during development.

Now that our environment is running, we are ready to start building our components.

Votes from Twitter

In your `$GOPATH/src` folder, alongside other projects, create a new folder called `socialpoll` for this chapter. This folder won't be a Go package or program by itself, but will contain our three component programs. Inside `socialpoll`, create a new folder called `twittervotes` and add the obligatory `main.go` template (this is important as `main` packages without a `main` function won't compile):

```
package main
func main(){}
```

Our `twittervotes` program is going to:

- Load all polls from the MongoDB database using `mgo`, and collect all options from the `options` array in each document

- Open and maintain a connection to Twitter's streaming APIs looking for any mention of the options

- For each tweet that matches the filter, figure out which option is mentioned and push that option through to NSQ

- If the connection to Twitter is dropped (which is common in long-running connections as it is actually part of Twitter's streaming API specification) after a short delay (so we do not bombard Twitter with connection requests), reconnect and continue

- Periodically re-query MongoDB for the latest polls and refresh the connection to Twitter to make sure we are always looking out for the right options

- When the user terminates the program by hitting *Ctrl + C*, it will gracefully stop itself

Authorization with Twitter

In order to use the streaming API, we will need authentication credentials from Twitter's Application Management console, much in the same way we did for our Gomniauth service providers in *Chapter 3, Three Ways to Implement Profile Pictures*. Head over to `https://apps.twitter.com` and create a new app called something like `SocialPoll` (the names have to be unique, so you can have some fun here; the choice of name doesn't affect the code either way). When your app has been created, visit the **API Keys** tab and locate the **Your access token** section where you need to create a new access token. After a short delay, refresh the page and notice that you in fact have two sets of keys and secrets; an API key and a secret, and an access token and the corresponding secret. Following good coding practices, we are going to set these values as environment variables so that our program can have access to them without us having to hardcode them in our source files.

The keys we will use in this chapter are:

- `SP_TWITTER_KEY`
- `SP_TWITTER_SECRET`
- `SP_TWITTER_ACCESSTOKEN`
- `SP_TWITTER_ACCESSSECRET`

You can set the environment variables however you like, but since the app relies on them in order to work, creating a new file called `setup.sh` (for bash shells) or `setup.bat` (on Windows) is a good idea since you can check such files into your source code repository. Insert the following code in `setup.sh` or `setup.bat` by copying the appropriate values from the Twitter app page:

```
#!/bin/bash
export SP_TWITTER_KEY=yCwwKKnuBnUBrelyTN...
export SP_TWITTER_SECRET=6on0YRYniT1sI3f...
export SP_TWITTER_ACCESSTOKEN=2427-13677...
export SP_TWITTER_ACCESSSECRET=SpnZf336u...
```

Run the file with the source or call commands to have the values appropriately set, or add them to your `.bashrc` or `C:\cmdauto.cmd` files to save you running them every time you open a new terminal window.

Extracting the connection

The Twitter streaming API supports HTTP connections that stay open for a long time, and given the design of our solution, we are going to need to access the `net.Conn` object in order to close it from outside of the goroutine in which requests occur. We can achieve this by providing our own `dial` method to an `http.Transport` object that we will create.

Create a new file called `twitter.go` inside `twittervotes` (which is where all things Twitter-related will live), and insert the following code:

```
var conn net.Conn
func dial(netw, addr string) (net.Conn, error) {
  if conn != nil {
    conn.Close()
    conn = nil
  }
  netc, err := net.DialTimeout(netw, addr, 5*time.Second)
  if err != nil {
```

```
    return nil, err
  }
  conn = netc
  return netc, nil
}
```

Our bespoke `dial` function first ensures `conn` is closed, and then opens a new connection keeping the `conn` variable updated with the current connection. If a connection dies (Twitter's API will do this from time to time) or is closed by us, we can redial without worrying about zombie connections.

We will periodically close the connection ourselves and initiate a new one, because we want to reload the options from the database at regular intervals. To do this, we need a function that closes the connection, and also closes an `io.ReadCloser` that we will use to read the body of the responses. Add the following code to `twitter.go`:

```
var reader io.ReadCloser
func closeConn() {
  if conn != nil {
    conn.Close()
  }
  if reader != nil {
    reader.Close()
  }
}
```

Now we can call `closeConn` at any time to break the ongoing connection with Twitter and tidy things up. In most cases, our code will load the options from the database again and open a new connection right away, but if we're shutting the program down (in response to a *Ctrl + C* hit) then we can call `closeConn` just before we exit.

Reading environment variables

Next we are going to write a function that will read the environment variables and set up the `OAuth` objects we'll need in order to authenticate the requests. Add the following code in the `twitter.go` file:

```
var (
  authClient *oauth.Client
  creds *oauth.Credentials
)
```

```
func setupTwitterAuth() {
  var ts struct {
    ConsumerKey     string `env:"SP_TWITTER_KEY,required"`
    ConsumerSecret  string `env:"SP_TWITTER_SECRET,required"`
    AccessToken     string `env:"SP_TWITTER_ACCESSTOKEN,required"`
    AccessSecret    string `env:"SP_TWITTER_ACCESSSECRET,required"`
  }
  if err := envdecode.Decode(&ts); err != nil {
    log.Fatalln(err)
  }
  creds = &oauth.Credentials{
    Token:  ts.AccessToken,
    Secret: ts.AccessSecret,
  }
  authClient = &oauth.Client{
    Credentials: oauth.Credentials{
      Token:  ts.ConsumerKey,
      Secret: ts.ConsumerSecret,
    },
  }
}
```

Here we define a `struct` type to store the environment variables that we need to authenticate with Twitter. Since we don't need to use the type elsewhere, we define it inline and creating a variable called `ts` of this anonymous type (that's why we have the somewhat unusual `var ts struct...` code). We then use Joe Shaw's elegant `envdecode` package to pull in those environment variables for us. You will need to run `go get github.com/joeshaw/envdecode` and also import the `log` package. Our program will try to load appropriate values for all the fields marked `required`, and return an error if it fails to do so, which reminds people that the program won't work without Twitter credentials.

The strings inside the back ticks alongside each field in `struct` are called tags, and are available through a reflection interface, which is how `envdecode` knows which variables to look for. Tyler Bunnell and I added the required argument to this package, which indicates that it is an error for any of the environment variables to be missing (or empty).

Once we have the keys, we use them to create `oauth.Credentials` and an `oauth.Client` object from Gary Burd's `go-oauth` package, which will allow us to authorize requests with Twitter.

Now that we have the ability to control the underlying connection and authorize requests, we are ready to write the code that will actually build the authorized request, and return the response. In `twitter.go`, add the following code:

```
var (
  authSetupOnce sync.Once
  httpClient    *http.Client
)
func makeRequest(req *http.Request, params url.Values) (*http.
Response, error) {
  authSetupOnce.Do(func() {
    setupTwitterAuth()
    httpClient = &http.Client{
      Transport: &http.Transport{
        Dial: dial,
      },
    }
  })
  formEnc := params.Encode()
  req.Header.Set("Content-Type", "application/x-www-form-
urlencoded")
  req.Header.Set("Content-Length", strconv.Itoa(len(formEnc)))
  req.Header.Set("Authorization",
authClient.AuthorizationHeader(creds, "POST", req.URL, params))
  return httpClient.Do(req)
}
```

We use `sync.Once` to ensure our initialization code only gets run once despite the number of times we call `makeRequest`. After calling the `setupTwitterAuth` method, we create a new `http.Client` using an `http.Transport` that uses our custom `dial` method. We then set the appropriate headers needed for authorization with Twitter by encoding the specified `params` object that will contain the options we are querying for.

Reading from MongoDB

In order to load the polls, and therefore the options to search Twitter for, we need to connect to and query MongoDB. In `main.go`, add the two functions `dialdb` and `closedb`:

```
var db *mgo.Session
func dialdb() error {
  var err error
  log.Println("dialing mongodb: localhost")
  db, err = mgo.Dial("localhost")
  return err
```

```
}
func closedb() {
  db.Close()
  log.Println("closed database connection")
}
```

These two functions will connect to and disconnect from the locally running MongoDB instance using the mgo package, and store mgo.Session (the database connection object) in a global variable called db.

> As an additional assignment, see if you can find an elegant way to make the location of the MongoDB instance configurable so that you don't need to run it locally.

Assuming MongoDB is running and our code is able to connect, we need to load the poll objects and extract all the options from the documents, which we will then use to search Twitter. Add the following Options function to main.go:

```
type poll struct {
  Options []string
}
func loadOptions() ([]string, error) {
  var options []string
  iter := db.DB("ballots").C("polls").Find(nil).Iter()
  var p poll
  for iter.Next(&p) {
    options = append(options, p.Options...)
  }
  iter.Close()
  return options, iter.Err()
}
```

Our poll document contains more than just Options, but our program doesn't care about anything else, so there's no need for us to bloat our poll struct. We use the db variable to access the polls collection from the ballots database, and call the mgo package's fluent Find method, passing nil (meaning no filtering).

> A fluent interface (first coined by Eric Evans and Martin Fowler) refers to an API design that aims to make the code more readable by allowing you to chain together method calls. This is achieved by each method returning the context object itself, so that another method can be called directly afterwards. For example, mgo allows you to write queries such as this:
> ```
> query := col.Find(q).Sort("field").Limit(10).Skip(10)
> ```

We then get an iterator by calling the `Iter` method, which allows us to access each poll one by one. This is a very memory-efficient way of reading the poll data, because it only ever uses a single `poll` object. If we were to use the `All` method instead, the amount of memory we'd use would depend on the number of polls we had in our database, which would be out of our control.

When we have a poll, we use the `append` method to build up the options slice. Of course, with millions of polls in the database, this slice too would grow large and unwieldy. For that kind of scale, we would probably run multiple `twittervotes` programs, each dedicated to a portion of the poll data. A simple way to do this would be to break polls into groups based on the letters the titles begin with, such as group A-N and O-Z. A somewhat more sophisticated approach would be to add a field to the `poll` document grouping it up in a more controlled manner, perhaps based on the stats for the other groups so that we are able to balance the load across many `twittervotes` instances.

 The `append` built-in function is actually a `variadic` function, which means you can pass multiple elements for it to append. If you have a slice of the correct type, you can add `...` to the end, which simulates the passing of each item of the slice as a different argument.

Finally, we close the iterator and clean up any used memory before returning the options and any errors that occurred while iterating (by calling the `Err` method on the `mgo.Iter` object).

Reading from Twitter

Now we are able to load the options and make authorized requests to the Twitter API. We are thus ready to write the code that initiates the connection, and continuously reads from the stream until either we call our `closeConn` method, or Twitter closes the connection for one reason or another. The structure contained in the stream is a complex one containing all kinds of information about the tweet—who made it and when, and even what links or mentions of users occur in the body (see Twitter's API documentation for more details). However, we are only interested in the tweet text itself so you need not worry about all the other noise; add the following structure to `twitter.go`:

```
type tweet struct {
  Text string
}
```

This may feel incomplete, but think about how clear it makes our intentions to other programmers who might see our code: a tweet has some text, and that is all we care about.

Using this new structure, in `twitter.go`, add the following `readFromTwitter` function that takes a send-only channel called `votes`; this is how this function will inform the rest of our program that it has noticed a vote on twitter:

```go
func readFromTwitter(votes chan<- string) {
  options, err := loadOptions()
  if err != nil {
    log.Println("failed to load options:", err)
    return
  }
  u, err := url.Parse("https://stream.twitter.com/1.1/statuses/filter.
json")
  if err != nil {
    log.Println("creating filter request failed:", err)
    return
  }
  query := make(url.Values)
  query.Set("track", strings.Join(options, ","))
  req, err := http.NewRequest("POST", u.String(), strings.
NewReader(query.Encode()))
  if err != nil {
    log.Println("creating filter request failed:", err)
    return
  }
  resp, err := makeRequest(req, query)
  if err != nil {
    log.Println("making request failed:", err)
    return
  }
  reader := resp.Body
  decoder := json.NewDecoder(reader)
  for {
    var tweet tweet
    if err := decoder.Decode(&tweet); err != nil {
      break
    }
    for _, option := range options {
      if strings.Contains(
        strings.ToLower(tweet.Text),
```

```
            strings.ToLower(option),
        ) {
            log.Println("vote:", option)
            votes <- option
        }
      }
    }
  }
}
```

In the preceding code, after loading the options from all the polls data (by calling the loadOptions function), we use url.Parse to create a url.URL object describing the appropriate endpoint on Twitter. We build a url.Values object called query, and set the options as a comma-separated list. As per the API, we make a new POST request using the encoded url.Values object as the body, and pass it to makeRequest along with the query object itself. All being well, we make a new json.Decoder from the body of the request, and keep reading inside an infinite for loop by calling the Decode method. If there is an error (probably due to the connection being closed), we simply break the loop and exit the function. If there is a tweet to read, it will be decoded into the tweet variable, which will give us access to the Text property (the 140 characters of the tweet itself). We then iterate over all possible options, and if the tweet has mentioned it, we send it on the votes channel. This technique also allows a tweet to contain many votes at the same time, something you may or may not decide to change based on the rules of the election.

> The votes channel is **send-only** (which means we cannot receive on it), since it is of the type chan<- string. Think of the little "arrow" telling us which way messages will flow: either into the channel or out of it. This is a great way to express intent—it's clear that we never intend to read votes using our readFromTwitter function; rather we will only send them on that channel.

Terminating the program whenever Decode returns an error doesn't provide a very robust solution. This is because the Twitter API documentation states that the connection will drop from time to time, and clients should consider this when consuming the services. And remember, we are going to terminate the connection periodically too, so we need to think about a way to reconnect once the connection is dropped.

Signal channels

A great use of channels in Go is to signal events between code running in different goroutines. We are going to see a real-world example of this when we write our next function.

The purpose of the function is to start a goroutine that continually calls the `readFromTwitter` function (with the specified `votes` channel to receive the votes on), until we signal that we want it to stop. And once it has stopped, we want to be notified through another signal channel. The return of the function will be a channel of `struct{}`; a signal channel.

Signal channels have some interesting properties that are worth taking a closer look at. Firstly, the type sent down the channels is an empty `struct{}`, instances of which actually take up zero bytes, since it has no fields. So `struct{}{}` is a great memory-efficient option for signaling events. Some people use `bool` types, which is also fine, although `true` and `false` both take up a byte of memory.

> Head over to `http://play.golang.org` and try this out for yourself.
> The size of a `bool` is 1:
>
> ```
> fmt.Println(reflect.TypeOf(true).Size())
> = 1
> ```
>
> Whereas the size of `struct{}{}` is 0:
>
> ```
> fmt.Println(reflect.TypeOf(struct{}{}).Size())
> = 0
> ```

The signal channels also have a buffer size of 1, which means that execution will not block until something reads the signal from the channel.

We are going to employ two signal channels in our code, one that we pass into our function that tells our goroutine that it should stop, and another (provided by the function) that signals once stopping is complete.

In `twitter.go`, add the following function:

```go
func startTwitterStream(stopchan <-chan struct{}, votes chan<- string)
<-chan struct{} {
  stoppedchan := make(chan struct{}, 1)
  go func() {
    defer func() {
      stoppedchan <- struct{}{}
    }()
    for {
      select {
      case <-stopchan:
        log.Println("stopping Twitter...")
        return
      default:
```

```
        log.Println("Querying Twitter...")
        readFromTwitter(votes)
        log.Println("  (waiting)")
        time.Sleep(10 * time.Second) // wait before reconnecting
      }
    }
  }()
  return stoppedchan
}
```

In the preceding code, the first argument `stopchan` is a channel of type `<-chan struct{}`, a **receive-only** signal channel. It is this channel that, outside the code, will signal on, which will tell our goroutine to stop. Remember that it's receive-only inside this function, the actual channel itself will be capable of sending. The second argument is the `votes` channel on which votes will be sent. The return type of our function is also a signal channel of type `<-chan struct{}`; a receive-only channel that we will use to indicate that we have stopped.

These channels are necessary because our function triggers its own goroutine, and immediately returns, so without this, calling code would have no idea if the spawned code were still running or not.

The first thing we do in the `startTwitterStream` function is make our `stoppedchan`, and defer the sending of a `struct{}{}` to indicate that we have finished when our function exits. Notice that `stoppedchan` is a normal channel so even though it is returned as a receive-only, we will be able to send on it from within this function.

We then start an infinite `for` loop in which we select from one of two channels. The first is the `stopchan` (the first argument), which would indicate that it was time to stop, and return (thus triggering the deferred signaling on `stoppedchan`). If that hasn't happened, we will call `readFromTwitter` (passing in the `votes` channel), which will go and load the options from the database and open the connection to Twitter.

When the Twitter connection dies, our code will return here where we sleep for ten seconds using the `time.Sleep` function. This is to give the Twitter API a rest in case it closed the connection due to overuse. Once we've rested, we re-enter the loop and check again on the `stopchan` channel to see if the calling code wants us to stop or not.

To make this flow clear, we are logging out key statements that will not only help us debug our code, but also let us peek into the inner workings of this somewhat complicated mechanism.

Publishing to NSQ

Once our code is successfully noticing votes on Twitter and sending them down the votes channel, we need a way to publish them into an NSQ topic; after all, this is the point of the `twittervotes` program.

We will write a function called `publishVotes` that will take the votes channel, this time of type `<-chan string` (a receive-only channel) and publish each string that is received from it.

> In our previous functions, the votes channel was of type `chan<-string`, but this time it's of the type `<-chan string`. You might think this is a mistake, or even that it means we cannot use the same channel for both but you would be wrong. The channel we create later will be made with `make(chan string)`, neither receive or only send, and can act in both cases. The reason for using the `<-` operator on a channel in arguments is to make clear the intent of what the channel will be used for; or in the case where it is the return type, to prevent users from accidentally sending on channels intended for receiving or vice versa. The compiler will actually produce an error if they use such a channel incorrectly.

Once the votes channel is closed (this is how external code will tell our function to stop working), we will stop publishing and send a signal down the returned stop signal channel.

Add the `publishVotes` function to `main.go`:

```
func publishVotes(votes <-chan string) <-chan struct{} {
  stopchan := make(chan struct{}, 1)
  pub, _ := nsq.NewProducer("localhost:4150", nsq.NewConfig())
  go func() {
    for vote := range votes {
      pub.Publish("votes", []byte(vote)) // publish vote
    }
    log.Println("Publisher: Stopping")
    pub.Stop()
    log.Println("Publisher: Stopped")
    stopchan <- struct{}{}
  }()
  return stopchan
}
```

Again the first thing we do is to create the `stopchan`, which we later return, this time not deferring the signaling but doing it inline by sending a `struct{}{}` down `stopchan`.

> The difference is to show alternative options: within one codebase you should pick a style you like and stick with it, until a standard emerges within the community; in which case we should all go with that.

We then create an NSQ producer by calling `NewProducer` and connecting to the default NSQ port on `localhost`, using a default configuration. We start a goroutine, which uses another great built-in feature of the Go language that lets us continually pull values from a channel (in our case the `votes` channel) just by doing a normal `for...range` operation on it. Whenever the channel has no values, execution will be blocked until a value comes down the line. If the `votes` channel is closed, the `for` loop will exit.

> To learn more about the power of channels in Go, it is highly recommended that you seek out blog posts and videos by John Graham-Cumming, in particular one entitled *A Channel Compendium* that he presented at Gophercon 2014 and which contains a brief history of channels, including their origin. (Interestingly, John was also the guy who successfully petitioned the British Government to officially apologize for its treatment of Alan Turing.)

When the loop exits (after the `votes` channel is closed) the publisher is stopped, following which the `stopchan` signal is sent.

Gracefully starting and stopping

When our program is terminated, we want to do a few things before actually exiting; namely closing our connection to Twitter and stopping the NSQ publisher (which actually deregisters its interest in the queue). To achieve this, we have to override the default *Ctrl + C* behavior.

> The upcoming code blocks all go inside the main function; they are broken up so we can discuss each section before continuing.

Add the following code inside the `main` function:

```
var stoplock sync.Mutex
stop := false
stopChan := make(chan struct{}, 1)
```

```
signalChan := make(chan os.Signal, 1)
go func() {
  <-signalChan
  stoplock.Lock()
  stop = true
  stoplock.Unlock()
  log.Println("Stopping...")
  stopChan <- struct{}{}
  closeConn()
}()
signal.Notify(signalChan, syscall.SIGINT, syscall.SIGTERM)
```

Here we create a stop `bool` with an associated `sync.Mutex` so that we can access it
from many goroutines at the same time. We then create two more signal channels,
`stopChan` and `signalChan`, and use `signal.Notify` to ask Go to send the signal
down the `signalChan` when someone tries to halt the program (either with the
SIGINT interrupt, or the SIGTERM termination POSIX signals). The `stopChan` is how
we indicate that we want our processes to terminate, and we pass it as an argument
to `startTwitterStream` later.

We then run a goroutine that blocks waiting for the signal by trying to read from
`signalChan`; this is what the `<-` operator does in this case (it's trying to read from
the channel). Since we don't care about the type of signal, we don't bother capturing
the object returned on the channel. Once a signal is received, we set `stop` to `true`,
and close the connection. Only when one of the specified signals is sent will the
rest of the goroutine code run, which is how we are able to perform teardown code
before exiting the program.

Add the following piece of code (inside the main function) to open and defer the
closing of the database connection:

```
if err := dialdb(); err != nil {
  log.Fatalln("failed to dial MongoDB:", err)
}
defer closedb()
```

Since the `readFromTwitter` method reloads the options from the database each
time, and because we want to keep our program updated without having to restart
it, we are going to introduce one final goroutine. This goroutine will simply call
`closeConn` every minute, causing the connection to die, and cause `readFromTwitter`
to be called over again. Insert the following code at the bottom of the `main` function
to start all of these processes, and then wait for them to gracefully stop:

```
// start things
votes := make(chan string) // chan for votes
```

```
publisherStoppedChan := publishVotes(votes)
twitterStoppedChan := startTwitterStream(stopChan, votes)
go func() {
  for {
    time.Sleep(1 * time.Minute)
    closeConn()
    stoplock.Lock()
    if stop {
      stoplock.Unlock()
      break
    }
    stoplock.Unlock()
  }
}()
<-twitterStoppedChan
close(votes)
<-publisherStoppedChan
```

First we make the `votes` channel that we have been talking about throughout this section, which is a simple channel of string. Notice that it is neither a send (`chan<-`) or receive (`<-chan`) channel; in fact, making such channels makes little sense. We then call `publishVotes`, passing in the `votes` channel for it to receive from, and capturing the returned stop signal channel as `publisherStoppedChan`. Similarly, we call `startTwitterStream` passing in our `stopChan` from the beginning of the `main` function, and the `votes` channel for it to send to, while capturing the resulting stop signal channel as `twitterStoppedChan`.

We then start our refresher goroutine, which immediately enters an infinite `for` loop before sleeping for a minute and closing the connection via the call to `closeConn`. If the stop `bool` has been set to true (in that previous goroutine), we will `break` the loop and exit, otherwise we will loop around and wait another minute before closing the connection again. The use of the `stoplock` is important because we have two goroutines that might try to access the stop variable at the same time but we want to avoid collisions.

Once the goroutine has started, we then block on the `twitterStoppedChan` by attempting to read from it. When successful (which means the signal was sent on the `stopChan`), we close the `votes` channel which will cause the publisher's `for...range` loop to exit, and the publisher itself to stop, after which the signal will be sent on the `publisherStoppedChan`, which we wait for before exiting.

Testing

To make sure our program works, we need to do two things: first we need to create a poll in the database, and second, we need to peer inside the messaging queue to see if the messages are indeed being generated by `twittervotes`.

In a terminal, run the `mongo` command to open a database shell that allows us to interact with MongoDB. Then enter the following commands to add a test poll:

```
> use ballots
switched to db ballots

> db.polls.insert({"title":"Test poll","options":["happy","sad","fail","w
in"]})
```

The preceding commands add a new item to the `polls` collection in the `ballots` database. We are using some common words for options that are likely to be mentioned by people on Twitter so that we can observe real tweets being translated into messages. You might notice that our poll object is missing the `results` field; this is fine since we are dealing with unstructured data where documents do not have to adhere to a strict schema. The `counter` program we are going to write in the next section will add and maintain the `results` data for us later.

Press *Ctrl + C* to exit the MongoDB shell and type the following command:

```
nsq_tail --topic="votes" --lookupd-http-address=localhost:4161
```

The `nsq_tail` tool connects to the specified messaging queue topic and outputs any messages that it notices. This is where we will validate that our `twittervotes` program is sending messages.

In a separate terminal window, let's build and run the `twittervotes` program:

```
go build -o twittervotes
./twittervotes
```

Now switch back to the window running `nsq_tail` and notice that messages are indeed being generated in response to live Twitter activity.

 If you aren't seeing much activity, try looking up trending hashtags on Twitter and adding another poll containing those options.

Counting votes

The second program we are going to implement is the `counter` tool, which will be responsible for watching out for votes in NSQ, counting them, and keeping MongoDB up to date with the latest numbers.

Create a new folder called `counter` alongside `twittervotes`, and add the following code to a new `main.go` file:

```
package main
import (
  "flag"
  "fmt"
  "os"
)
var fatalErr error
func fatal(e error) {
  fmt.Println(e)
  flag.PrintDefaults()
  fatalErr = e
}
func main() {
  defer func() {
    if fatalErr != nil {
      os.Exit(1)
    }
  }()
}
```

Normally when we encounter an error in our code, we use a call like `log.Fatal` or `os.Exit`, which immediately terminates the program. Exiting the program with a non-zero exit code is important, because it is our way of telling the operating system that something went wrong, and we didn't complete our task successfully. The problem with the normal approach is that any deferred functions we have scheduled (and therefore any tear down code we need to run), won't get a chance to execute.

The pattern employed in the preceding code snippet lets us call the `fatal` function to record that an error occurred. Note that only when our main function exits will the deferred function run, which in turn calls `os.Exit(1)` to exit the program with an exit code of 1. Because the deferred statements are run in LIFO (last in, first out) order, the first function we defer will be the last function to be executed, which is why the first thing we do in the `main` function is to defer the exiting code. This allows us to be sure that other functions we defer will be called *before* the program exits. We'll use this feature to ensure our database connection gets closed regardless of any errors.

Connecting to the database

The best time to think about cleaning up resources, such as database connections, is immediately after you have successfully obtained the resource; Go's `defer` keyword makes this easy. At the bottom of the main function, add the following code:

```
log.Println("Connecting to database...")
db, err := mgo.Dial("localhost")
if err != nil {
  fatal(err)
  return
}
defer func() {
  log.Println("Closing database connection...")
  db.Close()
}()
pollData := db.DB("ballots").C("polls")
```

This code uses the familiar `mgo.Dial` method to open a session to the locally running MongoDB instance and immediately defers a function that closes the session. We can be sure that this code will run before our previously deferred statement containing the exit code (because deferred functions are run in the reverse order in which they were called). Therefore, whatever happens in our program, we know that the database session will definitely and properly close.

> The log statements are optional, but will help us see what's going on when we run and exit our program.

At the end of the snippet, we use the `mgo` fluent API to keep a reference of the `ballots.polls` data collection in the `pollData` variable, which we will use later to make queries.

Consuming messages in NSQ

In order to count the votes, we need to consume the messages on the `votes` topic in NSQ, and we'll need a place to store them. Add the following variables to the `main` function:

```
var counts map[string]int
var countsLock sync.Mutex
```

A map and a lock (sync.Mutex) is a common combination in Go, because we will have multiple goroutines trying to access the same map and we need to avoid corrupting it by trying to modify or read it at the same time.

Add the following code to the main function:

```
log.Println("Connecting to nsq...")
q, err := nsq.NewConsumer("votes", "counter", nsq.NewConfig())
if err != nil {
  fatal(err)
  return
}
```

The NewConsumer function allows us to set up an object that will listen on the votes NSQ topic, so when twittervotes publishes a vote on that topic, we can handle it in this program. If NewConsumer returns an error, we'll use our fatal function to record it and return.

Next we are going to add the code that handles messages (votes) from NSQ:

```
q.AddHandler(nsq.HandlerFunc(func(m *nsq.Message) error {
  countsLock.Lock()
  defer countsLock.Unlock()
  if counts == nil {
    counts = make(map[string]int)
  }
  vote := string(m.Body)
  counts[vote]++
  return nil
}))
```

We call the AddHandler method on nsq.Consumer and pass it a function that will be called for every message received on the votes topic.

When a vote comes in, the first thing we do is lock the countsLock mutex. Next we defer the unlocking of the mutex for when the function exits. This allows us to be sure that while NewConsumer is running, we are the only ones allowed to modify the map; others will have to wait until our function exits before they can use it. Calls to the Lock method block execution while the lock is in place, and it only continues when the lock is released by a call to Unlock. This is why it's vital that every Lock call has an Unlock counterpart, otherwise we will deadlock our program.

Every time we receive a vote, we check if counts is nil and make a new map if it is, because once the database has been updated with the latest results, we want to reset everything and start at zero. Finally we increase the int value by one for the given key, and return nil indicating no errors.

Although we have created our NSQ consumer, and added our handler function, we still need to connect to the NSQ service, which we will do by adding the following code:

```
if err := q.ConnectToNSQLookupd("localhost:4161"); err != nil {
  fatal(err)
  return
}
```

It is important to note that we are actually connecting to the HTTP port of the `nsqlookupd` instance, rather than NSQ instances; this abstraction means that our program doesn't need to know *where* the messages are coming from in order to consume them. If we fail to connect to the server (for instance if we forget to start it), we'll get an error, which we report to our fatal function before immediately returning.

Keeping the database updated

Our code will listen out for votes, and keep a map of the results in memory, but that information is so far trapped inside our program. Next, we need to add the code that will periodically push the results to the database:

```
log.Println("Waiting for votes on nsq...")
var updater *time.Timer
updater = time.AfterFunc(updateDuration, func() {
  countsLock.Lock()
  defer countsLock.Unlock()
  if len(counts) == 0 {
    log.Println("No new votes, skipping database update")
  } else {
    log.Println("Updating database...")
    log.Println(counts)
    ok := true
    for option, count := range counts {
      sel := bson.M{"options": bson.M{"$in": []string{option}}}
      up := bson.M{"$inc": bson.M{"results." + option: count}}
      if _, err := pollData.UpdateAll(sel, up); err != nil {
        log.Println("failed to update:", err)
        ok = false
      }
    }
    if ok {
      log.Println("Finished updating database...")
```

```
        counts = nil // reset counts
    }
  }
  updater.Reset(updateDuration)
})
```

The `time.AfterFunc` function calls the function after the specified duration in a goroutine of its own. At the end we call `Reset`, which starts the process again; this allows us to schedule our update code to run at regular intervals.

When our update function runs, the first thing we do is lock the `countsLock`, and defer its unlocking. We then check to see if there are any values in the counts map. If there aren't, we just log that we're skipping the update and wait for next time.

If there are some votes, we iterate over the `counts` map pulling out the option and number of votes (since the last update), and use some MongoDB magic to update the results.

 MongoDB stores BSON (short for Binary JSON) documents internally, which are easier to traverse than normal JSON documents, and is why the `mgo` package comes with `mgo/bson` encoding package. When using `mgo`, we will often use `bson` types, such as the `bson.M` map to describe concepts for MongoDB.

We first create the selector for our update operation using the `bson.M` shortcut type, which is similar to creating `map[string]interface{}` types. The selector we create will look something like this:

```
{
  "options": {
    "$in": ["happy"]
  }
}
```

In MongoDB, the preceding BSON specifies that we want to select polls where `"happy"` is one of the items in the `options` array.

Next, we use the same technique to generate the update operation, which looks something like this:

```
{
  "$inc": {
    "results.happy": 3
  }
}
```

In MongoDB, the preceding BSON specifies that we want to increase the `results.happy` field by 3. If there is no `results` map in the poll, one will be created, and if there is no `happy` key inside `results`, 0 will be assumed.

We then call the `UpdateAll` method on our `pollsData` query to issue the command to the database, which will in turn update every poll that matches the selector (contrast this to the `Update` method, which will update only one). If something goes wrong, we report it and set the `ok` Boolean to false. If all goes well, we set the `counts` map to nil, since we want to reset the counter.

We are going to specify the `updateDuration` as a constant at the top of the file, which will make it easy for us to change when we are testing our program. Add the following code above the `main` function:

```
const updateDuration = 1 * time.Second
```

Responding to Ctrl + C

The last thing to do before our program is ready is to make sure our `main` function waits for operations to complete before exiting, like we did in our `twittervotes` program. Add the following code at the end of the `main` function:

```
termChan := make(chan os.Signal, 1)
signal.Notify(termChan, syscall.SIGINT, syscall.SIGTERM, syscall.
SIGHUP)
for {
  select {
  case <-termChan:
    updater.Stop()
    q.Stop()
  case <-q.StopChan:
    // finished
    return
  }
}
```

Here we have employed a slightly different tactic than before. We trap the termination event, which will cause a signal to go down `termChan` when we hit *Ctrl + C*. Next we start an infinite loop, inside which we use Go's `select` structure to allow us to run code if we receive something on either `termChan`, or the `StopChan` of the consumer.

In fact, we will only ever get a `termChan` signal first in response to a `Ctrl+C`-press, at which point we stop the `updater` timer and ask the consumer to stop listening for votes. Execution then re-enters the loop and will block until the consumer reports that it has indeed stopped by signaling on its `StopChan`. When that happens, we're done and we exit, at which point our deferred statement runs, which, if you remember, tidies up the database session.

Running our solution

It's time to see our code in action. Be sure to have `nsqlookupd`, `nsqd`, and `mongod` running in separate terminal windows with:

```
nsqlookupd
nsqd --lookupd-tcp-address=127.0.0.1:4160
mongod --dbpath ./db
```

If you haven't already done so, make sure the `twittervotes` program is running too. Then in the `counter` folder, build and run our counting program:

```
go build -o counter
./counter
```

You should see periodic output describing what work `counter` is doing, such as:

```
No new votes, skipping database update
Updating database...
map[win:2 happy:2 fail:1]
Finished updating database...
No new votes, skipping database update
Updating database...
map[win:3]
Finished updating database...
```

 The output will of course vary since we are actually responding to real live activity on Twitter.

We can see that our program is receiving vote data from NSQ, and reports to be updating the database with the results. We can confirm this by opening the MongoDB shell and querying the poll data to see if the `results` map is being updated. In another terminal window, open the MongoDB shell:

```
mongo
```

Ask it to use the ballots database:

```
> use ballots
switched to db ballots
```

Use the find method with no arguments to get all polls (add the `pretty` method to the end to get nicely formatted JSON):

```
> db.polls.find().pretty()
{
        "_id" : ObjectId("53e2a3afffbff195c2e09a02"),
        "options" : [
                "happy","sad","fail","win"
        ],
        "results" : {
                "fail" : 159, "win" : 711,
                "happy" : 233, "sad" : 166,
        },
        "title" : "Test poll"
}
```

The `results` map is indeed being updated, and at any point in time contains the total number of votes for each option.

Summary

In this chapter we covered a lot of ground. We learned different techniques for gracefully shutting down programs using signaling channels, which is especially important when our code has some work to do before it can exit. We saw that deferring the reporting of fatal errors at the start of our program can give our other deferred functions a chance to execute before the process ends.

We also discovered how easy it is to interact with MongoDB using the `mgo` package, and how to use BSON types when describing concepts for the database. The `bson.M` alternative to `map[string]interface{}` helps us keep our code more concise, while still providing all the flexibility we need when working with unstructured or schemaless data.

We learned about message queues and how they allow us to break apart the components of a system into isolated and specialized micro-services. We started an instance of NSQ by first running the lookup daemon `nsqlookupd`, before running a single `nsqd` instance and connecting them together via a TCP interface. We were then able to publish votes to the queue in `twittervotes`, and connect to the lookup daemon to run a handler function for every vote sent in our `counter` program.

While our solution is actually performing a pretty simple task, the architecture we have put together in this chapter is capable of doing some pretty great things.

- We eliminated the need for our `twittervotes` and `counter` programs to run on the same machine—as long as they can both connect to the appropriate NSQ, they will function as expected regardless of where they are running.

- We can distribute our MongoDB and NSQ nodes across many physical machines which would mean our system is capable of gigantic scale—whenever resources start running low, we can add new boxes to cope with the demand.

- When we add other applications that need to query and read the results from polls, we can be sure that our database services are highly available and capable of delivering.

- We can spread our database across geographical expanses replicating data for backup so we don't lose anything when disaster strikes.

- We can build a multi-node, fault tolerant NSQ environment, which means when our `twittervotes` program learns of interesting tweets, there will always be somewhere to send the data.

- We could write many more programs that generate votes from different sources; the only requirement is that they know how to put messages into NSQ.

- In the next chapter, we will build a RESTful data service of our own, through which we will expose the functionality of our social polling application. We will also build a web interface that lets users create their own polls, and visualize the results.

6
Exposing Data and Functionality through a RESTful Data Web Service API

In the previous chapter, we built a service that reads tweets from Twitter, counts the hashtag votes, and stores the results in a MongoDB database. We also used the MongoDB shell to add polls and see the poll results. This approach is fine if we are the only ones using our solution, but it would be madness if we released our project and expected users to connect directly to our MongoDB instance in order to use the service we built.

Therefore, in this chapter, we are going to build a RESTful data service through which the data and functionality will be exposed. We will also put together a simple website that consumes the new API. Users may then either use our website to create and monitor polls or build their own application on top of the web services we release.

 The code in this chapter depends on the code in *Chapter 5, Building Distributed Systems and Working with Flexible Data*, so it is recommended that you complete that chapter first, especially since it covers setting up the environment that the code in this chapter runs on.

Specifically, you will learn:

- How wrapping `http.HandlerFunc` types can give us a simple but powerful pipeline of execution for our HTTP requests
- How to safely share data between HTTP handlers

- Best practices for writing handlers responsible for exposing data
- Where small abstractions can allow us to write the simplest possible implementations now, but leave room to improve them later without changing the interface
- How adding simple helper functions and types to our project will prevent us from (or at least defer) adding dependencies on external packages

RESTful API design

For an API to be considered RESTful, it must adhere to a few principles that stay true to the original concepts behind the Web, and are already known to most developers. Such an approach allows us to make sure we aren't building anything strange or unusual into our API while also giving our users a head start towards consuming it, since they are already familiar with its concepts.

Some of the most important RESTful design concepts are:

- HTTP methods describe the kind of action to take, for example, GET methods will only ever *read* data, while POST requests will *create* something
- Data is expressed as a collection of resources
- Actions are expressed as changes to data
- URLs are used to refer to specific data
- HTTP headers are used to describe the kind of representation coming into and going out of the server

 For an in-depth overview of these and other details of RESTful designs, see the Wikipedia article at http://en.wikipedia.org/wiki/ Representational_state_transfer.

The following table shows the HTTP methods and URLs that represent the actions that we will support in our API, along with a brief description and an example use case of how we intend the call to be used:

Request	Description	Use case
GET /polls/	Read all polls	Show a list of polls to the users
GET /polls/{id}	Read the poll	Show details or results of a specific poll
POST /polls/	Create a poll	Create a new poll
DELETE /polls/{id}	Delete a poll	Delete a specific poll

The {id} placeholder represents where in the path the unique ID for a poll will go.

Sharing data between handlers

If we want to keep our handlers as pure as the `http.Handler` interface from the Go standard library, while still extracting common functionality into our own methods, we need a way of sharing data between handlers. The `HandlerFunc` signature that follows tells us that we are only allowed to pass in an `http.ResponseWriter` object and an `http.Request` object, and nothing else:

```
type HandlerFunc func(http.ResponseWriter, *http.Request)
```

This means that we cannot create and manage database session objects in one place and pass them into our handlers, which is ideally what we want to do.

Instead, we are going to implement an in-memory map of per-request data, and provide an easy way for handlers to access it. Alongside the `twittervotes` and `counter` folders, create a new folder called `api` and create a new file called `vars.go` inside it. Add the following code to the file:

```
package main
import (
  "net/http"
  "sync"
)
var vars map[*http.Request]map[string]interface{}
var varsLock sync.RWMutex
```

Here we declare a `vars` map that has a pointer to an `http.Request` type as its key, and another map as the value. We will store the map of variables keyed with the request instances that the variables belong to. The `varsLock` mutex is important, as our handlers will all be trying to access and change the `vars` map at the same time as handling many concurrent HTTP requests, and we need to ensure that they do this safely.

Next we are going to add the `OpenVars` function that allows us to prepare the `vars` map to hold variables for a particular request:

```
func OpenVars(r *http.Request) {
  varsLock.Lock()
  if vars == nil {
    vars = map[*http.Request]map[string]interface{}{}
  }
  vars[r] = map[string]interface{}{}
  varsLock.Unlock()
}
```

This function first locks the mutex so that we can safely modify the map, before ensuring that vars contains a non-nil map, which would otherwise cause a panic when we try to access its data. Finally, it assigns a new empty map value using the specified http.Request pointer as the key, before unlocking the mutex and therefore freeing other handlers to interact with it.

Once we have finished handling the request, we need a way to clean up the memory that we are using here; otherwise the memory footprint of our code would continuously increase (also known as a memory leak). We do this by adding a CloseVars function:

```
func CloseVars(r *http.Request) {
  varsLock.Lock()
  delete(vars, r)
  varsLock.Unlock()
}
```

This function safely deletes the entry in the vars map for the request. As long as we call OpenVars before we try to interact with the variables, and CloseVars when we have finished, we will be free to safely store and retrieve data for each request. However, we don't want our handler code to have to worry about locking and unlocking the map whenever it needs to get or set some data, so let's add two helper functions, GetVar and SetVar:

```
func GetVar(r *http.Request, key string) interface{} {
  varsLock.RLock()
  value := vars[r][key]
  varsLock.RUnlock()
  return value
}
func SetVar(r *http.Request, key string, value interface{}) {
  varsLock.Lock()
  vars[r][key] = value
  varsLock.Unlock()
}
```

The GetVar function will make it easy for us to get a variable from the map for the specified request, and SetVar allows us to set one. Notice that the GetVar function calls RLock and RUnlock rather than Lock and Unlock; this is because we're using sync.RWMutex, which means it's safe for many reads to occur at the same time, as long as a write isn't happening. This is good for performance on items that are safe to concurrently read from. With a normal mutex, Lock would block execution—waiting for the thing that has locked it to unlock it—while RLock will not.

Wrapping handler functions

One of the most valuable patterns to learn when building web services and websites in Go is one we already utilized in *Chapter 2, Adding Authentication*, where we decorated `http.Handler` types by wrapping them with other `http.Handler` types. For our RESTful API, we are going to apply this same technique to `http.HandlerFunc` functions, to deliver an extremely powerful way of modularizing our code without breaking the standard `func(w http.ResponseWriter, r *http.Request)` interface.

API key

Most web APIs require clients to register an API key for their application, which they are asked to send along with every request. Such keys have many purposes, ranging from simply identifying which app the requests are coming from to addressing authorization concerns in situations where some apps are only able to do limited things based on what a user has allowed. While we don't actually need to implement API keys for our application, we are going to ask clients to provide one, which will allow us to add an implementation later while keeping the interface constant.

Add the essential `main.go` file inside your `api` folder:

```
package main
func main(){}
```

Next we are going to add our first `HandlerFunc` wrapper function called `withAPIKey` to the bottom of `main.go`:

```
func withAPIKey(fn http.HandlerFunc) http.HandlerFunc {
  return func(w http.ResponseWriter, r *http.Request) {
    if !isValidAPIKey(r.URL.Query().Get("key")) {
      respondErr(w, r, http.StatusUnauthorized, "invalid API key")
      return
    }
    fn(w, r)
  }
}
```

As you can see, our `withAPIKey` function both takes an `http.HandlerFunc` type as an argument and returns one; this is what we mean by wrapping in this context. The `withAPIKey` function relies on a number of other functions that we are yet to write, but you can clearly see what's going on. Our function immediately returns a new `http.HandlerFunc` type that performs a check for the query parameter `key` by calling `isValidAPIKey`. If the key is deemed invalid (by the return of `false`), we respond with an `invalid API key` error. To use this wrapper, we simply pass an `http.HandlerFunc` type into this function to enable the `key` parameter check. Since it returns an `http.HandlerFunc` type too, the result can then be passed into other wrappers or given directly to the `http.HandleFunc` function to actually register it as the handler for a particular path pattern.

Let's add our `isValidAPIKey` function next:

```
func isValidAPIKey(key string) bool {
    return key == "abc123"
}
```

For now, we are simply going to hardcode the API key as `abc123`; anything else will return `false` and therefore be considered invalid. Later we could modify this function to consult a configuration file or database to check the authenticity of a key without affecting how we use the `isValidAPIKey` method, or indeed the `withAPIKey` wrapper.

Database session

Now that we can be sure a request has a valid API key, we must consider how handlers will connect to the database. One option is to have each handler dial its own connection, but this isn't very **DRY (Don't Repeat Yourself)**, and leaves room for potentially erroneous code, such as code that forgets to close a database session once it is finished with it. Instead, we will create another `HandlerFunc` wrapper that manages the database session for us. In `main.go`, add the following function:

```
func withData(d *mgo.Session, f http.HandlerFunc) http.HandlerFunc {
    return func(w http.ResponseWriter, r *http.Request) {
        thisDb := d.Copy()
        defer thisDb.Close()
```

```
      SetVar(r, "db", thisDb.DB("ballots"))
      f(w, r)
    }
}
```

The `withData` function takes a MongoDB session representation using the `mgo` package, and another handler as per the pattern. The returned `http.HandlerFunc` type will copy the database session, defer the closing of that copy, and set a reference to the `ballots` database as the `db` variable using our `SetVar` helper, before finally calling the next `HandlerFunc`. This means that any handlers that get executed after this one will have access to a managed database session via the `GetVar` function. Once the handlers have finished executing, the deferred closing of the session will occur, which will clean up any memory used by the request without the individual handlers having to worry about it.

Per request variables

Our pattern allows us to very easily perform common tasks on behalf of our actual handlers. Notice that one of the handlers is calling `OpenVars` and `CloseVars` so that `GetVar` and `SetVar` may be used without individual handlers having to concern themselves with setting things up and tearing them down. The function will return an `http.HandlerFunc` that first calls `OpenVars` for the request, defers the calling of `CloseVars`, and calls the specified handler function. Any handlers wrapped with `withVars` will be able to use `GetVar` and `SetVar`.

Add the following code to `main.go`:

```
func withVars(fn http.HandlerFunc) http.HandlerFunc {
  return func(w http.ResponseWriter, r *http.Request) {
    OpenVars(r)
    defer CloseVars(r)
    fn(w, r)
  }
}
```

There are lots of other problems that can be addressed using this pattern; and whenever you find yourself duplicating common tasks inside handlers, it's worth considering whether a handler wrapper function could help simplify code.

Cross-browser resource sharing

The same-origin security policy mandates that AJAX requests in web browsers be only allowed for services hosted on the same domain, which would make our API fairly limited since we won't be necessarily hosting all of the websites that use our web service. The CORS technique circumnavigates the same-origin policy, allowing us to build a service capable of serving websites hosted on other domains. To do this, we simply have to set the `Access-Control-Allow-Origin` header in response to `*`. While we're at it—since we're using the `Location` header in our create poll call—we'll allow that header to be accessible by the client too, which can be done by listing it in the `Access-Control-Expose-Headers` header. Add the following code to `main.go`:

```go
func withCORS(fn http.HandlerFunc) http.HandlerFunc {
  return func(w http.ResponseWriter, r *http.Request) {
    w.Header().Set("Access-Control-Allow-Origin", "*")
    w.Header().Set("Access-Control-Expose-Headers", "Location")
    fn(w, r)
  }
}
```

This is the simplest wrapper function yet; it just sets the appropriate header on the `ResponseWriter` type and calls the specified `http.HandlerFunc` type.

 In this chapter, we are handling CORS explicitly so we can understand exactly what is going on; for real production code, you should consider employing an open source solution such as `https://github.com/fasterness/cors`.

Responding

A big part of any API is responding to requests with a combination of status codes, data, errors, and sometimes headers—the `net/http` package makes all of this very easy to do. One option we have, which remains the best option for tiny projects or even the early stages of big projects, is to just build the response code directly inside the handler. As the number of handlers grows, however, we would end up duplicating a lot of code and sprinkling representation decisions all over our project. A more scalable approach is to abstract the response code into helper functions.

For the first version of our API, we are going to speak only JSON, but we want the flexibility to add other representations later if we need to.

Create a new file called `respond.go`, and add the following code:

```
func decodeBody(r *http.Request, v interface{}) error {
  defer r.Body.Close()
  return json.NewDecoder(r.Body).Decode(v)
}
func encodeBody(w http.ResponseWriter, r *http.Request, v
interface{}) error {
  return json.NewEncoder(w).Encode(v)
}
```

These two functions abstract the decoding and encoding of data from and to the `Request` and `ResponseWriter` objects respectively. The decoder also closes the request body, which is recommended. Although we haven't added much functionality here, it means that we do not need to mention JSON anywhere else in our code, and if we decide to add support for other representations or switch to a binary protocol instead, we need only touch these two functions.

Next we are going to add a few more helpers that will make responding even easier. In `respond.go`, add the following code:

```
func respond(w http.ResponseWriter, r *http.Request,
  status int, data interface{},
) {
  w.WriteHeader(status)
  if data != nil {
    encodeBody(w, r, data)
  }
}
```

This function makes it easy to write the status code and some data to the `ResponseWriter` object using our `encodeBody` helper.

Handling errors is another important aspect that is worth abstracting. Add the following `respondErr` helper:

```
func respondErr(w http.ResponseWriter, r *http.Request,
  status int, args ...interface{},
) {
  respond(w, r, status, map[string]interface{}{
    "error": map[string]interface{}{
      "message": fmt.Sprint(args...),
    },
  })
}
```

This method gives us an interface similar to the respond function, but the data written will be enveloped in an error object, to make it clear that something went wrong. Finally, we can add an HTTP error-specific helper that will generate the correct message for us by using the http.StatusText function from the Go standard library:

```go
func respondHTTPErr(w http.ResponseWriter, r *http.Request,
    status int,
) {
    respondErr(w, r, status, http.StatusText(status))
}
```

Notice that these functions are all dogfooding, which means they use each other (as in, eating your own dog food), which is important since we want actual responding to only happen in one place, for if (or more likely, when) we need to make changes.

Understanding the request

The http.Request object gives us access to every piece of information we might need about the underlying HTTP request, and therefore it is worth glancing through the net/http documentation to really get a feel for its power. Examples include, but are not limited to:

- URL, path and query string
- HTTP method
- Cookies
- Files
- Form values
- Referrer and user agent of requester
- Basic authentication details
- Request body
- Header information

There are a few things it doesn't address, which we need to either solve ourselves or look to an external package to help us with. URL path parsing is one such example—while we can access a path (such as /people/1/books/2) as a string via the http.Request type's URL.Path field, there is no easy way to pull out the data encoded in the path such as the people ID of 1, or the books ID of 2.

A few projects do a good job of addressing this problem, such as Goweb or Gorillz's `mux` package. They let you map path patterns that contain placeholders for values that they then pull out of the original string and make available to your code. For example, you can map a pattern of `/users/{userID}/comments/{commentID}`, which will map paths such as `/users/1/comments/2`. In your handler code, you can then get the values by the names placed inside the curly braces, rather than having to parse the path yourself.

Since our needs are simple, we are going to knock together a simple path-parsing utility; we can always use a different package later if we have to, but that would mean adding a dependency to our project.

Create a new file called `path.go`, and insert the following code:

```go
package main
import (
  "strings"
)
const PathSeparator = "/"
type Path struct {
  Path string
  ID   string
}
func NewPath(p string) *Path {
  var id string
  p = strings.Trim(p, PathSeparator)
  s := strings.Split(p, PathSeparator)
  if len(s) > 1 {
    id = s[len(s)-1]
    p = strings.Join(s[:len(s)-1], PathSeparator)
  }
  return &Path{Path: p, ID: id}
}
func (p *Path) HasID() bool {
  return len(p.ID) > 0
}
```

This simple parser provides a `NewPath` function that parses the specified path string and returns a new instance of the `Path` type. Leading and trailing slashes are trimmed (using `strings.Trim`) and the remaining path is split (using `strings.Split`) by the `PathSeparator` constant that is just a forward slash. If there is more than one segment (`len(s) > 1`), the last one is considered to be the ID. We re-slice the slice of strings to select the last item for the ID using `s[len(s)-1]`, and the rest of the items for the remainder of the path using `s[:len(s)-1]`. On the same lines, we also re-join the path segments with the `PathSeparator` constant to form a single string containing the path without the ID.

This supports any `collection/id` pair, which is all we need for our API. The following table shows the state of the `Path` type for the given original path string:

Original path string	Path	ID	HasID
/	/	nil	false
/people/	people	nil	false
/people/1/	people	1	true

A simple main function to serve our API

A web service is nothing more than a simple Go program that binds to a specific HTTP address and port and serves requests, so we get to use all our command-line tool-writing knowledge and techniques.

 We also want to ensure that our `main` function is as simple and modest as possible, which is always a goal of coding, especially in Go.

Before we write our `main` function, let's look at a few design goals of our API program:

- We should be able to specify the HTTP address and port to which our API listens and the address of the MongoDB instances without having to recompile the program (through command-line flags)

- We want the program to gracefully shut down when we terminate it, allowing the in-flight requests (requests that are still being processed when the termination signal is sent to our program) to complete

- We want the program to log out status updates and report errors properly

Atop the `main.go` file, replace the `main` function placeholder with the following code:

```go
func main() {
  var (
    addr  = flag.String("addr", ":8080", "endpoint address")
    mongo = flag.String("mongo", "localhost", "mongodb address")
  )
  flag.Parse()
  log.Println("Dialing mongo", *mongo)
  db, err := mgo.Dial(*mongo)
  if err != nil {
    log.Fatalln("failed to connect to mongo:", err)
  }
  defer db.Close()
  mux := http.NewServeMux()
  mux.HandleFunc("/polls/", withCORS(withVars(withData(db,
withAPIKey(handlePolls)))))
  log.Println("Starting web server on", *addr)
  graceful.Run(*addr, 1*time.Second, mux)
  log.Println("Stopping...")
}
```

This function is the entirety of our API `main` function, and even as our API grows, there is just a little bloat we would need to add to this.

The first thing we do is to specify two command-line flags, `addr` and `mongo`, with some sensible defaults, and to ask the `flag` package to parse them. We then attempt to dial the MongoDB database at the specified address. If we are unsuccessful, we abort with a call to `log.Fatalln`. Assuming the database is running and we are able to connect, we store the reference in the `db` variable before deferring the closing of the connection. This ensures our program properly disconnects and tidies up after itself when it ends.

We then create a new `http.ServeMux` object, which is a request multiplexer provided by the Go standard library, and register a single handler for all requests that begin with the path `/polls/`.

Finally, we make use of Tyler Bunnell's excellent `Graceful` package, which can be found at `https://github.com/stretchr/graceful` to start the server. This package allows us to specify `time.Duration` when running any `http.Handler` (such as our `ServeMux` handler), which will allow any in-flight requests some time to complete before the function exits. The `Run` function will block until the program is terminated (for example, when someone presses *Ctrl + C*).

Using handler function wrappers

It is when we call `HandleFunc` on the `ServeMux` handler that we are making use of our handler function wrappers, with the line:

```
withCORS(withVars(withData(db, withAPIKey(handlePolls)))))
```

Since each function takes an `http.HandlerFunc` type as an argument and also returns one, we are able to chain the execution just by nesting the function calls as we have done previously. So when a request comes in with a path prefix of `/polls/`, the program will take the following execution path:

1. `withCORS` is called, which sets the appropriate header.

2. `withVars` is called, which calls `OpenVars` and defers `CloseVars` for the request.

3. `withData` is then called, which copies the database session provided as the first argument and defers the closing of that session.

4. `withAPIKey` is called next, which checks the request for an API key and aborts if it's invalid, or else calls the next handler function.

5. `handlePolls` is then called, which has access to variables and a database session, and which may use the helper functions in `respond.go` to write a response to the client.

6. Execution goes back to `withAPIKey` that just exits.

7. Execution goes back to `withData` that exits, therefore calling the deferred session `Close` function and clearing up the database session.

8. Execution goes back to `withVars` that exits, therefore calling `CloseVars` and tidying that up too.

9. Execution finally goes back to `withCORS` that just exits.

> The order that we nest the wrapper functions in is important, because `withData` puts the database session for each request in that request's variables map using `SetVar`. So `withVars` must be outside `withData`. If this isn't respected, the code will likely panic and you may want to add a check so that the panic is more meaningful to other developers.

Handling endpoints

The final piece of the puzzle is the `handlePolls` function that will use the helpers to understand the incoming request and access the database, and generate a meaningful response that will be sent back to the client. We also need to model the poll data that we were working with in the previous chapter.

Create a new file called `polls.go`, and add the following code:

```
package main
import "gopkg.in/mgo.v2/bson"
type poll struct {
  ID       bson.ObjectId  `bson:"_id" json:"id"`
  Title    string         `json":"title""`
  Options  []string       `json:"options"`
  Results  map[string]int `json:"results,omitempty"`
}
```

Here we define a structure called `poll` that has three fields that in turn describe the polls being created and maintained by the code we wrote in the previous chapter. Each field also has a tag (two in the `ID` case), which allows us to provide some extra metadata.

Using tags to add metadata to structs

Tags are strings that follow a field definition within a `struct` type on the same line of code. We use the back tick character to denote literal strings, which means we are free to use double quotes within the tag string itself. The `reflect` package allows us to pull out the value associated with any key; in our case, both `bson` and `json` are examples of keys, and they are each key/value-pair-separated by a space character. Both the `encoding/json` and `gopkg.in/mgo.v2/bson` packages allow you to use tags to specify the field name that will be used with encoding and decoding (along with some other properties), rather than having it infer the values from the name of the fields themselves. We are using BSON to talk with the MongoDB database and JSON to talk to the client, so we can actually specify different views of the same `struct` type. For example, consider the ID field:

```
ID bson.ObjectId `bson:"_id" json:"id"`
```

The name of the field in Go is `ID`, the JSON field is `id`, and the BSON field is `_id`, which is the special identifier field used in MongoDB.

Many operations with a single handler

Because our simple path-parsing solution cares only about the path, we have to do some extra work when looking at the kind of RESTful operation the client is making. Specifically, we need to consider the HTTP method so we know how to handle the request. For example, a GET call to our /polls/ path should read polls, where a POST call would create a new one. Some frameworks solve this problem for you, by allowing you to map handlers based on more than the path, such as the HTTP method or the presence of specific headers in the request. Since our case is ultra simple, we are going to use a simple switch case. In polls.go, add the handlePolls function:

```go
func handlePolls(w http.ResponseWriter, r *http.Request) {
  switch r.Method {
  case "GET":
    handlePollsGet(w, r)
    return
  case "POST":
    handlePollsPost(w, r)
    return
  case "DELETE":
    handlePollsDelete(w, r)
    return
  }
  // not found
  respondHTTPErr(w, r, http.StatusNotFound)
}
```

We switch on the HTTP method and branch our code depending on whether it is GET, POST, or DELETE. If the HTTP method is something else, we just respond with a 404 http.StatusNotFound error. To make this code compile, you can add the following function stubs underneath the handlePolls handler:

```go
func handlePollsGet(w http.ResponseWriter, r *http.Request) {
  respondErr(w, r, http.StatusInternalServerError, errors.New("not
implemented"))
}
func handlePollsPost(w http.ResponseWriter, r *http.Request) {
  respondErr(w, r, http.StatusInternalServerError, errors.New("not
implemented"))
}
func handlePollsDelete(w http.ResponseWriter, r *http.Request) {
  respondErr(w, r, http.StatusInternalServerError, errors.New("not
implemented"))
}
```

In this section, we learned how to manually parse elements of the requests (the HTTP method) and make decisions in code. This is great for simple cases, but it's worth looking at packages such as Goweb or Gorilla's `mux` package for some more powerful ways of solving these problems. Nevertheless, keeping external dependencies to a minimum is a core philosophy of writing good and contained Go code.

Reading polls

Now it's time to implement the functionality of our web service. Inside the GET case, add the following code:

```go
func handlePollsGet(w http.ResponseWriter, r *http.Request) {
  db := GetVar(r, "db").(*mgo.Database)
  c := db.C("polls")
  var q *mgo.Query
  p := NewPath(r.URL.Path)
  if p.HasID() {
    // get specific poll
    q = c.FindId(bson.ObjectIdHex(p.ID))
  } else {
    // get all polls
    q = c.Find(nil)
  }
  var result []*poll
  if err := q.All(&result); err != nil {
    respondErr(w, r, http.StatusInternalServerError, err)
    return
  }
  respond(w, r, http.StatusOK, &result)
}
```

The very first thing we do in each of our subhandler functions is to use `GetVar` to get the `mgo.Database` object that will allow us to interact with MongoDB. Since this handler was nested inside both `withVars` and `withData`, we know that the database will be available by the time execution reaches our handler. We then use `mgo` to create an object referring to the `polls` collection in the database—if you remember, this is where our polls live.

We then build up an `mgo.Query` object by parsing the path. If an ID is present, we use the `FindId` method on the `polls` collection, otherwise we pass `nil` to the `Find` method, which indicates that we want to select all the polls. We are converting the ID from a string to a `bson.ObjectId` type with the `ObjectIdHex` method so that we can refer to the polls with their numerical (hex) identifiers.

Since the `All` method expects to generate a collection of poll objects, we define the result as `[]*poll`, or a slice of pointers to poll types. Calling the `All` method on the query will cause `mgo` to use its connection to MongoDB to read all the polls and populate the `result` object.

For small scale projects, such as a small number of polls, this approach is fine, but as the number of polls grow, we would need to consider paging the results or even iterating over them using the `Iter` method on the query, so we do not try to load too much data into memory.

Now that we have added some functionality, let's try out our API for the first time. If you are using the same MongoDB instance that we set up in the previous chapter, you should already have some data in the `polls` collection; to see our API working properly, you should ensure there are at least two polls in the database.

If you need to add other polls to the database, in a terminal, run the `mongo` command to open a database shell that will allow you to interact with MongoDB. Then enter the following commands to add some test polls:

```
> use ballots
switched to db ballots
> db.polls.insert({"title":"Test
poll","options":["one","two","three"]})
> db.polls.insert({"title":"Test poll
two","options":["four","five","six"]})
```

In a terminal, navigate to your `api` folder, and build and run the project:

```
go build -o api
```
`./api`

Now make a `GET` request to the `/polls/` endpoint by navigating in your browser to `http://localhost:8080/polls/?key=abc123`; remember to include the trailing slash. The result will be an array of polls in JSON format.

Copy and paste one of the IDs from the polls list, and insert it before the `?` character in the browser to access the data for a specific poll; for example, `http://localhost:8080/polls/5415b060a02cd4adb487c3ae?key=abc123`. Notice that instead of returning all the polls, it only returns one.

Test the API key functionality by removing or changing the key parameter to see what the error looks like.

You might have also noticed that although we are only returning a single poll, this poll value is still nested inside an array. This is a deliberate design decision made for two reasons: the first and most important reason is that nesting makes it easier for users of the API to write code to consume the data. If users are always expecting a JSON array, they can write strong types that describe that expectation, rather than having one type for single polls and another for collections of polls. As an API designer, this is your decision to make. The second reason we left the object nested in an array is that it makes the API code simpler, allowing us to just change the `mgo.Query` object and to leave the rest of the code the same.

Creating a poll

Clients should be able to make a POST request to /polls/ to create a poll. Let's add the following code inside the POST case:

```
func handlePollsPost(w http.ResponseWriter, r *http.Request) {
  db := GetVar(r, "db").(*mgo.Database)
  c := db.C("polls")
  var p poll
  if err := decodeBody(r, &p); err != nil {
    respondErr(w, r, http.StatusBadRequest, "failed to read poll
from request", err)
    return
  }
  p.ID = bson.NewObjectId()
  if err := c.Insert(p); err != nil {
    respondErr(w, r, http.StatusInternalServerError, "failed to
insert poll", err)
    return
  }
  w.Header().Set("Location", "polls/"+p.ID.Hex())
  respond(w, r, http.StatusCreated, nil)
}
```

Here we first attempt to decode the body of the request that, according to RESTful principles, should contain a representation of the poll object the client wants to create. If an error occurs, we use the `respondErr` helper to write the error to the user, and immediately return the function. We then generate a new unique ID for the poll, and use the `mgo` package's `Insert` method to send it into the database. As per HTTP standards, we then set the `Location` header of the response and respond with a 201 `http.StatusCreated` message, pointing to the URL from which the newly created poll maybe accessed.

Deleting a poll

The final piece of functionality we are going to include in our API is the capability to delete polls. By making a request with the DELETE HTTP method to the URL of a poll (such as /polls/5415b060a02cd4adb487c3ae), we want to be able to remove the poll from the database and return a 200 Success response:

```
func handlePollsDelete(w http.ResponseWriter, r *http.Request) {
  db := GetVar(r, "db").(*mgo.Database)
  c := db.C("polls")
  p := NewPath(r.URL.Path)
  if !p.HasID() {
    respondErr(w, r, http.StatusMethodNotAllowed, "Cannot delete
all polls.")
    return
  }
  if err := c.RemoveId(bson.ObjectIdHex(p.ID)); err != nil {
    respondErr(w, r, http.StatusInternalServerError, "failed to
delete poll", err)
    return
  }
  respond(w, r, http.StatusOK, nil) // ok
}
```

Similar to the GET case, we parse the path, but this time we respond with an error if the path does not contain an ID. For now, we don't want people to be able to delete all polls with one request, and so use the suitable StatusMethodNotAllowed code. Then, using the same collection we used in the previous cases, we call RemoveId, passing in the ID in the path after converting it into a bson.ObjectId type. Assuming things go well, we respond with an http.StatusOK message, with no body.

CORS support

In order for our DELETE capability to work over CORS, we must do a little extra work to support the way CORS browsers handle some HTTP methods such as DELETE. A CORS browser will actually send a pre-flight request (with an HTTP method of OPTIONS) asking for permission to make a DELETE request (listed in the Access-Control-Request-Method request header), and the API must respond appropriately in order for the request to work. Add another case in the switch statement for OPTIONS:

```
case "OPTIONS":
  w.Header().Add("Access-Control-Allow-Methods", "DELETE")
  respond(w, r, http.StatusOK, nil)
  return
```

If the browser asks for permission to send a DELETE request, the API will respond by setting the `Access-Control-Allow-Methods` header to DELETE, thus overriding the default * value that we set in our `withCORS` wrapper handler. In the real world, the value for the `Access-Control-Allow-Methods` header will change in response to the request made, but since DELETE is the only case we are supporting, we can hardcode it for now.

> The details of CORS are out of the scope of this book, but it is recommended that you research the particulars online if you intend to build truly accessible web services and APIs. Head over to `http://enable-cors.org/` to get started.

Testing our API using curl

`curl` is a command-line tool that allows us to make HTTP requests to our service so that we can access it as though we were a real app or client consuming the service.

> Windows users do not have access to `curl` by default, and will need to seek an alternative. Check out `http://curl.haxx.se/dlwiz/?type=bin` or search the Web for "Windows `curl` alternative".

In a terminal, let's read all the polls in the database through our API. Navigate to your `api` folder and build and run the project, and also ensure MongoDB is running:

```
go build -o api
```

```
./api
```

We then perform the following steps:

1. Enter the following `curl` command that uses the `-X` flag to denote we want to make a GET request to the specified URL:

   ```
   curl -X GET http://localhost:8080/polls/?key=abc123
   ```

2. The output is printed after you hit *Enter*:

   ```
   [{"id":"541727b08ea48e5e5d5bb189","title":"Best
   Beatle?","options":["john","paul","george","ringo"]},{"id":"54
   1728728ea48e5e5d5bb18a","title":"Favorite
   language?","options":["go","java","javascript","ruby"]}]
   ```

3. While it isn't pretty, you can see that the API returns the polls from your database. Issue the following command to create a new poll:

   ```
   curl --data '{"title":"test","options":["one","two","three"]}'
   -X POST http://localhost:8080/polls/?key=abc123
   ```

4. Get the list again to see the new poll included:

```
curl -X GET http://localhost:8080/polls/?key=abc123
```

5. Copy and paste one of the IDs, and adjust the URL to refer specifically to that poll:

```
curl -X GET
http://localhost:8080/polls/541727b08ea48e5e5d5bb189?key=abc12
3

[{"id":"541727b08ea48e5e5d5bb189",",","title":"Best
Beatle?","options":["john","paul","george","ringo"]}]
```

6. Now we see only the selected poll, `Best Beatle`. Let's make a `DELETE` request to remove the poll:

```
curl -X DELETE
http://localhost:8080/polls/541727b08ea48e5e5d5bb189?key=abc12
3
```

7. Now when we get all the polls again, we'll see that the `Best Beatle` poll has gone:

```
curl -X GET http://localhost:8080/polls/?key=abc123

[{"id":"541728728ea48e5e5d5bb18a","title":"Favorite
language?","options":["go","java","javascript","ruby"]}]
```

So now that we know that our API is working as expected, it's time to build something that consumes the API properly.

A web client that consumes the API

We are going to put together an ultra-simple web client that consumes the capabilities and data exposed through our API, allowing users to interact with the polling system we built in the previous chapter and earlier in this chapter. Our client will be made up of three web pages:

- An `index.html` page that shows all the polls
- A `view.html` page that shows the results of a specific poll
- A `new.html` page that allows users to create new polls

Create a new folder called `web` alongside the `api` folder, and add the following content to the `main.go` file:

```
package main
```

```
import (
  "flag"
  "log"
  "net/http"
)
func main() {
  var addr = flag.String("addr", ":8081", "website address")
  flag.Parse()
  mux := http.NewServeMux()
  mux.Handle("/", http.StripPrefix("/",
    http.FileServer(http.Dir("public"))))
  log.Println("Serving website at:", *addr)
  http.ListenAndServe(*addr, mux)
}
```

These few lines of Go code really highlight the beauty of the language and the Go standard library. They represent a complete, highly scalable, static website hosting program. The program takes an `addr` flag and uses the familiar `http.ServeMux` type to serve static files from a folder called `public`.

Building the next few pages—while we're building the UI—consists of writing a lot of HTML and JavaScript code. Since this is not Go code, if you'd rather not type it all out, feel free to head over to the GitHub repository for this book and copy and paste it from `https://github.com/matryer/goblueprints`.

An index page showing a list of polls

Create the `public` folder inside `web` and add the `index.html` file after writing the following HTML code in it:

```
<!DOCTYPE html>
<html>
<head>
  <title>Polls</title>
  <link rel="stylesheet"
    href="//maxcdn.bootstrapcdn.com/bootstrap/3.2.0/css/
    bootstrap.min.css">
</head>
<body>
</body>
</html>
```

We will use Bootstrap again to make our simple UI look nice, but we need to add two additional sections to the `body` tag of the HTML page. First, add the DOM elements that will display the list of polls:

```
<div class="container">
  <div class="col-md-4"></div>
  <div class="col-md-4">
    <h1>Polls</h1>
    <ul id="polls"></ul>
    <a href="new.html" class="btn btn-primary">Create new poll</a>
  </div>
  <div class="col-md-4"></div>
</div>
```

Here we are using Bootstrap's grid system to center-align our content that is made up of a list of polls and a link to `new.html`, where users can create new polls.

Next, add the following `script` tags and JavaScript underneath the previous code:

```
<script
src="//ajax.googleapis.com/ajax/libs/jquery/2.1.1/jquery.min.js"><
/script>
<script
src="//maxcdn.bootstrapcdn.com/bootstrap/3.2.0/js/bootstrap.min.js
"></script>
<script>
  $(function(){
    var update = function(){
      $.get("http://localhost:8080/polls/?key=abc123", null, null,
"json")
        .done(function(polls){
          $("#polls").empty();
          for (var p in polls) {
            var poll = polls[p];
            $("#polls").append(
              $("<li>").append(
                $("<a>")
                  .attr("href", "view.html?poll=polls/" + poll.id)
                  .text(poll.title)
              )
            )
          }
        }
      );
```

```
          window.setTimeout(update, 10000);
      }
      update();
  });
</script>
```

We are using jQuery's `$.get` function to make an AJAX request to our web service.
We are also hardcoding the API URL. In practice, you might decide against this, but
you should at least use a domain name to abstract it. Once the polls have loaded,
we use jQuery to build up a list containing hyperlinks to the `view.html` page,
passing the ID of the poll as a query parameter.

A page to create a new poll

To allow users to create a new poll, create a file called `new.html` inside the `public`
folder, and add the following HTML code to the file:

```
<!DOCTYPE html>
<html>
<head>
  <title>Create Poll</title>
  <link rel="stylesheet"
    href="//maxcdn.bootstrapcdn.com/bootstrap/3.2.0/css/
    bootstrap.min.css">
</head>
<body>
  <script
src="//ajax.googleapis.com/ajax/libs/jquery/2.1.1/jquery.min.js"><
/script>
  <script
src="//maxcdn.bootstrapcdn.com/bootstrap/3.2.0/js/bootstrap.min.js
"></script>
</body>
</html>
```

We are going to add the elements for an HTML form that will capture the information
we need when creating a new poll, namely the title of the poll and the options. Add the
following code inside the `body` tags:

```
<div class="container">
  <div class="col-md-4"></div>
  <form id="poll" role="form" class="col-md-4">
    <h2>Create Poll</h2>
    <div class="form-group">
      <label for="title">Title</label>
```

```
      <input type="text" class="form-control" id="title"
placeholder="Title">
    </div>
    <div class="form-group">
      <label for="options">Options</label>
      <input type="text" class="form-control" id="options"
placeholder="Options">
      <p class="help-block">Comma separated</p>
    </div>
    <button type="submit" class="btn btn-primary">Create
Poll</button> or <a href="/">cancel</a>
  </form>
  <div class="col-md-4"></div>
</div>
```

Since our API speaks JSON, we need to do a bit of work to turn the HTML form into a JSON-encoded string, and also break the comma-separated options string into an array of options. Add the following `script` tag:

```
<script>
  $(function(){
    var form = $("form#poll");
    form.submit(function(e){
      e.preventDefault();
      var title = form.find("input[id='title']").val();
      var options = form.find("input[id='options']").val();
      options = options.split(",");
      for (var opt in options) {
        options[opt] = options[opt].trim();
      }
      $.post("http://localhost:8080/polls/?key=abc123",
        JSON.stringify({
          title: title, options: options
        })
      ).done(function(d, s, r){
        location.href = "view.html?poll=" +
r.getResponseHeader("Location");
      });
    });
  });
</script>
```

Here we add a listener to the submit event of our form, and use jQuery's val method to collect the input values. We split the options with a comma, and trim the spaces away before using the $.post method to make the POST request to the appropriate API endpoint. JSON.stringify allows us to turn the data object into a JSON string, and we use that string as the body of the request, as expected by the API. On success, we pull out the Location header and redirect the user to the view.html page, passing a reference to the newly created poll as the parameter.

A page to show details of the poll

The final page of our app we need to complete is the view.html page where users can see the details and live results of the poll. Create a new file called view.html inside the public folder, and add the following HTML code to it:

```
<!DOCTYPE html>
<html>
<head>
  <title>View Poll</title>
  <link rel="stylesheet"
href="//maxcdn.bootstrapcdn.com/bootstrap/3.2.0/css/bootstrap.min.
css">
</head>
<body>
  <div class="container">
    <div class="col-md-4"></div>
    <div class="col-md-4">
      <h1 data-field="title">...</h1>
      <ul id="options"></ul>
      <div id="chart"></div>
      <div>
        <button class="btn btn-sm" id="delete">Delete this
poll</button>
      </div>
    </div>
    <div class="col-md-4"></div>
  </div>
</body>
</html>
```

This page is mostly similar to the other pages; it contains elements for presenting the title of the poll, the options, and a pie chart. We will be mashing up Google's Visualization API with our API to present the results. Underneath the final `div` tag in `view.html` (and above the closing `body` tag), add the following `script` tags:

```
<script src="//www.google.com/jsapi"></script>
<script
src="//ajax.googleapis.com/ajax/libs/jquery/2.1.1/jquery.min.js"><
/script>
<script
src="//maxcdn.bootstrapcdn.com/bootstrap/3.2.0/js/bootstrap.min.js
"></script>
<script>
google.load('visualization', '1.0', {'packages':['corechart']});
google.setOnLoadCallback(function(){
  $(function(){
    var chart;
    var poll = location.href.split("poll=")[1];
    var update = function(){
      $.get("http://localhost:8080/"+poll+"?key=abc123", null,
null, "json")
        .done(function(polls){
          var poll = polls[0];
          $('[data-field="title"]').text(poll.title);
          $("#options").empty();
          for (var o in poll.results) {
            $("#options").append(
              $("<li>").append(
                $("<small>").addClass("label label-
default").text(poll.results[o]),
                " ", o
              )
            )
          }
          if (poll.results) {
            var data = new google.visualization.DataTable();
            data.addColumn("string","Option");
            data.addColumn("number","Votes");
            for (var o in poll.results) {
              data.addRow([o, poll.results[o]])
            }
            if (!chart) {
              chart = new
google.visualization.PieChart(document.getElementById('chart'));
            }
```

```
                    chart.draw(data, {is3D: true});
                }
            }
        );
        window.setTimeout(update, 1000);
    };
    update();
    $("#delete").click(function(){
        if (confirm("Sure?")) {
            $.ajax({
                url:"http://localhost:8080/"+poll+"?key=abc123",
                type:"DELETE"
            })
            .done(function(){
                location.href = "/";
            })
        }
    });
});
});
</script>
```

We include the dependencies we will need to power our page, jQuery and Bootstrap, and also the Google JavaScript API. The code loads the appropriate visualization libraries from Google, and waits for the DOM elements to load before extracting the poll ID from the URL by splitting it on `poll=`. We then create a variable called `update` that represents a function responsible for generating the view of the page. This approach is taken to make it easy for us to use `window.setTimeout` to issue regular calls to update the view. Inside the `update` function, we use `$.get` to make a GET request to our `/polls/{id}` endpoint, replacing `{id}` with the actual ID we extracted from the URL earlier. Once the poll has loaded, we update the title on the page and iterate over the options to add them to the list. If there are results (remember in the previous chapter, the `results` map was only added to the data as votes start being counted), we create a new `google.visualization.PieChart` object and build a `google.visualization.DataTable` object containing the results. Calling `draw` on the chart causes it to render the data, and thus update the chart with the latest numbers. We then use `setTimeout` to tell our code to call `update` again in another second.

Finally, we bind to the `click` event of the `delete` button we added to our page, and after asking the user if they are sure, make a DELETE request to the polls URL and then redirect them back to the home page. It is this request that will actually cause the OPTIONS request to be made first, asking for permission, which is why we added explicit support for it in our `handlePolls` function earlier.

Running the solution

We have built many components over the last two chapters, and it is now time to see them all working together. This section contains everything you need to get all the items running, assuming you have the environment set up properly as described at the beginning of the previous chapter. This section assumes you have a single folder that contains four subfolders: api, counter, twittervotes, and web.

Assuming nothing is running, take the following steps (each step in its own terminal window):

1. In the top-level folder, start the nsqlookupd daemon:

   ```
   nsqlookupd
   ```

2. In the same directory, start the nsqd daemon:

   ```
   nsqd --lookupd-tcp-address=localhost:4160
   ```

3. Start the MongoDB daemon:

   ```
   mongod
   ```

4. Navigate to the counter folder and build and run it:

   ```
   cd counter
   go build -o counter
   ./counter
   ```

5. Navigate to the twittervotes folder and build and run it. Be sure that you have the appropriate environment variables set, otherwise you will see errors when you run the program:

   ```
   cd ../twittervotes
   go build -o twittervotes
   ./twittervotes
   ```

6. Navigate to the api folder and build and run it:

   ```
   cd ../api
   go build -o api
   ./api
   ```

7. Navigate to the web folder and build and run it:

   ```
   cd ../web
   go build -o web
   ./web
   ```

Now that everything is running, open a browser and head to `http://localhost:8081/`. Using the user interface, create a poll called `Moods` and input the options as `happy`, `sad`, `fail`, and `success`. These are common enough words that we are likely to see some relevant activity on Twitter.

Once you have created your poll, you will be taken to the view page where you will start to see the results coming in. Wait for a few seconds, and enjoy the fruits of your hard work as the UI updates in real time showing live, real-time results.

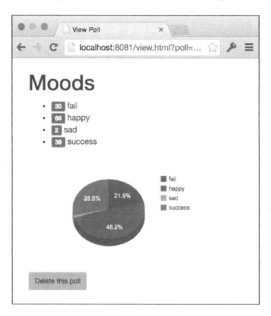

Summary

In this chapter, we exposed the data for our social polling solution through a highly scalable RESTful API and built a simple website that consumes the API to provide an intuitive way for users to interact with it. The website consists of static content only, with no server-side processing (since the API does the heavy lifting for us). This allows us to host the website very cheaply on static hosting sites such as `bitballoon.com`, or to distribute the files to content delivery networks.

Within our API service, we learned how to share data between handlers without breaking or obfuscating the handler pattern from the standard library. We also saw how writing wrapped handler functions allows us to build a pipeline of functionality in a very simple and intuitive way.

We wrote some basic encoding and decoding functions that—while only simply wrapping their counterparts from the encoding/json package for now—could be improved later to support a range of different data representations without changing the internal interface to our code. We wrote a few simple helper functions that make responding to data requests easy, while providing the same kind of abstraction that would allow us to evolve our API later.

We saw how, for simple cases, switching on to HTTP methods is an elegant way to support many functions for a single endpoint. We also saw how, with a few extra lines of code, we are able to build in support for CORS to allow applications running on different domains to interact with our services—without the need for hacks like JSONP.

The code in this chapter, combined with the work we did in the previous chapter, provides a real-world, production-ready solution that implements the following flow:

1. The user clicks on the **Create Poll** button on the website, and enters the title and options for a poll.

2. The JavaScript running in the browser encodes the data as a JSON string and sends it in the body of a POST request to our API.

3. The API receives the request, and after validating the API key, setting up a database session, and storing it in our variables map, calls the handlePolls function that processes the request and stores the new poll in the MongoDB database.

4. The API redirects the user to the view.html page for the newly created poll.

5. Meanwhile, the twittervotes program loads all polls from the database, including the new one, and opens a connection to Twitter filtering on the hashtags that represent options from the polls.

6. As votes come in, twittervotes pushes them to NSQ.

7. The counter program is listening in on the appropriate channel and notices the votes coming in, counting each one and periodically making updates to the database.

8. The user sees the results displayed (and refreshed) on the view.html page as the website continually makes GET requests to the API endpoint for the selected poll.

In the next chapter, we will evolve our API and web skills to build a brand new start-up app called Meander. We'll see how we can write a full, static web server in just a few lines of Go code, and explore an interesting way of representing enumerators in a language that doesn't officially support them!

7
Random Recommendations Web Service

The concept behind the project that we will build in this chapter is a simple one: we want users to be able to generate random recommendations for things to do in specific geographical locations based on a predefined set of journey types that we will expose through the API. We will give our project the codename Meander.

Often on projects in the real world, you are responsible for the full stack; somebody else builds the website, a different person still might write the iOS app, and maybe an outsourced company builds the desktop version. On more successful API projects, you might not even know who the consumers of your API are, especially if it's a public API.

In this chapter, we will simulate this reality by designing and agreeing a minimal API design with a fictional partner up front before going on to implement the API. Once we have finished our side of the project, we will download a user interface built by our teammates to see the two work together to produce the final application.

In this chapter, you will:

- Learn to express the general goals of a project using short and simple Agile user stories
- Discover that you can agree a meeting point in a project by agreeing on the design of an API, which allows many people to work in parallel
- See how early versions of code can actually have data fixtures written in code and compiled into the program, allowing us to change the implementation later without touching the interface
- Learn a strategy that allows structs (and other types) to represent a public version of themselves for cases when we want to hide or transform internal representations

- Learn to use embedded structs to represent nested data, while keeping the interface of our types simple

- Learn to use `http.Get` to make external API requests, specifically to the Google Places API, with no code bloat

- Learn to effectively implement enumerators in Go, even though they aren't really a language feature

- Experience a real-world example of TDD

- See how the `math/rand` package makes it easy to select an item from a slice at random

- Learn an easy way to grab data from the URL parameters of the `http.Request` type

Project overview

Following Agile methodologies, let's write two user stories that describe the functionality of our project. User stories shouldn't be comprehensive documents describing the entire set of features of an application; rather small cards are perfect for not only describing what the user is trying to do, but why. Also, we should do this without trying to design the whole system up front or delve too deep into implementation details.

First we need a story about seeing the different journey types from which our users may select:

As a	traveler
I want	to see the different types of journeys I can get recommendations for
So that	I can decide what kind of evening to take my partner on

Secondly, we need a story about providing random recommendations for a selected journey type:

As a	traveler
I want	to see a random recommendation for my selected journey type
So that	I know where to go, and what the evening will entail

These two stories represent the two core capabilities that our API needs to provide, and actually ends up representing two endpoints.

In order to discover places around specified locations, we are going to make use of the Google Places API, which allows us to search for listings of businesses with given types, such as `bar`, `café`, or `movie_theater`. We will then use Go's `math/rand` package to pick from those places at random, building up a complete journey for our users.

 The Google Places API supports many business types; see `https://developers.google.com/places/documentation/supported_types` for the complete list.

Project design specifics

In order to turn our stories into an interactive application, we are going to provide two JSON endpoints; one to deliver the kinds of journeys users will be able to select in the application, and another to actually generate the random recommendations for the selected journey type.

```
GET /journeys
```

The above call should return a list such as the following:

```
[
  {
    name: "Romantic",
    journey: "park|bar|movie_theater|restaurant|florist"
  },
  {
    name: "Shopping",
    journey: "department_store|clothing_store|jewelry_store"
  }
]
```

The `name` field is a human-readable label for the type of recommendations the app generates, and the `journey` field is a pipe-separated list of supported journey types. It is the journey value that we will pass, as a URL parameter, into our other endpoint, which generates the actual recommendations:

```
GET /recommendations?
    lat=1&lng=2&journey=bar|cafe&radius=10&cost=$...$$$$$
```

This endpoint is responsible for querying the Google Places API and generating the recommendations before returning an array of place objects. We will use the parameters in the URL to control the kind of query to make as per the HTTP specification. The lat and lng parameters, representing latitude and longitude, respectively, tell our API where in the world we want recommendations from, and the radius parameter represents the distance in meters around the point in which we are interested in. The cost value is a human-readable way of representing the price range for places that the API returns. It is made up of two values: a lower and upper range separated by three dots. The number of dollar characters represents the price level, with $ being the most affordable and $$$$$ being the most expensive. Using this pattern, a value of $...$$ would represent very low cost recommendations, where $$$$...$$$$$ would represent a pretty expensive experience.

 Some programmers might insist the cost range is represented by numerical values, but since our API is going to be consumed by people, why not make things a little more interesting?

An example payload for this call might look something like this:

```
[
  {
    icon: "http://maps.gstatic.com/mapfiles/place_api/icons/cafe-
71.png",
    lat: 51.519583, lng: -0.146251,
    vicinity: "63 New Cavendish St, London",
    name: "Asia House",
    photos: [{
      url:
"https://maps.googleapis.com/maps/api/place/photo?maxwidth=400&pho
toreference=CnRnAAAAyLRN"
    }]
  }, ...
]
```

The array returned contains a place object representing a random recommendation for each segment in the journey, in the appropriate order. The preceding example is a café in London. The data fields are fairly self-explanatory; the lat and lng fields represent the location of the place (they're short for latitude and longitude), the name and vicinity fields tell us what and where the business is, and the photos array gives us a list of relevant photographs from Google's servers. The vicinity and icon fields will help us deliver a richer experience to our users.

Representing data in code

We are first going to expose the journeys that users can select from, so create a new folder called `meander` in GOPATH, and add the following `journeys.go` code:

```
package meander
type j struct {
  Name       string
  PlaceTypes []string
}
var Journeys = []interface{}{
  &j{Name: "Romantic", PlaceTypes: []string{"park", "bar",
"movie_theater", "restaurant", "florist", "taxi_stand"}},
  &j{Name: "Shopping", PlaceTypes: []string{"department_store",
"cafe", "clothing_store", "jewelry_store", "shoe_store"}},
  &j{Name: "Night Out", PlaceTypes: []string{"bar", "casino",
"food", "bar", "night_club", "bar", "bar", "hospital"}},
  &j{Name: "Culture", PlaceTypes: []string{"museum", "cafe",
"cemetery", "library", "art_gallery"}},
  &j{Name: "Pamper", PlaceTypes: []string{"hair_care",
"beauty_salon", "cafe", "spa"}},
}
```

Here we define an internal type called `j` inside the `meander` package, which we then use to describe the journeys by creating instances of them inside the `Journeys` slice. This approach is an ultra-simple way of representing data in the code, without building in a dependency on an external data store.

As an additional assignment, why not see if you can keep `golint` happy throughout this process? Every time you add some code, run `golint` for the packages and satisfy any suggestions that emerge. It cares a lot about exported items having no documentation, so adding simple comments in the correct format will keep it happy. To learn more about `golint`, see `https://github.com/golang/lint`.

Of course, this would likely evolve into just that later, maybe even with the ability for users to create and share their own journeys. Since we are exposing our data via an API, we are free to change the internal implementation without affecting the interface, so this approach is great for a version 1.0.

We are using a slice of type `[]interface{}` because we will later implement a general way of exposing public data regardless of actual types.

A romantic journey consists of a visit first to a park, then a bar, a movie theater, then a restaurant, before a visit to a florist, and finally a taxi ride home; you get the general idea. Feel free to get creative and add others by consulting the supported types in the Google Places API.

You might have noticed that since we are containing our code inside a package called meander (rather than main), our code can never be run as a tool like the other APIs we have written so far. Create a new folder called cmd inside meander; this will house the actual command-line tool that exposes the meander package's capabilities via an HTTP endpoint.

Inside the cmd folder, add the following code to the main.go file:

```
package main
func main() {
  runtime.GOMAXPROCS(runtime.NumCPU())
  //meander.APIKey = "TODO"
  http.HandleFunc("/journeys", func(w http.ResponseWriter, r
*http.Request) {
    respond(w, r, meander.Journeys)
  })
  http.ListenAndServe(":8080", http.DefaultServeMux)
}
func respond(w http.ResponseWriter, r *http.Request, data
[]interface{}) error {
  return json.NewEncoder(w).Encode(data)
}
```

You will recognize this as a simple API endpoint program, mapping to the /journeys endpoint.

 You'll have to import the encoding/json, net/http, and runtime packages, along with the meander package you created earlier.

The runtime.GOMAXPROCS call sets the maximum number of CPUs that our program can use, and we tell it to use them all. We then set the value of APIKey in the meander package (which is commented out for now, since we have yet to implement it) before calling the familiar HandleFunc function on the net/http package to bind our endpoint, which then just responds with the meander.Journeys variable. We borrow the abstract responding concept from the previous chapter by providing a respond function that encodes the specified data to the http.ResponseWriter type.

Let's run our API program by navigating to the cmd folder in a terminal and using go run. We don't need to build this into an executable file at this stage since it's just a single file:

```
go run main.go
```

Hit the http://localhost:8080/journeys endpoint, and notice that our Journeys data payload is served, which looks like this:

```
[{
  Name: "Romantic",
  PlaceTypes: [
    "park",
    "bar",
    "movie_theater",
    "restaurant",
    "florist",
    "taxi_stand"
  ]
}]
```

This is perfectly acceptable, but there is one major flaw: it exposes internals about our implementation. If we changed the PlaceTypes field name to Types, our API would change and it's important that we avoid this.

Projects evolve and change over time, especially successful ones, and as developers we should do what we can to protect our customers from the impact of the evolution. Abstracting interfaces is a great way to do this, as is taking ownership of the public-facing view of our data objects.

Public views of Go structs

In order to control the public view of structs in Go, we need to invent a way to allow individual journey types to tell us how they want to be exposed. In the meander folder, create a new file called public.go, and add the following code:

```
package meander
type Facade interface {
  Public() interface{}
}
func Public(o interface{}) interface{} {
  if p, ok := o.(Facade); ok {
    return p.Public()
  }
  return o
}
```

The `Facade` interface exposes a single `Public` method, which will return the public view of a struct. The `Public` function takes any object and checks to see whether it implements the `Facade` interface (does it have a `Public() interface{}` method?); and if it is implemented, calls the method and returns the result—otherwise it just returns the original object untouched. This allows us to pass anything through the `Public` function before writing the result to the `ResponseWriter` object, allowing individual structs to control their public appearance.

Let's implement a `Public` method for our `j` type by adding the following code to `journeys.go`:

```
func (j *j) Public() interface{} {
  return map[string]interface{}{
    "name":    j.Name,
    "journey": strings.Join(j.PlaceTypes, "|"),
  }
}
```

The public view of our `j` type joins the `PlaceTypes` field into a single string separated by the pipe character, as per our API design.

Head back to `cmd/main.go` and replace the `respond` method with one that makes use of our new `Public` function:

```
func respond(w http.ResponseWriter, r *http.Request, data []
interface{}) error {
  publicData := make([]interface{}, len(data))
  for i, d := range data {
    publicData[i] = meander.Public(d)
  }
  return json.NewEncoder(w).Encode(publicData)
}
```

Here we iterate over the data slice calling the `meander.Public` function for each item, building the results into a new slice of the same size. In the case of our `j` type, its `Public` method will be called to serve the public view of the data, rather than the default view. In a terminal, navigate to the `cmd` folder again and run `go run main.go` before hitting `http://localhost:8080/journeys` again. Notice that the same data has now changed to a new structure:

```
[{
  journey: "park|bar|movie_theater|restaurant|florist|taxi_stand",
  name: "Romantic"
}, ...]
```

Generating random recommendations

In order to obtain the places from which our code will randomly build up recommendations, we need to query the Google Places API. In the `meander` folder, add the following `query.go` file:

```go
package meander
type Place struct {
  *googleGeometry `json:"geometry"`
  Name            string        `json:"name"`
  Icon            string        `json:"icon"`
  Photos          []*googlePhoto `json:"photos"`
  Vicinity        string        `json:"vicinity"`
}
type googleResponse struct {
  Results []*Place `json:"results"`
}
type googleGeometry struct {
  *googleLocation `json:"location"`
}
type googleLocation struct {
  Lat float64 `json:"lat"`
  Lng float64 `json:"lng"`
}
type googlePhoto struct {
  PhotoRef string `json:"photo_reference"`
  URL      string `json:"url"`
}
```

This code defines the structures we will need to parse the JSON response from the Google Places API into usable objects.

 Head over to the Google Places API documentation for an example of the response we are expecting. See `http://developers.google. com/places/documentation/search`.

Most of the preceding code will be obvious, but it's worth noticing that the `Place` type embeds the `googleGeometry` type, which allows us to represent the nested data as per the API, while essentially flattening it in our code. We do the same with `googleLocation` inside `googleGeometry`, which means that we will be able to access the `Lat` and `Lng` values directly on a `Place` object, even though they're technically nested in other structures.

Because we want to control how a `Place` object appears publically, let's give this type the following `Public` method:

```go
func (p *Place) Public() interface{} {
  return map[string]interface{}{
    "name":     p.Name,
    "icon":     p.Icon,
    "photos":   p.Photos,
    "vicinity": p.Vicinity,
    "lat":      p.Lat,
    "lng":      p.Lng,
  }
}
```

Remember to run `golint` on this code to see which comments need to be added to the exported items.

Google Places API key

Like with most APIs, we will need an API key in order to access the remote services. Head over to the Google APIs Console, sign in with a Google account, and create a key for the Google Places API. For more detailed instructions, see the documentation on Google's developer website.

Once you have your key, let's make a variable inside the `meander` package that can hold it. At the top of `query.go`, add the following definition:

```go
var APIKey string
```

Now nip back into `main.go`, remove the double slash `//` from the `APIKey` line, and replace the `TODO` value with the actual key provided by the Google APIs console.

Enumerators in Go

To handle the various cost ranges for our API, it makes sense to use an enumerator (or **enum**) to denote the various values and to handle conversions to and from string representations. Go doesn't explicitly provide enumerators, but there is a neat way of implementing them, which we will explore in this section.

A simple flexible checklist for writing enumerators in Go is:

- Define a new type, based on a primitive integer type
- Use that type whenever you need users to specify one of the appropriate values
- Use the `iota` keyword to set the values in a `const` block, disregarding the first zero value
- Implement a map of sensible string representations to the values of your enumerator
- Implement a `String` method on the type that returns the appropriate string representation from the map
- Implement a `ParseType` function that converts from a string to your type using the map

Now we will write an enumerator to represent the cost levels in our API. Create a new file called `cost_level.go` inside the `meander` folder and add the following code:

```
package meander
type Cost int8
const (
  _ Cost = iota
  Cost1
  Cost2
  Cost3
  Cost4
  Cost5
)
```

Here we define the type of our enumerator, which we have called `Cost`, and since we only need to represent a few values, we have based it on an `int8` range. For enumerators where we need larger values, you are free to use any of the integer types that work with `iota`. The `Cost` type is now a real type in its own right, and we can use it wherever we need to represent one of the supported values—for example, we can specify a `Cost` type as an argument in functions, or use it as the type for a field in a struct.

We then define a list of constants of that type, and use the `iota` keyword to indicate that we want incrementing values for the constants. By disregarding the first `iota` value (which is always zero), we indicate that one of the specified constants must be explicitly used, rather than the zero value.

To provide a string representation of our enumerator, we need only add a String method to the Cost type. This is a useful exercise even if you don't need to use the strings in your code, because whenever you use the print calls from the Go standard library (such as fmt.Println), the numerical values will be used by default. Often those values are meaningless and will require you to look them up, and even count the lines to determine the numerical value for each item.

For more information about the String() method in Go, see the Stringer and GoStringer interfaces in the fmt package at http://golang.org/pkg/fmt/#Stringer.

Test-driven enumerator

To be sure that our enumerator code is working correctly, we are going to write unit tests that make some assertions about expected behavior.

Alongside cost_level.go, add a new file called cost_level_test.go, and add the following unit test:

```
package meander_test
import (
  "testing"
  "github.com/cheekybits/is"
  "path/to/meander"
)
func TestCostValues(t *testing.T) {
  is := is.New(t)
  is.Equal(int(meander.Cost1), 1)
  is.Equal(int(meander.Cost2), 2)
  is.Equal(int(meander.Cost3), 3)
  is.Equal(int(meander.Cost4), 4)
  is.Equal(int(meander.Cost5), 5)
}
```

You will need to run go get to get the CheekyBits' is package (from github.com/cheekybits/is).

The is package is an alternative testing helper package, but this one is ultra-simple and deliberately bare-bones. You get to pick your favorite when you write your own projects.

Normally, we wouldn't worry about the actual integer value of constants in our enumerator, but since the Google Places API uses numerical values to represent the same thing, we need to care about the values.

> You might have noticed something strange about this test file that breaks from convention. Although it is inside the meander folder, it is not a part of the meander package; rather it's in meander_test.
>
> In Go, this is an error in every case except for tests. Because we are putting our test code into its own package, it means that we no longer have access to the internals of the meander package—notice how we have to use the package prefix. This may seem like a disadvantage, but in fact it allows us to be sure that we are testing the package as though we were a real user of it. We may only call exported methods and only have visibility into exported types; just like our users.

Run the tests by running go test in a terminal, and notice that it passes.

Let's add another test to make assertions about the string representations for each Cost constant. In cost_level_test.go, add the following unit test:

```go
func TestCostString(t *testing.T) {
    is := is.New(t)
    is.Equal(meander.Cost1.String(), "$")
    is.Equal(meander.Cost2.String(), "$$")
    is.Equal(meander.Cost3.String(), "$$$")
    is.Equal(meander.Cost4.String(), "$$$$")
    is.Equal(meander.Cost5.String(), "$$$$$")
}
```

This test asserts that calling the String method for each constant yields the expected value. Running these tests will of course fail, because we haven't yet implemented the String method.

Underneath the Cost constants, add the following map and the String method:

```go
var costStrings = map[string]Cost{
    "$":     Cost1,
    "$$":    Cost2,
    "$$$":   Cost3,
    "$$$$":  Cost4,
    "$$$$$": Cost5,
}
func (l Cost) String() string {
```

```go
    for s, v := range costStrings {
      if l == v {
        return s
      }
    }
    return "invalid"
}
```

The `map[string]Cost` variable maps the cost values to the string representation, and the `String` method iterates over the map to return the appropriate value.

 In our case, a simple return `strings.Repeat("$", int(l))` would work just as well (and wins because it's simpler code), but it often won't, therefore this section explores the general approach.

Now if we were to print out the `Cost3` value, we would actually see $$$, which is much more useful than numerical vales. However, since we do want to use these strings in our API, we are also going to add a `ParseCost` method.

In `cost_value_test.go`, add the following unit test:

```go
func TestParseCost(t *testing.T) {
  is := is.New(t)
  is.Equal(meander.Cost1, meander.ParseCost("$"))
  is.Equal(meander.Cost2, meander.ParseCost("$$"))
  is.Equal(meander.Cost3, meander.ParseCost("$$$"))
  is.Equal(meander.Cost4, meander.ParseCost("$$$$"))
  is.Equal(meander.Cost5, meander.ParseCost("$$$$$"))
}
```

Here we assert that calling `ParseCost` will in fact yield the appropriate value depending on the input string.

In `cost_value.go`, add the following implementation code:

```go
func ParseCost(s string) Cost {
  return costStrings[s]
}
```

Parsing a `Cost` string is very simple since this is how our map is laid out.

As we need to represent a range of cost values, let's imagine a `CostRange` type, and write the tests out for how we intend to use it. Add the following tests to `cost_value_test.go`:

```go
func TestParseCostRange(t *testing.T) {
  is := is.New(t)
  var l *meander.CostRange
  l = meander.ParseCostRange("$$...$$$")
  is.Equal(l.From, meander.Cost2)
  is.Equal(l.To, meander.Cost3)
  l = meander.ParseCostRange("$...$$$$$")
  is.Equal(l.From, meander.Cost1)
  is.Equal(l.To, meander.Cost5)
}
func TestCostRangeString(t *testing.T) {
  is := is.New(t)
  is.Equal("$$...$$$$", (&meander.CostRange{
    From: meander.Cost2,
    To:   meander.Cost4,
  }).String())
}
```

We specify that passing in a string with two dollar characters first, followed by three dots and then three dollar characters should create a new `meander.CostRange` type that has `From` set to `meander.Cost2`, and `To` set to `meander.Cost3`. The second test does the reverse by testing that the `CostRange.String` method returns the appropriate value.

To make our tests pass, add the following `CostRange` type and associated `String` and `ParseString` functions:

```go
type CostRange struct {
  From Cost
  To   Cost
}
func (r CostRange) String() string {
  return r.From.String() + "..." + r.To.String()
}
func ParseCostRange(s string) *CostRange {
  segs := strings.Split(s, "...")
```

```
      return &CostRange{
    From: ParseCost(segs[0]),
    To:   ParseCost(segs[1]),
  }
}
```

This allows us to convert a string such as $...$$$$$ to a structure that contains two Cost values; a From and To set and vice versa.

Querying the Google Places API

Now that we are capable of representing the results of the API, we need a way to represent and initiate the actual query. Add the following structure to query.go:

```
type Query struct {
  Lat          float64
  Lng          float64
  Journey      []string
  Radius       int
  CostRangeStr string
}
```

This structure contains all the information we will need to build up the query, all of which will actually come from the URL parameters in the requests from the client. Next, add the following find method, which will be responsible for making the actual request to Google's servers:

```
func (q *Query) find(types string) (*googleResponse, error) {
  u :=
"https://maps.googleapis.com/maps/api/place/nearbysearch/json"
  vals := make(url.Values)
  vals.Set("location", fmt.Sprintf("%g,%g", q.Lat, q.Lng))
  vals.Set("radius", fmt.Sprintf("%d", q.Radius))
  vals.Set("types", types)
  vals.Set("key", APIKey)
  if len(q.CostRangeStr) > 0 {
    r := ParseCostRange(q.CostRangeStr)
    vals.Set("minprice", fmt.Sprintf("%d", int(r.From)-1))
    vals.Set("maxprice", fmt.Sprintf("%d", int(r.To)-1))
  }
```

```
res, err := http.Get(u + "?" + vals.Encode())
if err != nil {
  return nil, err
}
defer res.Body.Close()
var response googleResponse
if err := json.NewDecoder(res.Body).Decode(&response); err !=
nil {
  return nil, err
}
return &response, nil
}
```

First we build the request URL as per the Google Places API specification, by appending the `url.Values` encoded string of the data for `lat`, `lng`, `radius`, and of course the `APIKey` values.

 The `url.Values` type is actually a `map[string][]string` type, which is why we use `make` rather than `new`.

The `types` value we specify as an argument represents the kind of business to look for. If there is a `CostRangeStr`, we parse it and set the `minprice` and `maxprice` values, before finally calling `http.Get` to actually make the request. If the request is successful, we defer the closing of the response body and use a `json.Decoder` method to decode the JSON that comes back from the API into our `googleResponse` type.

Building recommendations

Next we need to write a method that will allow us to make many calls to find, for the different steps in a journey. Underneath the `find` method, add the following `Run` method to the `Query` struct:

```
// Run runs the query concurrently, and returns the results.
func (q *Query) Run() []interface{} {
  rand.Seed(time.Now().UnixNano())
  var w sync.WaitGroup
  var l sync.Mutex
  places := make([]interface{}, len(q.Journey))
```

```
    for i, r := range q.Journey {
      w.Add(1)
      go func(types string, i int) {
        defer w.Done()
        response, err := q.find(types)
        if err != nil {
          log.Println("Failed to find places:", err)
          return
        }
        if len(response.Results) == 0 {
          log.Println("No places found for", types)
          return
        }
        for _, result := range response.Results {
          for _, photo := range result.Photos {
            photo.URL =
"https://maps.googleapis.com/maps/api/place/photo?" +
              "maxwidth=1000&photoreference=" + photo.PhotoRef +
"&key=" + APIKey
          }
        }
        randI := rand.Intn(len(response.Results))
        l.Lock()
        places[i] = response.Results[randI]
        l.Unlock()
      }(r, i)
    }
    w.Wait() // wait for everything to finish
    return places
}
```

The first thing we do is set the random seed to the current time in nanoseconds past since January 1, 1970 UTC. This ensures that every time we call the Run method and use the rand package, the results will be different. If we didn't do this, our code would suggest the same recommendations every time, which defeats the object.

Since we need to make many requests to Google — and since we want to make sure this is as quick as possible — we are going to run all the queries at the same time by making concurrent calls to our Query.find method. So we next create a sync.WaitGroup method, and a map to hold the selected places along with a sync.Mutex method to allow many go routines to access the map concurrently.

We then iterate over each item in the `Journey` slice, which might be `bar`, `cafe`, `movie_theater`. For each item, we add 1 to the `WaitGroup` object, and call a goroutine. Inside the routine, we first defer the `w.Done` call informing the `WaitGroup` object that this request has completed, before calling our `find` method to make the actual request. Assuming no errors occurred, and it was indeed able to find some places, we iterate over the results and build up a usable URL for any photos that might be present. According to the Google Places API, we are given a `photoreference` key, which we can use in another API call to get the actual image. To save our clients from having to have knowledge of the Google Places API at all, we build the complete URL for them.

We then lock the map locker and with a call to `rand.Intn`, pick one of the options at random and insert it into the right position in the `places` slice, before unlocking the `sync.Mutex` method.

Finally, we wait for all goroutines to complete with a call to `w.Wait`, before returning the places.

Handlers that use query parameters

Now we need to wire up our `/recommendations` call, so head back to `main.go` in the `cmd` folder, and add the following code inside the `main` function:

```
http.HandleFunc("/recommendations", func(w http.ResponseWriter, r
*http.Request) {
  q := &meander.Query{
    Journey: strings.Split(r.URL.Query().Get("journey"), "|"),
  }
  q.Lat, _ = strconv.ParseFloat(r.URL.Query().Get("lat"), 64)
  q.Lng, _ = strconv.ParseFloat(r.URL.Query().Get("lng"), 64)
  q.Radius, _ = strconv.Atoi(r.URL.Query().Get("radius"))
  q.CostRangeStr = r.URL.Query().Get("cost")
  places := q.Run()
  respond(w, r, places)
})
```

This handler is responsible for preparing the `meander.Query` object and calling its `Run` method, before responding with the results. The `http.Request` type's URL value exposes the `Query` data that provides a `Get` method that, in turn, looks up a value for a given key.

The journey string is translated from the `bar|cafe|movie_theater` format to a slice of strings, by splitting on the pipe character. Then a few calls to functions in the `strconv` package turn the string latitude, longitude, and radius values into numerical types.

CORS

The final piece of the first version of our API will be to implement CORS as we did in the previous chapter. See if you can solve this problem yourself before reading on to the solution in the next section.

 If you are going to tackle this yourself, remember that your aim is to set the `Access-Control-Allow-Origin` response header to `*`. Also consider the `http.HandlerFunc` wrapping we did in the previous chapter. The best place for this code is probably in the cmd program, since that is what exposes the functionality through an HTTP endpoint.

In `main.go`, add the following `cors` function:

```
func cors(f http.HandlerFunc) http.HandlerFunc {
  return func(w http.ResponseWriter, r *http.Request) {
    w.Header().Set("Access-Control-Allow-Origin", "*")
    f(w, r)
  }
}
```

This familiar pattern takes in an `http.HandlerFunc` type and returns a new one that sets the appropriate header before calling the passed-in function. Now we can modify our code to make sure the `cors` function gets called for both of our endpoints. Update the appropriate lines in the `main` function:

```
func main() {
  runtime.GOMAXPROCS(runtime.NumCPU())
  meander.APIKey = "YOUR_API_KEY"
  http.HandleFunc("/journeys", cors(func(w http.ResponseWriter, r
*http.Request) {
    respond(w, r, meander.Journeys)
  }))
  http.HandleFunc("/recommendations", cors(func(w
http.ResponseWriter, r *http.Request) {
    q := &meander.Query{
      Journey: strings.Split(r.URL.Query().Get("journey"), "|"),
    }
```

```
    q.Lat, _ = strconv.ParseFloat(r.URL.Query().Get("lat"), 64)
    q.Lng, _ = strconv.ParseFloat(r.URL.Query().Get("lng"), 64)
    q.Radius, _ = strconv.Atoi(r.URL.Query().Get("radius"))
    q.CostRangeStr = r.URL.Query().Get("cost")
    places := q.Run()
    respond(w, r, places)
  }))
  http.ListenAndServe(":8080", http.DefaultServeMux)
}
```

Now calls to our API will be allowed from any domain without a cross-origin error occurring.

Testing our API

Now that we are ready to test our API, head to a console and navigate to the cmd folder. Because our program imports the meander package, building the program will automatically build our meander package too.

Build and run the program:

```
go build -o meanderapi
```

```
./meanderapi
```

To see meaningful results from our API, let's take a minute to find your actual latitude and longitude. Head over to http://mygeoposition.com/ and use the web tools to get the x, y values for a location you are familiar with.

Or pick from these popular cities:

- London, England: 51.520707 x 0.153809
- New York, USA: 40.7127840 x -74.0059410
- Tokyo, Japan: 35.6894870 x 139.6917060
- San Francisco, USA: 37.7749290 x -122.4194160

Now open a web browser and access the /recommendations endpoint with some appropriate values for the fields:

```
http://localhost:8080/recommendations?
  lat=51.520707&lng=-0.153809&radius=5000&
  journey=cafe|bar|casino|restaurant&
  cost=$...$$$
```

The following screenshot shows what a sample recommendation around London might look like:

Feel free to play around with the values in the URL to see how powerful the simple API is by trying various journey strings, tweaking the locations, and trying different cost range value strings.

Web application

We are going to download a complete web application built to the same API specifications, and point it at our implementation to see it come to life before our eyes. Head over to https://github.com/matryer/goblueprints/tree/master/chapter7/meanderweb and download the meanderweb project into your GOPATH.

In a terminal, navigate to the meanderweb folder, and build and run it:

```
go build -o meanderweb
./meanderweb
```

This will start a website running on `localhost:8081`, which is hardcoded to look for the API running at `localhost:8080`. Because we added the CORS support, this won't be a problem despite them running on different domains.

Open a browser to `http://localhost:8081/` and interact with the application, while somebody else built the UI it would be pretty useless without the API that we built powering it.

Summary

In this chapter, we built an API that consumes and abstracts the Google Places API to provide a fun and interesting way of letting users plan their days and evenings.

We started by writing some simple and short user stories that described at a really high level what we wanted to achieve, without trying to design the implementation up front. In order to parallelize the project, we agreed the meeting point of the project as the API design, and we built towards it (as would our partners).

We embedded data directly in code, avoiding the need to investigate, design, and implement a data store in the early stages of a project. By caring instead about how that data is accessed (via the API endpoint), we allowed our future selves to completely change how and where the data is stored, without breaking any apps that have been written to our API.

We implemented the `Facade` interface, which allows our structs and other types to provide public representations of them, without revealing messy or sensitive details about our implementation.

Our foray into enumerators gave us a useful starting point to build enumerated types, even though there is no official support for them in the language. The `iota` keyword that we used lets us specify constants of our own numerical type, with incrementing values. The common `String` method that we implemented showed us how to make sure our enumerated types don't become obscure numbers in our logs. At the same time, we also saw a real-world example of TDD, and red/green programming where we wrote unit tests that first fail, but which we then go on to make pass by writing the implementation code.

8
Filesystem Backup

There are many solutions that provide filesystem backup capabilities. These include everything from apps such as Dropbox, Box, Carbonite to hardware solutions such as Apple's Time Machine, Seagate, or network-attached storage products, to name a few. Most consumer tools provide some key automatic functionality, along with an app or website for you to manage your policies and content. Often, especially for developers, these tools don't quite do the things we need them to. However, thanks to Go's standard library (that includes packages such as `ioutil` and `os`) we have everything we need to build a backup solution that behaves exactly as we need it to.

For our final project, we will build a simple filesystem backup for our source code projects that archive specified folders and save a snapshot of them every time we make a change. The change could be when we tweak a file and save it, or if we add new files and folders, or even if we delete a file. We want to be able to go back to any point in time to retrieve old files.

Specifically in this chapter, you will learn:

- How to structure projects that consist of packages and command-line tools
- A pragmatic approach to persisting simple data across tool executions
- How the `os` package allows you to interact with a filesystem
- How to run code in an infinite timed loop, while respecting *Ctrl + C*
- How to use `filepath.Walk` to iterate over files and folders
- How to quickly determine if the contents of a directory have changed
- How to use the `archive/zip` package to zip files
- How to build tools that care about a combination of command-line flags and normal arguments

Solution design

We will start by listing some high-level acceptance criteria for our solution and the approach we want to take:

- The solution should create a snapshot of our files at regular intervals, as we make changes to our source code projects

- We want to control the interval at which the directories are checked for changes

- Code projects are primarily text-based, so zipping the directories to generate archives will save a lot of space

- We will build this project quickly, while keeping a close watch over where we might want to make improvements later

- Any implementation decisions we make should be easily modified if we decide to change our implementation in the future

- We will build two command-line tools, the backend daemon that does the work, and a user interaction utility that will let us list, add, and remove paths from the backup service

Project structure

It is common in Go solutions to have, in a single project, both a package that allows other Go programmers to use your capabilities, and a command-line tool that allows end users to use your code.

A convention is emerging to structure the project by having the package in the main project folder, and the command-line tool inside a subfolder called `cmd`, or `cmds` if you have multiple commands. Because all packages (regardless of the directory tree) are equal in Go, you can import the main package from the subpackages, knowing you'll never need to import the commands from the main package. This may seem like an unnecessary abstraction, but is actually quite a common pattern and can be seen in the standard Go tool chain with examples such as `gofmt` and `goimports`.

For example, for our project we are going to write a package called `backup`, and two command-line tools: the daemon and the user interaction tool. We will structure our project in the following way:

```
/backup - package
/backup/cmds/backup - user interaction tool
/backup/cmds/backupd - worker daemon
```

Backup package

We are first going to write the backup package, of which we will become the first customer when we write the associated tools. The package will be responsible for deciding whether directories have changed and need backing up or not, as well as actually performing the backup procedure too.

Obvious interfaces?

The first thing to think about when embarking on a new Go program is whether any interfaces stand out to you. We don't want to over-abstract or waste too much time up front designing something that we know will change as we start to code, but that doesn't mean we shouldn't look for obvious concepts that are worth pulling out. Since our code will archive files, the Archiver interface pops out as a candidate.

Create a new folder inside your GOPATH called backup, and add the following archiver.go code:

```
package backup

type Archiver interface {
  Archive(src, dest string) error
}
```

An Archiver interface will specify a method called Archive that takes source and destination paths and returns an error. Implementations of this interface will be responsible for archiving the source folder, and storing it in the destination path.

> Defining an interface up front is a nice way to get some concepts out of our heads and into code; it doesn't mean this interface can't change as we evolve our solution as long as we remember the power of simple interfaces. Also, remember that most of the I/O interfaces in the io package expose only a single method.

From the very beginning, we have made the case that while we are going to implement ZIP files as our archive format, we could easily swap this out later with another kind of Archiver format.

Implementing ZIP

Now that we have the interface for our `Archiver` types, we are going to implement one that uses the ZIP file format.

Add the following `struct` definition to `archiver.go`:

```
type zipper struct{}
```

We are not going to export this type, which might make you jump to the conclusion that users outside of the package won't be able to make use of it. In fact, we are going to provide them with an instance of the type for them to use, to save them from having to worry about creating and managing their own types.

Add the following exported implementation:

```
// Zip is an Archiver that zips and unzips files.
var ZIP Archiver = (*zipper)(nil)
```

This curious snippet of Go voodoo is actually a very interesting way of exposing the intent to the compiler, without using any memory (literally 0 bytes). We are defining a variable called `ZIP` of type `Archiver`, so from outside the package it's pretty clear that we can use that variable wherever `Archiver` is needed—if you want to zip things. Then we assign it with `nil` cast to the type `*zipper`. We know that `nil` takes no memory, but since it's cast to a `zipper` pointer, and given that our `zipper` struct has no fields, it's an appropriate way of solving a problem, which hides the complexity of code (and indeed the actual implementation) from outside users. There is no reason anybody outside of the package needs to know about our `zipper` type at all, which frees us up to change the internals without touching the externals at any time; the true power of interfaces.

Another handy side benefit to this trick is that the compiler will now be checking whether our zipper type properly implements the `Archiver` interface or not, so if you try to build this code you'll get a compiler error:

```
./archiver.go:10: cannot use (*zipper)(nil) (type *zipper) as type
Archiver in assignment:
   *zipper does not implement Archiver (missing Archive method)
```

We see that our `zipper` type does not implement the `Archive` method as mandated in the interface.

You can also use the `Archive` method in test code to ensure that your types implement the interfaces they should. If you don't need to use the variable, you can always throw it away by using an underscore and you'll still get the compiler help:

```
var _ Interface = (*Implementation)(nil)
```

To make the compiler happy, we are going to add the implementation of the `Archive` method for our `zipper` type.

Add the following code to `archiver.go`:

```go
func (z *zipper) Archive(src, dest string) error {
  if err := os.MkdirAll(filepath.Dir(dest), 0777); err != nil {
    return err
  }
  out, err := os.Create(dest)
  if err != nil {
    return err
  }
  defer out.Close()
  w := zip.NewWriter(out)
  defer w.Close()
  return filepath.Walk(src, func(path string, info os.FileInfo,
err error) error {
    if info.IsDir() {
      return nil // skip
    }
    if err != nil {
      return err
    }
    in, err := os.Open(path)
    if err != nil {
      return err
    }
    defer in.Close()
    f, err := w.Create(path)
    if err != nil {
      return err
    }
    io.Copy(f, in)
    return nil
  })
}
```

You will have to also import the `archive/zip` package from the Go standard library. In our `Archive` method, we take the following steps to prepare writing to a ZIP file:

- Use `os.MkdirAll` to ensure the destination directory exists. The `0777` code represents the file permissions with which to create any missing directories.

- Use `os.Create` to create a new file as specified by the `dest` path.

- If the file is created without error, defer the closing of the file with `defer out.Close()`.

- Use `zip.NewWriter` to create a new `zip.Writer` type that will write to the file we just created, and defer the closing of the writer.

Once we have a `zip.Writer` type ready to go, we use the `filepath.Walk` function to iterate over the source directory `src`.

The `filepath.Walk` function takes two arguments: the root path, and a callback function `func` to be called for every item (files and folders) it encounters while iterating over the file system. The `filepath.Walk` function is recursive, so it will travel deep into subfolders too. The callback function itself takes three arguments: the full path of the file, the `os.FileInfo` object that describes the file or folder itself, and an error (it also returns an error in case something goes wrong). If any calls to the callback function result in an error being returned, the operation will be aborted and `filepath.Walk` returns that error. We simply pass that up to the caller of `Archive` and let them worry about it, since there's nothing more we can do.

For each item in the tree, our code takes the following steps:

- If the `info.IsDir` method tells us that the item is a folder, we just return `nil`, effectively skipping it. There is no reason to add folders to ZIP archives, because anyway the path of the files will encode that information for us.

- If an error is passed in (via the third argument), it means something went wrong when trying to access information about the file. This is uncommon, so we just return the error, which will eventually be passed out to the caller of `Archive`.

- Use `os.Open` to open the source file for reading, and if successful defer its closing.

- Call `Create` on the `ZipWriter` object to indicate that we want to create a new compressed file, and give it the full path of the file, which includes the directories it is nested inside.

- Use `io.Copy` to read all of the bytes from the source file, and write them through the `ZipWriter` object to the ZIP file we opened earlier.

- Return `nil` to indicate no errors.

This chapter will not cover unit testing or **Test-driven Development** (TDD) practices, but feel free to write a test to ensure that our implementation does what it is meant to do.

 Since we are writing a package, spend some time commenting the exported pieces so far. You can use `golint` to help you find any exported pieces you may have missed.

Has the filesystem changed?

One of the biggest problems our backup system has is deciding whether a folder has changed or not in a cross-platform, predictable, and reliable way. A few things spring to mind when we think about this problem: should we just check the last modified date on the top-level folder? Should we use system notifications to be informed whenever a file we care about changes? There are problems with both of these approaches, and it turns out it's not a trivial problem to solve.

We are instead going to generate an MD5 hash made up of all of the information that we care about when considering whether something has changed or not.

Looking at the `os.FileInfo` type, we can see that we can find out a lot of information about a file:

```
type FileInfo interface {
  Name() string        // base name of the file
  Size() int64         // length in bytes for regular files;
                       //   system-dependent for others
  Mode() FileMode      // file mode bits
  ModTime() time.Time  // modification time
  IsDir() bool         // abbreviation for Mode().IsDir()
  Sys() interface{}    // underlying data source (can return nil)
}
```

To ensure we are aware of a variety of changes to any file in a folder, the hash will be made up of the filename and path (so if they rename a file, the hash will be different), size (if a file changes size, it's obviously different), last modified date, whether the item is a file or folder, and file mode bits. Even though we won't be archiving the folders, we still care about their names and the tree structure of the folder.

Create a new file called `dirhash.go` and add the following function:

```
package backup
import (
  "crypto/md5"
```

```
    "fmt"
    "io"
    "os"
    "path/filepath"
)
func DirHash(path string) (string, error) {
  hash := md5.New()
  err := filepath.Walk(path, func(path string, info os.FileInfo, err
error) error {
    if err != nil {
      return err
    }
    io.WriteString(hash, path)
    fmt.Fprintf(hash, "%v", info.IsDir())
    fmt.Fprintf(hash, "%v", info.ModTime())
    fmt.Fprintf(hash, "%v", info.Mode())
    fmt.Fprintf(hash, "%v", info.Name())
    fmt.Fprintf(hash, "%v", info.Size())
    return nil
  })
  if err != nil {
    return "", err
  }
  return fmt.Sprintf("%x", hash.Sum(nil)), nil
}
```

We first create a new `hash.Hash` that knows how to calculate MD5s, before using `filepath.Walk` to iterate over all of the files and folders inside the specified path directory. For each item, assuming there are no errors, we write the differential information to the hash generator using `io.WriteString`, which lets us write a string to an `io.Writer`, and `fmt.Fprintf`, which does the same but exposes formatting capabilities at the same time, allowing us to generate the default value format for each item using the `%v` format verb.

Once each file has been processed, and assuming no errors occurred, we then use `fmt.Sprintf` to generate the result string. The `Sum` method on a `hash.Hash` calculates the final hash value with the specified values appended. In our case, we do not want to append anything since we've already added all of the information we care about, so we just pass `nil`. The `%x` format verb indicates that we want the value to be represented in hex (base 16) with lowercase letters. This is the usual way of representing an MD5 hash.

Checking for changes and initiating a backup

Now that we have the ability to hash a folder, and to perform a backup, we are going to put the two together in a new type called `Monitor`. The `Monitor` type will have a map of paths with their associated hashes, a reference to any `Archiver` type (of course, we'll use `backup.ZIP` for now), and a destination string representing where to put the archives.

Create a new file called `monitor.go` and add the following definition:

```
type Monitor struct {
  Paths        map[string]string
  Archiver     Archiver
  Destination  string
}
```

In order to trigger a check for changes, we are going to add the following `Now` method:

```
func (m *Monitor) Now() (int, error) {
  var counter int
  for path, lastHash := range m.Paths {
    newHash, err := DirHash(path)
    if err != nil {
      return 0, err
    }
    if newHash != lastHash {
      err := m.act(path)
      if err != nil {
        return counter, err
      }
      m.Paths[path] = newHash // update the hash
      counter++
    }
  }
  return counter, nil
}
```

The `Now` method iterates over every path in the map and generates the latest hash of that folder. If the hash does not match the hash from the map (generated the last time it checked), then it is considered to have changed, and needs backing up again. We do this with a call to the as yet unwritten `act` method, before then updating the hash in the map with this new hash.

To give our users a high-level indication of what happened when they called Now, we are also maintaining a counter which we increment every time we back up a folder. We will use this later to keep our end users up-to-date on what the system is doing without bombarding them with information.

```
m.act undefined (type *Monitor has no field or method act)
```

The compiler is helping us again and reminding us that we have yet to add the act method:

```
func (m *Monitor) act(path string) error {
  dirname := filepath.Base(path)
  filename := fmt.Sprintf("%d.zip", time.Now().UnixNano())
  return m.Archiver.Archive(path, filepath.Join(m.Destination,
dirname, filename))
}
```

Because we have done the heavy lifting in our ZIP Archiver type, all we have to do here is generate a filename, decide where the archive will go, and call the Archive method.

> If the Archive method returns an error, the act method and then the Now method will each return it. This mechanism of passing errors up the chain is very common in Go and allows you to either handle cases where you can do something useful to recover, or else defer the problem to somebody else.

The act method in the preceding code uses time.Now().UnixNano() to generate a timestamp filename and hardcodes the .zip extension.

Hardcoding is OK for a short while

Hardcoding the file extension like we have is OK in the beginning, but if you think about it we have blended concerns a little here. If we change the Archiver implementation to use RAR or a compression format of our making, the .zip extension would no longer be appropriate.

> Before reading on, think about what steps you might take to avoid hardcoding. Where does the filename extension decision live? What changes would you need to make in order to avoid hardcoding properly?

The right place for the filename extensions decision is probably in the `Archiver` interface, since it knows the kind of archiving it will be doing. So we could add an `Ext()` string method and access that from our `act` method. But we can add a little extra power with not much extra work by instead allowing `Archiver` authors to specify the entire filename format, rather than just the extension.

Back in `archiver.go`, update the `Archiver` interface definition:

```
type Archiver interface {
  DestFmt() string
  Archive(src, dest string) error
}
```

Our `zipper` type needs to now implement this:

```
func (z *zipper) DestFmt() string {
  return "%d.zip"
}
```

Now that we can ask our `act` method to get the whole format string from the `Archiver` interface, update the `act` method:

```
func (m *Monitor) act(path string) error {
  dirname := filepath.Base(path)
  filename := fmt.Sprintf(m.Archiver.DestFmt(),
time.Now().UnixNano())
  return m.Archiver.Archive(path, filepath.Join(m.Destination,
dirname, filename))
}
```

The user command-line tool

The first of two tools we will build allows the user to add, list, and remove paths for the backup daemon tool (which we will write later). You could expose a web interface, or even use the binding packages for desktop user interface integration, but we are going to keep things simple and build ourselves a command-line tool.

Create a new folder called `cmds` inside the `backup` folder and create another `backup` folder inside that.

 It's good practice to name the folder of the command and the command binary itself the same.

Inside our new `backup` folder, add the following code to `main.go`:

```go
func main() {
  var fatalErr error
  defer func() {
    if fatalErr != nil {
      flag.PrintDefaults()
      log.Fatalln(fatalErr)
    }
  }()
  var (
    dbpath = flag.String("db", "./backupdata", "path to database
directory")
  )
  flag.Parse()
  args := flag.Args()
  if len(args) < 1 {
    fatalErr = errors.New("invalid usage; must specify command")
    return
  }
}
```

We first define our `fatalErr` variable and defer the function that checks to ensure that value is `nil`. If it is not, it will print the error along with flag defaults and exit with a non-zero status code. We then define a flag called `db` that expects the path to the `filedb` database directory, before parsing the flags and getting the remaining arguments and ensuring there is at least one.

Persisting small data

In order to keep track of the paths, and the hashes that we generate, we will need some kind of data storage mechanism that ideally works even when we stop and start our programs. We have lots of choices here: everything from a text file to a full horizontally scalable database solution. The Go ethos of simplicity tells us that building-in a database dependency to our little backup program would not be a great idea; rather we should ask what is the simplest way we can solve this problem?

The `github.com/matryer/filedb` package is an experimental solution for just this kind of problem. It lets you interact with the filesystem as though it were a very simple schemaless database. It takes its design lead from packages such as `mgo`, and can be used in the cases where data querying needs are very simple. In `filedb`, a database is a folder, and a collection is a file where each line represents a different record. Of course, this could all change as the `filedb` project evolves, but the interface hopefully won't.

Add the following code to the end of the `main` function:

```
db, err := filedb.Dial(*dbpath)
if err != nil {
  fatalErr = err
  return
}
defer db.Close()
col, err := db.C("paths")
if err != nil {
  fatalErr = err
  return
}
```

Here we use the `filedb.Dial` function to connect with the `filedb` database. In actuality, nothing much happens here except specifying where the database is, since there are no real database servers to connect to (although this might change in the future, which is why such provisions exist in the interface). If that was successful, we defer the closing of the database. Closing the database does actually do something, since files may be open that need to be cleaned up.

Following the `mgo` pattern, next we specify a collection using the `C` method and keep a reference to it in the `col` variable. If at any point an error occurs, we assign it to the `fatalErr` variable and return.

To store data, we are going to define a type called `path`, which will store the full path and the last hash value, and use JSON encoding to store this in our `filedb` database. Add the following `struct` definition above the `main` function:

```
type path struct {
  Path string
  Hash string
}
```

Parsing arguments

When we call `flag.Args` (as opposed to `os.Args`), we receive a slice of arguments excluding the flags. This allows us to mix flag arguments and non-flag arguments in the same tool.

We want our tool to be able to be used in the following ways:

- To add a path:
  ```
  backup -db=/path/to/db add {path} [paths...]
  ```

- To remove a path:

  ```
  backup -db=/path/to/db remove {path} [paths...]
  ```

- To list all paths:

  ```
  backup -db=/path/to/db list
  ```

To achieve this, since we have already dealt with flags, we must check the first (non-flag) argument.

Add the following code to the main function:

```
switch strings.ToLower(args[0]) {
case "list":
case "add":
case "remove":
}
```

Here we simply switch on the first argument, after setting it to lowercase (if the user types backup LIST, we still want it to work).

Listing the paths

To list the paths in the database, we are going to use a ForEach method on the path's col variable. Add the following code to the list case:

```
var path path
col.ForEach(func(i int, data []byte) bool {
  err := json.Unmarshal(data, &path)
  if err != nil {
    fatalErr = err
    return false
  }
  fmt.Printf("= %s\n", path)
  return false
})
```

We pass in a callback function to ForEach that will be called for every item in that collection. We then Unmarshal it from JSON, into our path type, and just print it out using fmt.Printf. We return false as per the filedb interface, which tells us that returning true would stop iterating and that we want to make sure we list them all.

String representations for your own types

If you print structs in Go in this way, using the %s format verbs, you can get some messy results that are difficult for users to read. If, however, the type implements a String() string method, that will be used instead and we can use this to control what gets printed. Below the path struct, add the following method:

```go
func (p path) String() string {
    return fmt.Sprintf("%s [%s]", p.Path, p.Hash)
}
```

This tells the path type how it should represent itself as a string.

Adding paths

To add a path, or many paths, we are going to iterate over the remaining arguments and call the InsertJSON method for each one. Add the following code to the add case:

```go
if len(args[1:]) == 0 {
    fatalErr = errors.New("must specify path to add")
    return
}
for _, p := range args[1:] {
    path := &path{Path: p, Hash: "Not yet archived"}
    if err := col.InsertJSON(path); err != nil {
        fatalErr = err
        return
    }
    fmt.Printf("+ %s\n", path)
}
```

If the user hasn't specified any additional arguments, like if they just called backup add without typing any paths, we will return a fatal error. Otherwise, we do the work and print out the path string (prefixed with a + symbol) to indicate that it was successfully added. By default, we'll set the hash to the Not yet archived string literal—this is an invalid hash but serves the dual purposes of letting the user know that it hasn't yet been archived, as well as indicating as such to our code (given that a hash of the folder will never equal that string).

Removing paths

To remove a path, or many paths, we use the RemoveEach method for the path's collection. Add the following code to the remove case:

```
var path path
col.RemoveEach(func(i int, data []byte) (bool, bool) {
  err := json.Unmarshal(data, &path)
  if err != nil {
    fatalErr = err
    return false, true
  }
  for _, p := range args[1:] {
    if path.Path == p {
      fmt.Printf("- %s\n", path)
      return true, false
    }
  }
  return false, false
})
```

The callback function we provide to RemoveEach expects us to return two bool types: the first one indicates whether the item should be removed or not, and the second one indicates whether we should stop iterating or not.

Using our new tool

We have completed our simple backup command-line tool. Let's see it in action. Create a folder called backupdata inside backup/cmds/backup; this will become the filedb database.

Build the tool in a terminal by navigating to the main.go file and running:

```
go build -o backup
```

If all is well, we can now add a path:

```
./backup -db=./backupdata add ./test ./test2
```

You should see the expected output:

```
+ ./test [Not yet archived]
+ ./test2 [Not yet archived]
```

Now let's add another path:

```
./backup -db=./backupdata add ./test3
```

You should now see the complete list:

```
./backup -db=./backupdata list
```

Our program should yield:

```
= ./test [Not yet archived]
= ./test2 [Not yet archived]
= ./test3 [Not yet archived]
```

Let's remove test3 to make sure the remove functionality is working:

```
./backup -db=./backupdata remove ./test3
./backup -db=./backupdata list
```

This will take us back to:

```
+ ./test [Not yet archived]
+ ./test2 [Not yet archived]
```

We are now able to interact with the filedb database in a way that makes sense for our use case. Next we build the daemon program that will actually use our backup package to do the work.

The daemon backup tool

The backup tool, which we will call backupd, will be responsible for periodically checking the paths listed in the filedb database, hashing the folders to see whether anything has changed, and using the backup package to actually perform the archiving of folders that need it.

Create a new folder called backupd alongside the backup/cmds/backup folder, and let's jump right into handling the fatal errors and flags:

```go
func main() {
  var fatalErr error
  defer func() {
    if fatalErr != nil {
```

```
         log.Fatalln(fatalErr)
      }
   }()
   var (
      interval = flag.Int("interval", 10, "interval between checks
(seconds)")
      archive  = flag.String("archive", "archive", "path to archive
location")
      dbpath   = flag.String("db", "./db", "path to filedb
database")
   )
   flag.Parse()
}
```

You must be quite used to seeing this kind of code by now. We defer the handling of fatal errors before specifying three flags: `interval`, `archive`, and `db`. The `interval` flag represents the number of seconds between checks to see whether folders have changed, the `archive` flag is the path to the archive location where ZIP files will go, and the `db` flag is the path to the same `filedb` database that the `backup` command is interacting with. The usual call to `flag.Parse` sets the variables up and validates whether we're ready to move on.

In order to check the hashes of the folders, we are going to need an instance of `Monitor` that we wrote earlier. Append the following code to the `main` function:

```
m := &backup.Monitor{
   Destination: *archive,
   Archiver:    backup.ZIP,
   Paths:       make(map[string]string),
}
```

Here we create a `backup.Monitor` method using the `archive` value as the `Destination` type. We'll use the `backup.ZIP` archiver and create a map ready for it to store the paths and hashes internally. At the start of the daemon, we want to load the paths from the database so that it doesn't archive unnecessarily as we stop and start things.

Add the following code to the `main` function:

```
db, err := filedb.Dial(*dbpath)
if err != nil {
   fatalErr = err
```

```
    return
  }
  defer db.Close()
  col, err := db.C("paths")
  if err != nil {
    fatalErr = err
    return
  }
```

You have seen this code before too; it dials the database and creates an object that allows us to interact with the `paths` collection. If anything fails, we set `fatalErr` and return.

Duplicated structures

Since we're going to use the same path structure as in our user command-line tool program, we need to include a definition of it for this program too. Insert the following structure above the `main` function:

```
type path struct {
  Path string
  Hash string
}
```

The object-oriented programmers out there are no doubt by now screaming at the pages demanding for this shared snippet to exist in one place only and not be duplicated in both programs. I urge you to resist this compulsion of early abstraction. These four lines of code hardly justify a new package and therefore dependency for our code, when they can just as easily exist in both programs with very little overhead. Consider also that we might want to add a `LastChecked` field to our `backupd` program so that we could add rules where each folder only gets archived at most once an hour. Our `backup` program doesn't care about this and will chug along perfectly happy with its view into what fields constitute a path.

Caching data

We can now query all existing paths and update the `Paths` map, which is a useful technique to increase the speed of a program, especially given slow or disconnected data stores. By loading the data into a cache (in our case, the `Paths` map), we can access it at lightening speeds without having to consult the files each time we need information.

Add the following code to the body of the `main` function:

```
var path path
col.ForEach(func(_ int, data []byte) bool {
  if err := json.Unmarshal(data, &path); err != nil {
    fatalErr = err
    return true
  }
  m.Paths[path.Path] = path.Hash
  return false // carry on
})
if fatalErr != nil {
  return
}
if len(m.Paths) < 1 {
  fatalErr = errors.New("no paths - use backup tool to add at
least one")
  return
}
```

Using the `ForEach` method again allows us to iterate over all the paths in the database. We `Unmarshal` the JSON bytes into the same path structure as we used in our other program and set the values in the `Paths` map. Assuming nothing goes wrong, we do a final check to make sure there is at least one path, and if not, return with an error.

 One limitation to our program is that it will not dynamically add paths once it has started. The daemon would need to be restarted. If this bothers you, you could always build in a mechanism that updates the `Paths` map periodically.

Infinite loops

The next thing we need to do is to perform a check on the hashes right away to see whether anything needs archiving, before entering into an infinite timed loop where we check again at regular specified intervals.

An infinite loop sounds like a bad idea; in fact to some it sounds like a bug. However, since we're talking about an infinite loop within this program, and since infinite loops can be easily broken with a simple `break` command, they're not as dramatic as they might sound.

In Go, to write an infinite loop is as simple as:

```
for {}
```

The instructions inside the braces get executed over and over again, as quickly as the machine running the code can execute them. Again this sounds like a bad plan, unless you're careful about what you're asking it to do. In our case, we are immediately initiating a `select` case on the two channels that will block safely until one of the channels has something interesting to say.

Add the following code:

```
check(m, col)
signalChan := make(chan os.Signal, 1)
signal.Notify(signalChan, syscall.SIGINT, syscall.SIGTERM)
for {
  select {
  case <-time.After(time.Duration(*interval) * time.Second):
    check(m, col)
  case <-signalChan:
    // stop
    fmt.Println()
    log.Printf("Stopping...")
    goto stop
  }
}
stop:
```

Of course, as responsible programmers, we care about what happens when the user terminates our programs. So after a call to the `check` method, which doesn't yet exist, we make a signal channel and use `signal.Notify` to ask for the termination signal to be given to the channel, rather than handled automatically. In our infinite `for` loop, we select on two possibilities: either the `timer` channel sends a message or the termination signal channel sends a message. If it's the `timer` channel message, we call `check` again, otherwise we go about terminating the program.

The `time.After` function returns a channel that will send a signal (actually the current time) after the specified time has elapsed. The somewhat confusing `time.Duration(*interval) * time.Second` code simply indicates the amount of time to wait before the signal is sent; the first `*` character is a dereference operator since the `flag.Int` method represents a pointer to an int, and not the int itself. The second `*` character multiplies the interval value by `time.Second`, which gives a value equivalent to the specified interval in seconds. Casting the `*interval int` to `time.Duration` is required so that the compiler knows we are dealing with numbers.

We take a short trip down the memory lane in the preceding code snippet by using the `goto` statement to jump out of the switch and to block loops. We could do away with the `goto` statement altogether and just return when a termination signal is received, but the pattern discussed here allows us to run non-deferred code after the `for` loop, should we wish to.

Updating filedb records

All that is left is for us to implement the `check` function that should call the `Now` method on the `Monitor` type and update the database with new hashes if there are any.

Underneath the `main` function, add the following code:

```go
func check(m *backup.Monitor, col *filedb.C) {
  log.Println("Checking...")
  counter, err := m.Now()
  if err != nil {
    log.Fatalln("failed to backup:", err)
  }
  if counter > 0 {
    log.Printf("  Archived %d directories\n", counter)
    // update hashes
    var path path
    col.SelectEach(func(_ int, data []byte) (bool, []byte, bool) {
      if err := json.Unmarshal(data, &path); err != nil {
        log.Println("failed to unmarshal data (skipping):", err)
        return true, data, false
      }
      path.Hash, _ = m.Paths[path.Path]
      newdata, err := json.Marshal(&path)
      if err != nil {
        log.Println("failed to marshal data (skipping):", err)
        return true, data, false
      }
      return true, newdata, false
    })
  } else {
    log.Println("  No changes")
  }
}
```

The check function first tells the user that a check is happening, before immediately calling Now. If the Monitor type did any work for us, which is to ask if it archived any files, we output them to the user and go on to update the database with the new values. The SelectEach method allows us to change each record in the collection if we so wish, by returning the replacement bytes. So we Unmarshal the bytes to get the path structure, update the hash value and return the marshaled bytes. This ensures that next time we start a backupd process, it will do so with the correct hash values.

Testing our solution

Let's see whether our two programs play nicely together and what affects the code inside our backup package. You may want to open two terminal windows for this, since we'll be running two programs.

We have already added some paths to the database, so let's use backup to see them:

```
./backup -db="./backupdata" list
```

You should see the two test folders; if you don't, refer back to the *Adding paths* section.

```
= ./test [Not yet archived]
= ./test2 [Not yet archived]
```

In another window, navigate to the backupd folder and create our two test folders called test and test2.

Build backupd using the usual method:

```
go build -o backupd
```

Assuming all is well, we can now start the backup process being sure to point the db path to the same path as we used for the backup program, and specify that we want to use a new folder called archive to store the ZIP files. For testing purposes, let's specify an interval of 5 seconds to save time:

```
./backupd -db="../backup/backupdata/" -archive="./archive" -
interval=5
```

Immediately, backupd should check the folders, calculate the hashes, notice that they are different (to Not yet archived), and initiate the archive process for both folders. It will print the output telling us this:

```
Checking...
Archived 2 directories
```

Open the newly created `archive` folder inside `backup/cmds/backupd` and notice it has created two subfolders: `test` and `test2`. Inside those are compressed archive versions of the empty folders. Feel free to unzip one and see; not very exciting so far.

Meanwhile, back in the terminal window, `backupd` has been checking the folders again for changes:

```
Checking...
   No changes
Checking...
   No changes
```

In your favorite text editor, create a new text file inside the `test2` folder containing the word `test`, and save it as `one.txt`. After a few seconds, you will see that `backupd` has noticed the new file and created another snapshot inside the `archive/test2` folder.

Of course, it has a different filename because the time is different, but if you unzip it you will notice that it has indeed created a compressed archive version of the folder.

Play around with the solution by taking the following actions:

- Change the contents of the `one.txt` file
- Add a file to the `test` folder too
- Delete a file

Summary

In this chapter, we successfully built a very powerful and flexible backup system for your code projects. You can see how simple it would be to extend or modify the behavior of these programs. The scope for potential problems that you could go on to solve is limitless.

Rather than having a local archive destination folder like we did in the previous section, imagine mounting a network storage device and using that instead. Suddenly, you have off-site (or at least off-machine) backups of those vital files. You could easily set a Dropbox folder as the archive destination, which would mean not only do you get access to the snapshots yourself, but also a copy is stored in the cloud and can even be shared with other users.

Extending the `Archiver` interface to support `Restore` operations (which would just use the `encoding/zip` package to unzip the files) allows you to build tools that can peer inside the archives and access the changes of individual files much like Time Machine allows you to do. Indexing the files gives you full search across the entire history of your code, much like GitHub does.

Since the filenames are timestamps, you could have backed up retiring old archives to less active storage mediums, or summarized the changes into a daily dump.

Obviously, backup software exists, is well tested, and used through the world and it may be a smart move to focus on solving problems that haven't yet been solved. But when it requires such little effort to write small programs to get things done, it is often worth doing because of the control it gives you. When you write the code, you can get exactly what you want without compromise, and it's down to each individual to make that call.

Specifically in this chapter, we explored how easy Go's standard library makes it to interact with the filesystem: opening files for reading, creating new files, and making directories. The os package mixed in with the powerful types from the io package, blended further with capabilities like encoding/zip and others, gives a clear example of how extremely simple Go interfaces can be composed to deliver very powerful results.

Good Practices for a Stable Go Environment

Writing Go code is a fun and enjoyable experience where compile-time errors —rather than being a pain—actually guide you to write robust, high-quality code. However, every now and again, you will encounter environmental issues that start to get in the way and break your flow. While you can usually resolve these issues after some searching and a little tweaking, setting up your development environment correctly goes a long way in reducing problems, allowing you to focus on building useful applications.

In this chapter, we are going to install Go from scratch on a new machine and discuss some of the environmental options we have and the impact they might have in the future. We will also consider how collaboration might influence some of our decisions, as well as what impact open sourcing our packages might have.

Specifically, we are going to:

- Get the Go source code and build it natively on your development machine
- Learn what the GOPATH environment variable is for, and discuss a sensible approach to its use
- Learn about the Go tools and how to use them to keep the quality of our code high
- Learn how to use a tool to automatically manage our imports
- Think about "on save" operations for our .go files, and how we can integrate the Go tools as part of our daily development

Installing Go

Go is an open source project written originally in C, which means we can compile our own version from the code easily; this remains the best option for installing Go for a variety of reasons. It allows us to navigate through the source if we need to look something up later, either in the standard library Go code, or in the C code of the tools. It also allows us to easily update to newer versions of Go or experiment with release candidates as they come out, just by pulling a different tag or branch from the code repository and building again. Of course, we can also easily roll back to earlier versions if we need to, and even fix bugs and generate pull requests to send to the Go core team for them to consider contributions to the project.

> A continually updated resource for installing Go from its source on a variety of platforms can be found online at http://golang.org/doc/install/source or by searching for Install Golang from source. This chapter will cover the same things, but if you encounter problems, the Internet is going to be your best friend in helping resolve issues.

Installing the C tools

Since the Go tool chain is written in C, we will actually be compiling C code when we build our Go installation. This may seem a little counter-intuitive; a programming language was written using a different programming language, but of course, Go didn't exist when the Go core team started writing Go, but C did. It is more accurate to say that the tools used to build and link Go programs are written in C. Either way, for now, we need to be able to compile the C source code.

> At the first ever Gophercon in Denver, Colorado in 2014, Rob Pike and the team expressed that one of their goals would be to replace the C tool chain with programs written in Go— so that the entire stack becomes Go. At the time of writing, this hasn't happened yet, so we will need the C tools.

To determine whether you need to install the C tools or not, open a terminal and try to use the gcc command:

```
gcc -v
```

If you receive a command not found error or similar, you will likely have to install the C tools. If, however, you see the output from gcc giving you version information (that's what the -v flag was for), you can likely skip this section.

Installing C tools differs for various platforms and could change over time, so this section should be treated only as a rough guide to help you get the tools you need.

The tools on a Mac running OS X are shipped with Xcode, which is available in App Store for free. Once you install Xcode, you open **Preferences** and navigate to the **Downloads** section. From there, you find the command-line tools that include the C tools you will need to build Go.

On Ubuntu and Debian systems, you can use `apt-get` to install the tools:

```
sudo apt-get install gcc libc6-dev
```

For RedHat and Centos 6 systems, you can use `yum` to install the tools:

```
sudo yum install gcc glibc-devel
```

For Windows, the MinGW project offers a Windows installer that will install the tools for you. Navigate to `http://www.mingw.org/` and follow the instructions there to get started.

Once you have successfully installed the tools and ensured the appropriate binaries are included in your `PATH` environment variable, you should be able to see some sensible output when running `gcc -v`:

```
Apple LLVM version 5.1 (clang-503.0.40) (based on LLVM 3.4svn)
Target: x86_64-apple-darwin13.2.0
Thread model: posix
```

The preceding snippet is the output on an Apple Mac computer, and the most important thing to look for is the lack of the `command not found` error.

Downloading and building Go from the source

The Go source code is hosted at Google Code in a Mercurial repository, so we will use the `hg` command to clone it in preparation for building.

 If you do not have the `hg` command, you can get Mercurial from the download page at `http://mercurial.selenic.com/downloads`.

In a terminal, to install Go, navigate to a suitable location such as `/opt` on Unix systems, or `C:\` on Windows.

Get the latest release of Go by typing the following command:

```
hg clone -u release https://code.google.com/p/go
```

After a while, the latest Go source code will download into a new `go` folder.

Navigate to the `go/src` folder that was just created and run the `all` script, which will build an instance of Go from the source code. On Unix systems this is `all.bash`, on Windows it's `all.bat`.

Once all the build steps are complete, you should notice that all the tests have successfully passed.

Configuring Go

Go is now installed, but in order to use the tools we must ensure it is properly configured. To make calling the tools easier, we need to add our `go/bin` path to the `PATH` environment variable.

> On Unix systems, you should add export `PATH=$PATH:/opt/go/bin` (make sure it is the path you chose when downloading the source) to your `.bashrc` file.
>
> On Windows, open **System Properties** (try right-clicking on **My Computer**) and under **Advanced**, click on the **Environment Variables** button and use the UI to ensure the `PATH` variable contains the path to your `go/bin` folder.

In a terminal (you may need to restart it for your changes to take effect), you can make sure this worked by printing the value of the `PATH` variable:

```
echo $PATH
```

Ensure the value printed contains the correct path to your `go/bin` folder, for example, on my machine it prints as:

```
/usr/local/bin:/usr/bin:/bin:/opt/go/bin
```

> The colons (semicolons on Windows) between the paths indicate that the `PATH` variable is actually a list of folders rather than just one folder. This indicates that each folder included will be searched when you enter commands in your terminal.

Now we can make sure the Go build we just made runs successfully:

```
go version
```

Executing the `go` command (that can be found in your `go/bin` location) like this will print out the current version for us. For example, for Go 1.3, you should see something similar to:

```
go version go1.3 darwin/amd64
```

Getting GOPATH right

`GOPATH` is another environment variable to a folder (like `PATH` in the previous section) that is used to specify the location for Go source code and compiled binary packages. Using the `import` command in your Go programs will cause the compiler to look in the `GOPATH` location to find the packages you are referring to. When using `go get` and other commands, projects are downloaded into the `GOPATH` folder.

While the `GOPATH` location can contain a list of colon-separated folders such as `PATH`, and you can even have a different value for `GOPATH` depending on which project you are working in, it is strongly recommended that you use a single `GOPATH` location for everything, and this is what we will assume you will do for the projects in this book.

Create a new folder called `go`, this time in your `Users` folder somewhere, perhaps in a `Work` subfolder. This will be our `GOPATH` target and is where all the third-party code and binaries will end up, as well as where we will write our Go programs and packages. Using the same technique you used when setting the `PATH` environment variable in the previous section, set the `GOPATH` variable to the new `go` folder. Let's open a terminal and use one of the newly installed commands to get a third-party package for us to use:

```
go get github.com/stretchr/powerwalk
```

Getting the `powerwalk` library from `Stretchr` will actually cause the following folder structure to be created; `$GOPATH/src/github.com/stretchr/powerwalk`. You can see that the path segments are important in how Go organizes things, which helps namespace projects and keeps them unique. For example, if you created your own package called `powerwalk`, you wouldn't keep it in the GitHub repository of `Stretchr`, so the path would be different.

When we create projects in this book, you should consider a sensible `GOPATH` root for them. For example, I used `github.com/matryer/goblueprints`, and if you were to `go get` that, you would actually get a complete copy of all the source code for this book in your `GOPATH` folder!

Go tools

An early decision made by the Go core team was that all Go code should look familiar and obvious to everybody who speaks Go rather than each code base requiring additional learning in order for new programmers to understand it or work on it. This is an especially sensible approach when you consider open source projects, some of which have hundreds of contributors coming and going all the time.

There is a range of tools that can assist us in achieving the high standards set by the Go core team, and we will see some of the tools in action in this section.

In your GOPATH location, create a new folder called `tooling` and create a new `main.go` file containing the following code verbatim:

```
package main
import (
"fmt"
)
func main() {
return
var name string
name = "Mat"
fmt.Println("Hello ", name)
}
```

The tight spaces and lack of indentation are deliberate as we are going to look at a very cool utility that comes with Go.

In a terminal, navigate to your new folder and run:

go fmt

 At Gophercon 2014 in Denver, Colorado, most people learned that rather than pronouncing this little triad as "format" or "f, m, t" it is actually pronounced as a word. Try saying it to yourself now: "fhumt"; it seems that computer programmers aren't weird enough without speaking an alien language to each other too!

You will notice that this little tool has actually tweaked our code file to ensure that the layout (or format) of our program matches Go standards. The new version is much easier to read:

```
package main

import (
```

```
    "fmt"
)

func main() {
  return
  var name string
  name = "Mat"
  fmt.Println("Hello ", name)
}
```

The `go fmt` command cares about indentation, code blocks, unnecessary whitespace, unnecessary extra line feeds, and more. Formatting your code in this way is a great practice to ensure that your Go code looks like all other Go code.

Next we are going to vet our program to make sure we haven't made any mistakes or decisions that might be confusing to our users; we can do this automatically with another great tool that we get for free:

go vet

The output for our little program points out an obvious and glaring mistake:

main.go:10: unreachable code

exit status 1

We are calling `return` at the top of our function and then trying to do other things afterwards. The `go vet` tool has noticed this and points out that we have unreachable code in our file.

> If you get an error running any Go tools, it usually means you have to get the command before you can use it. However, in the case of the vet tool, you just have to open a terminal and run:
>
> `go get code.google.com/p/go.tools/cmd/vet`

It isn't just silly mistakes like this that `go vet` will catch, it will also look for subtler aspects of your program that will guide you towards writing the best Go code you can. For an up-to-date list of what the vet tool will report on, check out the documentation at `https://godoc.org/code.google.com/p/go.tools/cmd/vet`.

The final tool we will play with is called goimports, and was written by Brad Fitzpatrick to automatically fix (add or remove) import statements for Go files. It is an error in Go to import a package and not use it, and obviously trying to use a package without importing it won't work either. The goimports tool will automatically rewrite our import statement based on the contents of our code file. First, let's install goimports with the familiar command:

```
go get code.google.com/p/go.tools/cmd/goimports
```

Update your program to import some packages that we are not going to use and remove the fmt package:

```
import (
  "net/http"
  "sync"
)
```

When we try to run our program by calling go run main.go, we will see that we get some errors:

```
./main.go:4: imported and not used: "net/http"
```

```
./main.go:5: imported and not used: "sync"
```

```
./main.go:13: undefined: fmt
```

These errors are telling us that we have imported packages that we are not using and missing the fmt package, and that in order to continue we need to make corrections. This is where goimports comes in:

```
goimports -w *.go
```

We are calling the goimports command with the -w write flag, which will save us the task of making corrections to all files ending with .go.

Have a look at your main.go file now and notice that the net/http and sync packages have been removed and the fmt package has been put back in.

You could argue that switching to a terminal to run these commands takes more time than just doing it manually, and you would probably be right in most cases, which is why it is highly recommended that you integrate the Go tools with your text editor.

Cleaning up, building, and running tests on save

Since the Go core team has provided us with such great tools as `fmt`, `vet`, `test`, and `goimports`, we are going to look at a development practice that has proven to be extremely useful. Whenever we save a `.go` file, we want to perform the following tasks automatically:

1. Use `goimports` and `fmt` to fix our imports and format the code.

2. Vet the code for any faux pas and tell us immediately.

3. Attempt to build the current package and output any build errors.

4. If the build is successful, run the tests for the package and output any failures.

Because Go code compiles so quickly (Rob Pike once actually said that it doesn't build quickly, but it's just not slow like everything else), we can comfortably build entire packages every time we save a file. The same is true for running tests, to help us if we are developing in a TDD style, and the experience is great. Every time we make changes to our code, we can immediately see if we have broken something or had an unexpected impact on some other part of our project. We'll never see package import errors again, because our `import` statement will have been fixed for us, and our code will be correctly formatted right in front of our eyes.

Some editors will likely not support running code in response to specific events, such as saving a file, which leaves you with two options; you can either switch to a better editor or write your own script file that runs in response to filesystem changes. The latter solution is out of scope for this book, instead we will focus on how to implement this functionality in a popular text editor.

Sublime Text 3

Sublime Text 3 is an excellent editor for writing Go code that runs on OS X, Linux, and Windows, and has an extremely powerful expansion model, which makes it easy to customize and extend. You can download Sublime Text from `http://www.sublimetext.com/` and trial-use it for free before deciding if you want to buy it or not.

Thanks to **DisposaBoy** (see `https://github.com/DisposaBoy`), there is already a Sublime expansion package for Go, which actually gives us a wealth of features and power that a lot of Go programmers actually miss out on. We are going to install this `GoSublime` package and then build upon it to add our desired on-save functionality.

Before we can install GoSublime, we need to install Package Control into Sublime Text. Head over to https://sublime.wbond.net/ and click on the **Installation** link for instructions on how to install Package Control. At the time of writing, it's simply a case of copying the single, albeit long, line command, and pasting it into the Sublime console which can be opened by navigating to **View | Show Console** from the menu.

Once that is complete, press *shift + command + P* and type Package Control: Install Package and press *return* when you have selected the option. After a short delay (where Package Control is updating its listings), a box will appear allowing you to search for and install GoSublime just by typing it in, selecting it, and pressing *return*. All being well, GoSublime will be installed and writing Go code has just become an order of magnitude easier.

Now that you have GoSublime installed, you can open a short help file containing the details of the package by pressing *command + ., command + 2* (the *command* key and period at the same time, followed by the *command* key and number 2).

Tyler Bunnell is another popular name in the Go open source community (see https://github.com/tylerb) and we are going to use his customizations to implement our on-save functionality.

Press *command + ., command + 5* to open the GoSublime settings and add the following entry to the object:

```
"on_save": [
  {
    "cmd": "gs9o_open",
    "args": {
      "run": ["sh", "go build . errors && go test -i && go test &&
go vet && golint"],
      "focus_view": false
    }
  }
]
```

Notice that the settings file is actually a JSON object, so be sure to add the on_save property without corrupting the file. For example, if you have properties before and after, ensure the appropriate commas are in place.

The preceding setting will tell Sublime Text to build the code looking for errors, install test dependencies, run tests, and vet the code whenever we save the file. Save the settings file (don't close it just yet), and let's see this in action.

Navigate to **Choose File | Open...** from the menu and select a folder to open—for now let's open our `tooling` folder. The simple user interface of Sublime Text makes it clear that we only have one file in our project right now, `main.go`. Click on the file, add some extra linefeeds, and add and remove some indenting. Then navigate to **File | Save** from the menu, or press *command + S*. Notice that the code is immediately cleaned up, and provided you haven't removed the oddly placed `return` statement from `main.go`, you will notice that the console has appeared, and it is reporting the issue thanks to `go vet`:

```
main.go:8: unreachable code
```

Holding down *command + shift* and double-clicking on the unreachable code line in the console will open the file and jump the cursor to the right line in question. You can see how helpful this feature is going to be as you continue to write Go code.

If you add an unwanted import to the file, you will notice that on using `on_save` you are told about the problem, but it wasn't automatically fixed. That's because we have another tweak to make. In the same settings file as you added the `on_save` property to, add the following property:

```
"fmt_cmd": ["goimports"]
```

This tells GoSublime to use the `goimports` command instead of `go fmt`. Save this file again and head back to `main.go`. Add `net/http` to the imports again, remove `fmt` import, and save the file. Notice that the unused package was removed and `fmt` was again put back.

Summary

In this appendix, we installed our own build of Go from the source code, which means we can easily use the `hg` command to keep our installation up to date, or to test our beta features before they are released. It's also nice to have the entire Go language code for us to browse on those lonely nights by the fire.

You learned about the `GOPATH` environment variable, and discovered a common practice of keeping one value for all projects. This approach dramatically simplifies working on Go projects, where otherwise you would likely continue to encounter tricky failures.

We discovered how the Go toolset can really help us to produce high quality, community-standards-compliant code that any other programmer could pick up and work on with little to no additional learning. And more importantly, we looked at how automating the use of these tools means we can truly get down to the business of writing applications and solving problems, which is all that developers really want to do.

Index

Thank you for buying
Go Programming Blueprints

About Packt Publishing

Packt, pronounced 'packed', published its first book, *Mastering phpMyAdmin for Effective MySQL Management*, in April 2004, and subsequently continued to specialize in publishing highly focused books on specific technologies and solutions.

Our books and publications share the experiences of your fellow IT professionals in adapting and customizing today's systems, applications, and frameworks. Our solution-based books give you the knowledge and power to customize the software and technologies you're using to get the job done. Packt books are more specific and less general than the IT books you have seen in the past. Our unique business model allows us to bring you more focused information, giving you more of what you need to know, and less of what you don't.

Packt is a modern yet unique publishing company that focuses on producing quality, cutting-edge books for communities of developers, administrators, and newbies alike. For more information, please visit our website at www.packtpub.com.

About Packt Open Source

In 2010, Packt launched two new brands, Packt Open Source and Packt Enterprise, in order to continue its focus on specialization. This book is part of the Packt Open Source brand, home to books published on software built around open source licenses, and offering information to anybody from advanced developers to budding web designers. The Open Source brand also runs Packt's Open Source Royalty Scheme, by which Packt gives a royalty to each open source project about whose software a book is sold.

Writing for Packt

We welcome all inquiries from people who are interested in authoring. Book proposals should be sent to author@packtpub.com. If your book idea is still at an early stage and you would like to discuss it first before writing a formal book proposal, then please contact us; one of our commissioning editors will get in touch with you.

We're not just looking for published authors; if you have strong technical skills but no writing experience, our experienced editors can help you develop a writing career, or simply get some additional reward for your expertise.

Mastering Concurrency in Go

ISBN: 978-1-78398-348-3   Paperback: 328 pages

Discover and harness Go's powerful concurrency features to develop and build fast, scalable network systems

1. Explore the core syntaxes and language features that enable concurrency in Go.

2. Understand when and where to use concurrency to keep data consistent and applications non-blocking, responsive, and reliable.

3. A practical approach to utilize application scaffolding to design highly-scalable programs that are deeply rooted in goroutines and channels.

Building Your First Application with Go [Video]

ISBN: 978-1-78328-381-1   Duration: 02:47 hrs

Get practical experience and learn basic skills while developing an application with Go

1. Learn the features and various aspects of Go programming.

2. Create a production-ready web application by the end of the course.

3. Master time-proven design patterns for creating highly reusable application components.

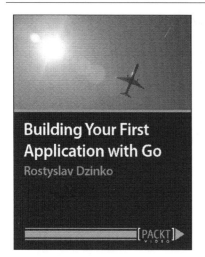

Please check **www.PacktPub.com** for information on our titles

iPad Enterprise Application Development BluePrints

ISBN: 978-1-84968-294-7   Paperback: 430 pages

Design and build your own enterprise applications for the iPad

1. Learn how to go about developing some simple yet powerful applications with ease.

2. Each chapter explains about the technology in-depth, while providing you with enough information and examples to help grasp the technology.

3. Get to grips with integrating Facebook, iCloud, Twitter, and Airplay into your applications.

Socket.IO Real-time Web Application Development

ISBN: 978-1-78216-078-6   Paperback: 140 pages

Build modern real-time web applications powered by Socket.IO

1. Understand the usage of various Socket.IO features such as rooms, namespaces, and sessions.

2. Secure the Socket.IO communication.

3. Deploy and scale your Socket.IO and Node.js applications in production.

4. A practical guide that quickly gets you up and running with Socket.IO.

Made in the USA
San Bernardino, CA
03 February 2016